The
Massachusetts
Legacy

The
Massachusetts
Legacy

150 Landmark Events
that Shaped Our Nation

Christopher Kenneally

To Kyle —
all best wishes
Christopher Kenneally

Adams Publishing
HOLBROOK, MASSACHUSETTS

To Sabine
for Claudia
who will make her own history.

Published by Adams Media Corporation
260 Center Street, Holbrook, MA 02343

ISBN: 1-55850-528-8
Printed in Canada.

First Edition
J   I   H   G   F   E   D   C   B   A

Library of Congress Cataloging-inPublication Data
Kenneally, Christopher.
The Massachusetts legacy : 150 landmark events that shaped our nation
/ Christopher Kenneally.
p.   cm.
Includes bibliographical references and index.
ISBN 1-55850-528-8 (hb)
1. Massachusetts—History—Anecdotes. I. Title.
F64.6.K46   1995
974.4—dc20   95-34507
CIP

Illustrations by Joanna Hudgens.

This book is available at quantity discounts for bulk purchases.
For information, call 1-800-872-5627.

Contents

Acknowledgments

PUNDITS LIKE TO SAY that Americans no longer know their history or have genuine interest in events older than a week ago. In my work on *The Massachusetts Legacy*, however, I was struck by the great attachment so many citizens in the state feel for their local history. From Boston to the Berkshires, the people of Massachusetts shared their knowledge of the past with me freely.

For invaluable research assistance, I owe a debt to librarians and staff at the Boston Public Library and Brookline Public Library; Christine Peterson, branch librarian, Jane Bickford, adult librarian, and the staff of the West Roxbury Branch of the Boston Public Library; Philip S. Bergen, librarian, Bostonian Society; Virginia H. Smith, reference librarian, Massachusetts Historical Society; Richard Johnson, The Sports Museum of New England; Richard J. Wolfe, curator of rare books and manuscripts, Harvard Medical School Library; Lisa Tuite and Kathleen Hennrikus, *Boston Globe* Library; Carolyn M. Kemmett, Unitarian Universalist Association of Congregations; Sylvia Watts McKinney, Museum of Afro-American History/African Meeting House; Tanya Bresinksky, librarian, Maria Mitchell Library; George Sanborn, State Transportation Library; Nancy Gaudette, librarian, Worcester Room, Worcester Public Library; Malcolm J. Flynn, Boston Latin School; Nantucket Chamber of Commerce; and Nancy Heywood, James Duncan Phillips Library, Essex Institute.

For their personal assistance, thanks to Robin Baker, director of education, Handel & Haydn Society; Kevin McCaffrey, Mount Holyoke College; Janet Heywood, Friends of Mount Auburn Cemetery; Alan Banks, park ranger, Frederick Law Olmsted National Historic Site; Lila S. Parrish, for information on William Stanley; Frances Gagnon, Springfield Historical Commission; Robin Jonathan Deutsch, Naismith Memorial Basketball Hall of Fame; Patricia Boudrot, Filene's Basement; Sonya

Latimere, Dimock Community Health Center; Chris Phillips, Ocean Spray Cranberries; Jeanne Blum Kissane, Worcester Foundation; Gloria Greis, Peabody Museum of Archaeology and Ethnology; Thomas Hutchinson, NYNEX; and Lori Moretti, CM Communications.

For providing me with their publications and materials of historical interest, thanks to the Saugus Iron Works National Historic Site; Perkins School for the Blind; Quincy Historical Society; Immigrant City Archives, Lawrence; and Old Dartmouth Historical Society Whaling Museum, New Bedford.

For their counsel, patience, and perseverance, thanks also to Pamela A. Liflander, my editor at Adams Media, and Alison Picard, my literary agent.

Introduction

GEORGIA HAS SWEET PEACHES, Florida has juicy oranges, Kansas has golden wheat. In Massachusetts, the bumper crop is history.

The Commonwealth of Massachusetts, as it is officially known, is largely undistinguished by geography. Mount Greylock, its highest point, rises only 3,487 feet. At 10,555 square miles, Massachusetts ranks forty-fourth of the fifty states in area. Six million people live in Massachusetts, which places it as the thirteenth most populous state, according to the 1990 federal census.

Massachusetts stands out, nevertheless, for its ongoing contribution to the life of the nation. In politics and social reform, science and medicine, education, the arts, sports, and many other fields, Massachusetts has given the nation and the world a disproportionate share of landmark events and historic achievements.

Certainly, the American character was indelibly shaped by the first European settlers of Massachusetts. The Pilgrims and the Puritans imparted to their descendants a rigorous work ethic; a genuine respect for education and self-improvement; and a system of citizen government that forms the foundation of our national democracy. Self-righteous and suspicious, frequently even intolerant, the residents of the Bible commonwealth also bequeathed us the blue law and the witch trial.

Anyone born or raised in Massachusetts inevitably acquires a native pride in the role played by the commonwealth's citizens in the American Revolution. Citizens of Lexington and Concord, Bunker Hill and Dorchester Heights can remain justifiably proud two centuries after those names were first enrolled in the ledger of historic places. But the Massachusetts legacy is not confined to the days of powdered wigs and buckled shoes.

Throughout the nineteenth century, Massachusetts led the country to expand its definition of liberty. The constitution of the commonwealth of

Massachusetts

Official name: . . . . Commonwealth of Massachusetts.

Origin of name: . . . . From Algonqian, for "large hill place."

Admitted to statehood: . February 6, 1788 (sixth).

Capital: . . . . Boston (founded 1630).

Motto: . . . . Ense Petit Placidam Sub Libertate Quietem
(By the Sword We Seek Peace, but Peace Only
under Liberty).

Area: . . . . 10,555 square miles (44th of 50 states).

Longitude/latitude: . . . . 72°W/42° 30'N.

Geographic center: . . . . Worcester, north part of city.

Length: . . . . 190 miles.

Width: . . . . 50 miles.

Highest point: . . . . Mt. Greylock (3,487 feet).

Mean elevation: . . . . 500 feet.

Population: . . . . 6,016,425 (1990 census; 13th largest).

**Highest/lowest recorded
temperature:** . . . . 107°F, August 2, 1975, at Chester and
New Bedford;
-35°F, January 12, 1981, at Chester.

Massachusetts, drafted by John Adams in 1780, included a Bill of Rights, and stated unequivocally, "All men are born free and equal." This was quickly interpreted as a bar to slavery. In Boston, abolitionists William Lloyd Garrison and Theodore Parker provided escaped slave Frederick Douglass with a platform for his thundering denunciations of the South's "peculiar institution." Robert Gould Shaw and men of the African-American 54th Massachusetts Regiment ultimately gave their lives on a Civil War battlefield for emancipation.

Massachusetts women also distinguished themselves. Maria Mitchell of Nantucket became the nation's first female astronomer and discovered a comet; Margaret Fuller served as editor of the influential Transcendalist publication *The Dial*; and novelist Louisa May Alcott created the enduring characters in *Little Women*.

In the twentieth century, the Massachusetts legacy is far-reaching. The launch of Robert Goddard's rocket, on a farm just outside Worcester, was the first small step toward exploration of the solar system. The election of John Fitzgerald Kennedy as the U.S. president created a Massachusetts political dynasty to rival the Adams family. The birth control pill and a successful method for organ transplants have shaped the destinies of countless men and women. Lowell's Jack Kerouac rides forever on the road with Dean Moriarty. And the record of Red Sox slugger Ted Williams, baseball's last man to hit .400, may stand just as long.

The Massachusetts legacy belongs not only to those living within the state's boundaries but also to the people of the world. In hospitals and town meetings; on the football field and the baseball diamond; in literature, the arts, and philosophy; at the town diner and the computer terminal, a man or a woman from Massachusetts hovers over us.

BOSTON
June, 1995

Massachusetts reemerges as Pleistocene ice sheet retreats (15,000–10,000 B.C.E.).

A MOOSE BENT ITS antlered head and sipped from a pond's soggy bank. Overhead, the sun shone and warmed the earth. The air temperature rose throughout the day, and life stirred everywhere. Deep in the pine woods, ice melted and dampened the forest floor, and patches of crusted snow lingered. The long winter of the last Pleistocene Ice Age was finally over.

No one knows for sure exactly when, but sometime between fifteen thousand and ten thousand years ago, Massachusetts and the rest of North America reemerged from under an ice sheet that had covered the land like the stone lid on a tomb. The landscape was resurrected and reinvigorated. Cranberry shrubs and mussels infiltrated its tidal marshes. Alewife and shad teemed in its pristine rivers. Deer grazed and bear hunted in its dense forests.

At its heaviest, the ice sheet rose nearly two miles high and weighed billions of tons. It reached as far south as the Missouri and Ohio River valleys. All of New England was buried along with New York State and northern Pennsylvania.

The massive ice sheet was not snowy white but dingy gray. When it descended from the north, the ice scraped across the surface of the earth like the blade of an awesome plow. The force carried off everything in its path—soil, stones, and boulders, down to the bedrock.

As it groaned forward, the ice sheet sculpted hills and rounded mountains; it etched deep grooves in exposed rock; and it sunk the earth where it was soft, like an artist's thumb pressing into clay. Without the ice sheet to shape it, Massachusetts as we know it would not exist. The history of the commonwealth can conceivably be traced to the formation of our planet 4.7 billion years ago, but Massachusetts before the Ice Age would be unrecognizable.

More than 200 million years ago, theropod beasts fifty feet from head to tail roamed the mud along the Connecticut River valley. Other, smaller dinosaurs—only about as large as a human being—shared the valley mud and the luxuriant tropical vegetation.

Long after dinosaurs disappeared, the earth swung wildly between chilly periods of "glaciation," some lasting millions of years, and relatively shorter warming periods or "interglacials." Whatever tall mountains and fuming volcanoes provided backdrop for the age of the theropods have all vanished under the unstoppable scouring action of ice sheets advancing and retreating.

When the most recent "interglacial" period began 15,000 years ago, the earth once more started to warm. The endangered ice sheet shrank back again toward the North Pole. Where chips of ice were trapped in depressed pockets of earth, they melted into pools, ponds, and lakes. As it retreated, the thawing glacier scattered a rubble of sand, rocks, and boulders. Where its gritty litter was piled hundreds of feet high, drumlins and moraines formed. The landscape of Massachusetts as we know it was created.

♣ ♥ ♣

Paleo-Indian hunters settle in Massachusetts (10,000–1500 B.C.E.).

AT LAST, A NAMELESS band of Paleo-Indian hunters crossed an imaginary line that today marks a border of the commonwealth. They were the first human beings to set foot in Massachusetts. A tribe of rugged nomads, they searched the tundra for food.

These first people were not alone. Caribou, mastodon, and mammoth roamed the land with them. The Paleo-Indians stalked these animals relentlessly. They dined on the great beasts' flesh; wore their thick skins for clothing; and from their bones, they fashioned weapons and crude tools.

When the ice sheet was entirely melted and all the heavy Pleistocene animals were extinct, the cultures that thrived in such an environment vanished, too. New England's Paleo-Indian population was probably never more than twenty-five thousand, and they left behind little evidence of their existence. At Bull Brook, near Ipswich, and at archaeological sites throughout the Connecticut River valley of Massachusetts, Paleo-Indian remains include burned bones, knives, drills, and their distinctive fluted spear points.

The ancient weapons-making techniques worked reasonably well. Extremely difficult to make and requiring painstaking carving work, fluted projectiles were designed to hold a spear point securely to a long wooden shaft. One theory on the relatively sudden disappearance of Paleo-Indians suggests that they may have hunted themselves out of existence by systematically killing off their food source in great orgies of bloodletting and feasting.

By 8000 B.C.E., forests had replaced tundra in Massachusetts. The native peoples of the "Archaic Period" wandered less than their nomadic ancestors. They settled into hunting territories where they fished and gathered wild strawberries and other fruits. These early inhabitants ate clam chowder seasoned with artichokes, and nuts and porridge made from ground corn mixed with milk and butter. They roasted turkey and boiled bear meat.

The descendants of the Archaic Period and the Algonquians, who arrived in Massachusetts after 2000 B.C.E., transformed the commonwealth's landscape over the passing generations. To clear land for the cultivation of corn, beans, and squash, they girdled trees to kill them and they burned the underbrush. With a high canopy overhead and open ground before them, they hunted deer with ease.

Seven native Indian tribes existed in the commonwealth at the time of contact with Europeans: the Wampanoags; the Nausets; the Pennacooks; the Nipmucks; the Pocumtucs; the Mohicans; and the Massachusetts, "the people of the Great Blue Hill," who lived on a crescent of land that curved around Boston Harbor from Salem to Braintree.

Leif Eriksson explores Martha's Vineyard and names it "Vinland" (A.D. 1000).

GIVEN HIS LATE TWENTIETH-century incarnation as the devil incarnate, it's difficult to imagine anyone wanting to emulate Christopher Columbus.

In the nineteenth century, nevertheless, the admiral of the ocean sea enjoyed a glittering reputation as discoverer of the New World. So important was the status of Christopher Columbus in American mythology, in fact, that jealous ethnic groups chafed under Italian chauvinism. They proposed a number of other discoverers who were said to have arrived in America long before Columbus. These pre-Columbian explorers included overextended Phoenician traders; evangelizing Irish monks; off-course Portuguese sailors; and an assortment of lost civilizations, beginning with the tribes of Israel.

Intentionally left off this list are the Norse or Vikings. Unlike the others, the case for their having set foot somewhere in North America is irrefutable. Those who advance the theory that Leif Eriksson and his men landed in Massachusetts, however, rely on theory rather than solid evidence.

"Vinland" is first mentioned in the *History of the Archbishops of Hamburg-Bremen*, written by Adam von Bremen in 1075. The story was later elaborated in the *Saga of the Greenlanders* and the *Saga of Eric the Red*, both written in the fourteenth century.

According to the tales, Leif Eriksson, son of Eric the Red, who discovered Greenland in 982, ventured with thirty-five men in A.D. 1000 or 1001 to verify sightings of land farther to the west. He stopped first at Helluland, a land of stone, and then at Markland, a land of wood. Finally, the wandering Viking reached a lush island he called "Vinland," after the "wine berries" found growing there in abundance.

Following Leif Eriksson's return to Iceland, merchant Thorfinn Karlsefni raised a colonizing expedition of 160 men and women as well as cattle. These "Vinlanders" stayed for three years until natives, whom they called "skraellings," attacked them and drove them off. The Viking colonists were bitter at the unfulfilled promises of wine and banquets.

Even if a temporarily warmer climate prevailed in the Northern Hemisphere in the eleventh century, as scientists now believe, grapes probably never grew in Vinland. In Norse language, "wine berries" can be taken as any fruit suitable for fermenting into wine. Viking scholars Helge Ingstad and Sven Søderberg have convincingly shown, in any case, that "Vinland" probably did not even mean "wineland" at all, but "grassland" or "pasture." Ingstad's own archaeological expeditions, undertaken between 1960 and 1969 at L'Anse aux Meadows on the northeastern tip of Newfoundland, uncovered eight Norse house sites and accompanying artifacts. Surrounding the site are the grasses Viking shepherds would have prized for their cattle and sheep.

L'Anse aux Meadows, a thousand miles from Massachusetts, is the only confirmed Viking settlement in North America. If the Norse did make their way farther south, no record of their passage has ever turned up. Yet no one has yet proposed a more idyllic location for the legendary island of Vinland.

♣ ♥ ♣

Bartholomew Gosnold explores the Massachusetts coast and names Cape Cod (1602).

IN THE CHAMBER OF the Massachusetts House of Representatives, an unusual totem hangs in the east gallery opposite the Speaker's chair. The "sacred cod," carved from a single block of pine, is an enduring legacy of the commonwealth's first industry and a reminder of the role cod once played as a powerful lure for Europeans to settle in Massachusetts.

In 1497 and 1498, Venetian-born explorer John Cabot sailed from

Newfoundland to the waters off New England now known as Georges Bank, making him the first documented European to view the commonwealth's shore. Cabot reported that the cod were so plentiful, his men pulled the fish from the sea in baskets. Not long afterward, Breton, Basque, and Portuguese fishermen arrived to profit from such an easy catch.

In 1524, Giovanni da Verrazano of Florence sailed from Florida to Newfoundland in a fruitless search for the Northwest Passage leading to China and India. He stopped at Narragansett Bay for two weeks and explored inland, probably along the Taunton River. The local country, wrote the explorer to his French sponsors, "we found as pleasing at it can be to narrate....The fields are from twenty-five to thirty leagues [seventy-five to ninety miles] wide, open and devoid of every impediment of trees, of such fertility that any seed in them would produce the best crops."

By 1578, at least four hundred European fishing vessels crowded Georges Bank, Massachusetts Bay, and the surrounding seas. Sailors landed and traded with the native people but did not seriously attempt to establish permanent settlements. Eventually France, England, and even the Netherlands all made claims to what is now Massachusetts.

In the area around Massachusetts Bay, early maps showed a pointed tip of land. Profit-minded English merchants sent Bartholomew Gosnold there in 1602 in search of sassafras. The plant's root, when made into tea, was popular as a cure for the "French pox" and other Elizabethan afflictions. Verrazano's account of New England a century earlier had described abundant sources of sassafras, but Gosnold could find none of it.

On May 18, 1602, Bartholomew Gosnold and his crew entered what is now Provincetown Harbor. The men fished while at anchor and caught so much cod that they were forced to throw many back into the sea. Gosnold marked the spot "Cape Cod." On the same voyage, he also landed on a nearby island where wild grapes were abundant. He name the island "Martha's Vineyard" after his daughter.

When Samuel de Champlain mapped the area in 1607, he named the same hooked peninsula Cap Blanc for its white, sandy beaches. English power soon predominated in the region, however. Today no one remembers "Cap Blanc."

Capt. John Smith maps the coastline between Cape Cod Bay and Penobscot and names the region "New England" (1614).

POCAHONTAS MAY NOT HAVE been on his mind as Capt. John Smith cruised through Cape Cod Bay in 1614. Of more immediate concern was the poor condition of the navigation charts he had brought from England as well as the unreliable descriptions of the region he had studied. He dismissed these accounts and the accompanying maps as "so differing from any true proportion or resemblance of the Countrey as they did mee no more good than so much waste paper, though they cost me more."

What Smith saw with his experienced explorer's eye persuaded him that the area was worth visiting. He paused to trade with local tribes and went away enriched handsomely. "We got for trifles near 1100 Bever skinnes, 100 martin [skins], and neer as many others."

Throughout the 1614 voyage, the first of two he would make to the seas north of Virginia, Captain Smith measured the water's depth; took note of dangerous sandbars and rocks; and finally, he drew up "a Map from Point to Point, Ile to Ile and Harbour to Harbour." The results Smith published at home two years later as "The Description of New England." The name stuck.

On his map, Smith recorded the native names for rivers and other features, but he cunningly turned the draft over for editing to Prince Charles, a potential patron. The fifteen-year-old's suggestions for changes were inspired by the names of his own family as well as that of English geography. Among the prince's lasting substitutions were Plymouth; Cape Anna (Cape Ann); and the River Charles, which the son named for his father.

♣ ♥ ♣

The *Mayflower,* carrying the Pilgrims, arrives in Cape Cod Bay (1620).

ON SEPTEMBER 6, 1620, the *Mayflower* sailed from Plymouth, England, with 101 passengers and crew. The "Pilgrims" crowded aboard were a strict Calvinist sect who had separated from the official Church of England and were severely persecuted for their beliefs.

After living for ten years in relative peace in Leyden, Holland, these "Separatists"—whom we call the Pilgrims—decided to resettle, in America. They read with longing in Captain Smith's "The Description of New England" of "many iles all planted with corne; groves, mulberries, salvage gardens and good harbours." Holding a charter from the Virginia Company of London, the Pilgrims planned to make a fresh start in an uncharted portion of "the Northern Parts of Virginia," where they hoped to practice their religion freely.

September was hurricane season in the North Atlantic. Unhappily for the Pilgrims, storms pounded the *Mayflower.* Whether the stout ship was blown off course, as is commonly believed, or whether the Pilgrims sailed toward Cape Cod Bay purposefully (even surreptitiously) is a matter of continuing argument for historians.

On November 11, the *Mayflower* landed near what is now Provincetown Harbor. The view from the small ship at anchor off Cape Cod in late November made a frightening prospect. Those who stood on deck had endured a sixty-five-day sea voyage. They saw they would now be tested further.

"For summer being done, all things stand upon them with a weather-beaten face," wrote one passenger, William Bradford, a native of Yorkshire. "The whole country, full of woods and thickets, represented a wild and savage hue." Such terror proved too great for Dorothy Bradford, William's wife. She threw herself overboard and was drowned.

In a boat he shared with Capt. Myles Standish and other Pilgrim men,

William Bradford made several visits to shore. These trips qualified as raids, for as Bradford wrote, the hungry Pilgrims came upon Indian stores of corn and "beans of various color, which they brought away, purposing to give them full satisfaction when they should meet with any of [the Indians]."

Aware that their position outside the limits of the Virginia Company's charter put them in a precarious situation with the royal authorities, the Pilgrims drew up a substitute patent for the one they had brought from England. In a brief "compact" of fewer than 250 words, the settlers declared their intentions. "We whose names are underwritten," runs the document, "do by these presents solemnly and mutually in the presence of God and one of another Covenant and Combine ourselves together into a Civil Body Politic for our better ordering and preservation."

The American tradition of self-government was thus born with the "*Mayflower* Compact."

♣ ♥ ♣

The Pilgrims celebrate the first Thanksgiving (1621).

OF THE 102 PILGRIMS WHO sailed from England in September 1620, 50 were dead by the following May. Among the dead was John Carver, first governor of the Pilgrims, but mortality was especially high among women. William Bradford was chosen Carver's successor and would be reelected thirty times before his death in 1657.

In spring 1621, the colonists planted seeds they had brought from England as well as those taken from Indian stores. English peas and wheat withered mysteriously, but native corn and other local vegetables grew well in the Plymouth soil. From the sea, the Pilgrims fished the plentiful cod and bass. With their muskets, they shot out of the air all manner of waterfowl and wild turkey. In the deep woods, they hunted deer.

The English enjoyed the peaceful welcome they received from the Wampanoag Indians. Throughout the worst of the first winter, the native people kept a distance from their uninvited guests. Indians occasionally showed themselves, though only indirectly: When a group of laboring colonists left behind their tools to eat dinner, the valuable instruments had vanished before the workmen returned.

Finally, a lone Indian walked fearlessly into Plymouth, in March 1621. The intruder, Samoset, stunned the Pilgrims even further when he spoke to them in broken English. An Algonquian from Pemaquid Point, in Maine, he explained that he had learned the white man's language from English fishermen and often worked with them as a guide and interpreter. When he next visited Plymouth, Samoset brought other Indians with him, as well as the missing set of tools.

Among Samoset's companions that second day was Squanto, who is remembered not only for his command of English but also for showing the colonists how to use fish as a fertilizer in their fields. A Pawtuxet Indian kidnapped by English sailors in 1605, Squanto lived in England until 1614, when Capt. John Smith agreed to return him home. Almost as soon as Smith left Squanto ashore, though, the hapless Indian was kidnapped again by a captain in Smith's fleet, who sold him into slavery in Spain.

Squanto managed to find his way home again in 1619. He discovered to his horror, however, that the Pawtuxets (who occupied the land where the Pilgrims later established Plymouth Plantation) were wiped out two years earlier by a plague. The last surviving member of his tribe was forced to take up with a nearby Wampanoag tribe led by Massasoit.

When harvest was completed and stores prepared for winter, the Pilgrims decided to show gratitude to their God. They invited Massasoit and about ninety of his people to rejoice with them and share a feast. After the first such celebration in 1621, other days for public "thanksgiving" were similarly observed at Plymouth in 1623 and 1630.

"Thanksgiving" was not officially made a holiday in the commonwealth until a century later. In 1723, Massachusetts governor William Dummer recognized "the many Instances of the Divine Goodness in the course of the Year past." He issued a proclamation "to order and appoint that Thursday the Twenty-eighth of November Currant be solemnly Observed as a Day of Publick Thanksgiving."

In 1789, President George Washington proclaimed the first national Thanksgiving in America. The campaign to make Thanksgiving a permanent holiday began in Boston in 1827, when Sarah Josepha Hall, editor of *Boston Ladies Magazine*, took up the cause. In 1863 President Lincoln put "Thanksgiving" forever on the calendar.

                  ♣   ♥   ♣

William Blackstone purchases Shawmut Peninsula, the future site of Boston, from the Indians (1623).

REV. WILLIAM BLACKSTONE, TWENTY-SEVEN, an ordained minister in the Anglican Church and a recent graduate of Emmanuel College, accompanied Capt. Robert Gorges to Massachusetts Bay in 1623. The Gorges expedition was intended to establish a colony based at Wessagusset, now called Weymouth. Blackstone was to be the settlement's assistant pastor.

As with so many other early attempts at colonies in North America, the Gorges expedition is remembered only for being a failure. The surviving members limped home in 1624, happy to be leaving with their lives.

Among those the Gorges colonists left behind were several men daring enough to make their solitary ways in the wilderness: Samuel Maverick, a trader, went to what is now East Boston; David Thompson took to an island in Boston Harbor later named for him; and the Rev. Blackstone purchased from the local Indians eight hundred acres of land on a bulb-shaped peninsula called "Shawmut" that jutted into Massachusetts Bay.

From all accounts, William Blackstone took to Shawmut like Henry David Thoreau later took to Walden Pond. Blackstone had a library of two hundred books and was a skilled farmer who tended a garden and an apple orchard. His house, presumably a simple log cabin, was situated near a spring with a view of the Charles River from the west slope of Beacon Hill.

Blackstone lived on peaceful terms with his Indian neighbors. Though he remained a minister, Blackstone made no attempt to preach the holy Scriptures to them or otherwise save their souls.

In 1630, the idyll Blackstone enjoyed was shattered when a fleet of English boats sailed into waters surrounding the Shawmut peninsula. If he did not notice from his own hilltop lookout, then he learned the news from his watchful friends among the local Indians. Settlers began to build new homes in Charlestown on land across a narrow channel from Shawmut. Too late, though, they realized that their chosen site had no reliable source of fresh water.

Shawmut's solitary dweller, perhaps reluctantly, emerged to help the newcomers. Blackstone told the thirsty Puritans about his clear spring, and they accepted a generous offer to resettle on his land. The Puritans were grateful enough to their benefactor: In appreciation for his actions, they graciously made him a member of their church and "gave" him fifty acres of his own land.

As he had grown weary of "the Lord Bishops" in England, William Blackstone soon grew tired of "the Lord Brethren." Preferring his own company, he sold his remaining land for £30, purchased a herd of cattle, and packed his books.

As he had done in 1624, Blackstone wandered blindly into the wilderness again. He made a new settlement by a river, now called the Blackstone, near the present-day border with Rhode Island. The first citizen of Boston returned from his "Study Hill" only once, twenty years later, when he courted and married Mary Stephenson, a widow with a sixteen-year-old daughter. When Blackstone charged into town riding on the back of a bull, he found that where he once planted his vegetables and orchard had been transformed into Boston Common, the first public park in America.

♣ ❦ ♣

John Winthrop leads the *Arbella* and ten other Puritan ships into Massachusetts Bay (1630).

A FLEET OF PURITAN ships sailed from England in March 1630, at what was then celebrated as the start of a new year. John Winthrop, recently elected governor of the Massachusetts Bay Company, commanded the fleet's flagship, *Arbella*. During a three-month voyage, the former lawyer and country squire began a journal in which he compared himself to Moses leading a new Exodus.

In England, Winthrops were prosperous members of the gentry and owned a five-hundred-acre estate, Groton Manor, in Suffolk. In 1603, fifteen-year-old John Winthrop attended Trinity College, Cambridge, but he left his studies in 1605 to wed Mary Forth, the first of his four wives. Later he became a justice of the peace, and he was admitted to the bar in 1628.

From an early age, Winthrop was keenly religious. As a devout Puritan, he eventually became convinced that God had chosen him a member of the Elect. In 1629, the same year Winthrop was driven from the bar for his Puritan beliefs, he signed on with the Massachusetts Bay Company.

When Winthrop spotted a loophole in the company's royal charter, his fellow colonist were delighted: By virtue of a significant oversight, meetings of the "General Court" were not required to be held in England. If the charter were transferred to New England, Winthrop suggested, the General Court could hold its sessions there and be free from oversight by the Crown. The other Puritans gave his plan their support and voted him governor. He would serve the people of Massachusetts in that office for the greater part of his life.

The Puritan fleet, carrying more than one thousand passengers altogether, first docked in June 1630, at Salem, where an advance guard led by John Endicott met them. They continued on to Charlestown, where they landed within site of the Shawmut peninsula. In September the colonists renamed William Blackstone's solitary settlement "Boston" after a town in Lincolnshire where many of them had previously lived.

In a contemporary portrait by the school of Sir Anthony Van Dyck, John Winthrop makes the archetypical Puritan figure with his neat beard, stiff accordion collar, and thin, arched eyebrows. A determined and humorless man who demanded from his peers and himself extraordinary self-discipline, Winthrop was also a fearless and inspiring leader who was deeply admired by his fellow colonists and even chastised by them for sometimes showing too great a leniency. More than any other first-generation Puritan, he was the colony's moral center.

The settlers of Boston and Charlestown endured an exceptionally brutal winter in their first year. At least two hundred died from exposure, malnutrition, and disease before spring. Within twelve months, yet another one hundred sailed home to England. By the decade's end, however, sixteen thousand English settlers had made the Great Migration to Massachusetts.

♣ ♥ ♣

Boston court officials create America's first police force (1631).

HARDLY A YEAR AFTER the Puritan settlement in Massachusetts Bay began, a need to protect citizens became apparent. Thieves and other criminals threatened the public safety as well as fires and assaults by Indians, bears, and wolves.

On April 12, 1631, the Boston court ordered that for the citizens' protection nighttime "watches" be maintained from sunset to sunrise. Such watches were not considered necessary in daylight because no crime was committed at those hours.

Boston watchmen were chosen by a draft system from the rolls of property-owning males age sixteen and over. The night watch consisted of six men and a constable designated the "officer in charge." The system derived from traditional English practices known as the "watch and ward." The constable and all those who served on watches were presumed to be well-known individuals to every Bostonian. A citizen was required to obey any orders they might give.

In 1701, presumably to help identify them to anyone who might not immediately recognize them, Boston watchmen were required to carry a "watch hook," a wooden staff with a metal spike and a hook at one end. A watchman might also carry a bell, which he rang to toll the hour, announce the weather, and declare the reassuring phrase "All's well."

As Boston grew from a rural outpost in the seventeenth century to a thriving port city in the eighteenth and early nineteenth centuries, the Watch and Ward evolved an increasingly professional character. The word "police" first appeared in city records on April 17, 1783, when the post of "inspector of police" was created. In 1838 Boston established the "Day Police," with a force of six officers who wore green leather badges and patrolled city streets and docks. The Night Watch remained, nevertheless, and was indeed an independent force with a not inconsiderable sense of rivalry toward the "Day Police."

On May 26, 1854, thirty-two years after Boston had received its city charter, the Boston Police Department was organized, uniting the Day Police and Night Watch at eight stations scattered throughout downtown, East Boston, and South Boston.

Finally, in 1855, night patrol officers of the Boston Police Department turned in their "watch hooks," used for a century and half, and traded them for fourteen-inch-long billy clubs. The Harbor Police, organized in 1853 to guard ships while at anchor, were already armed with revolvers. In a city of more than sixty thousand people, crime was committed at all hours, on land and on the water.

♣ ♥ ♣

Anne Hutchinson outrages Boston clergy (1634).

FROM THE PERSPECTIVE OF three and a half centuries, important religious disputes within the Puritan church appear greatly diminished. Arguments concerning the strict primacy of grace over works even verge on unintentional comedy to the contemporary mind, but these were hardly petty matters to the commonwealth's first citizens. Church and state were inseparable for them. A dispute in the former made for disturbing chaos in the latter.

When Anne Hutchinson began holding well-attended meetings in her Boston home in 1634, during which she challenged basic tenets of the prevailing Puritan orthodoxy, the authorities' response was accordingly quick and harsh.

A skilled nurse and midwife, Anne Marbury Hutchinson was raised in Lincolnshire, England. The daughter of an Anglican cleric who had overseen her thorough education, she was able to participate effortlessly in convoluted discussions of religious doctrine and to question established authority. In 1612, Anne, twenty-one, married William Hutchinson, a merchant. They would eventually have fifteen children.

In England, the Hutchinsons became followers of John Cotton, an Anglican minister with Puritan sympathies. When Cotton immigrated to the Massachusetts Bay Colony in 1634, the Hutchinsons went, too. Moving among mostly dour Puritan women, Anne Hutchinson immediately stood out on account of her education and for what John Winthrop later described as her "ready wit and bold spirit."

With the good wives of Boston gathered around her at her home, Hutchinson launched into pithy commentaries on the minister's Sunday sermons. She discussed "dark places of Scripture" and occasionally delivered a prophecy. At her most popular, Hutchinson attracted crowds of sixty to eighty men and women.

Hutchinson's most startling claim was that the voice of God spoke to her. This admission was considered a heresy among fundamentalist Puritans, who followed only the word of God written in the Bible. The sharp-tongued preacher's daughter made matters worse by declaring a soul was to be saved by an infusion of grace, not by works. This suggestion deeply offended many, especially John Winthrop, who believed such a "Covenant of Grace" abrogated the moral responsibility implied in a "Covenant of Works."

Finally, when Hutchinson dared to suggest in 1636 that only two of Boston's ministers were qualified to preach (John Cotton, of course, as well as John Wheelwright, her brother-in-law), she was instantly cast as a revolutionary. In 1638, Hutchinson was brought to trial before the General Court. Although she did not confess to any crime, Hutchinson did repeat her heresy that God's word was given directly to her. The court sentenced her to excommunication and banishment.

Hutchinson was first removed to Aquidneck Island, now Rhode Island, and later still farther from the Puritans, into Dutch-controlled territory on Long Island Sound. John Winthrop dogged her at each step. When Hutchinson and her family were murdered by Indians in 1643, Winthrop detected the clear hand of divine retribution.

♠ ❦ ♠

The first public school in America, the Boston Latin School, is founded (1635).

AUTOMOBILE BUMPER STICKERS FREQUENTLY exaggerate the truth, but not in the case of those for the Boston Latin. "Sumus primi," the stickers declare in bold purple script—"We are the first." Whatever the current fortunes of Latin's athletic teams or its students, the boast rings true in at least one sense: The Boston Latin School owns forever the title as the first public school founded in America.

In a region thick with costly private academies and exclusive boarding schools, Boston Latin is set apart as a free public school. Its college preparatory courses are open to all Boston schoolchildren, who are admitted according to academic merit.

For generations, Latin's high standards have allowed hardworking students of every ethnic background to compete for spaces at prestigious colleges and universities once reserved to the wealthy and the well-born. A large section of each year's graduating class regularly matriculates at Harvard College. Latin remains a required course at the Latin School, and the classical education includes instruction in ancient Greek and ancient history.

Covering nearly four centuries, a list of Latin School luminaries reads like a Who's Who in American history. A very abbreviated rendering of that roster includes theologian Cotton Mather; architect Charles Bulfinch; Revolutionary War Gen. Henry Knox; John Collins Warren, a founder of Massachusetts General Hospital; Transcendentalist Ralph Waldo Emerson; abolitionist Wendell Phillips; philosopher George Santayana; Ambassador Joseph P. Kennedy, Jr.; conductor Arthur Fiedler; composer Leonard Bernstein; and author Theodore White. Also among Boston Latin's graduates are five signers of the Declaration of Independence: John Hancock, Samuel Adams, Benjamin Franklin, Robert Treat Paine, and William Hooper.

Puritan Boston abounded in the sort of self-made type who considers education mostly in practical terms as a means to success. The country's oldest public school was created on April 13, 1635, by citizens attending "a Generall meeting upon publique notice." They voted to appoint Philemon Pormort "to become scholemaster for the teaching & nourtering of children" at what was first known as the Latin Grammar School.

Boston, then a five-year-old settlement on the Charles River, already held a large proportion of industrious college graduates from the English middle class. Naturally, these men (for only men were allowed to attend college) expected their sons to be likewise instructed in reading, writing, "cyphering," and spelling as well as Greek and Latin. That there were also classes in religion goes without saying.

The Puritans recognized that learning was an end in itself, yet they were not prepared to face the consequences of a strictly free public education. The early Latin School curriculum was rigidly proscribed, and its disciplinary code promised harsh punishment for any offenders. Puritan leaders such as John Winthrop demanded conformity of thought and stifled debate.

Philemon Pormort, appointed first "master" of the Latin School, was quickly run out of his job for poor pedagogic conduct. With many other prominent Bostonians, he had taken the side of Anne Hutchinson in her divisive religious quarrel with the Puritan theocrats. In 1638 Pormort chose to leave Boston for the new settlement of Exeter, New Hampshire. The exiled schoolmaster did not establish Exeter Academy in revenge. That well-known and very private college preparatory school opened in 1781.

♣ ♥ ♠

Roger Williams is banished from Massachusetts and establishes the settlement of Providence (1636).

GIVEN THE EVERLASTING EFFORTS of certain people to return prayer to the public schools, the question remains of how strict must be the separation between church and state.

The founders of the first settlements in the commonwealth, the Pilgrims and the Puritans, would have firmly answered that church and state are indivisible, two sides of a single coin. Those who thought otherwise met with serious rebuke.

In early January 1636 the patience of the Massachusetts Bay Puritans came to an end with one freethinker, Roger Williams. A court marshal was ordered to remove the nonconformist Salem pastor from his church and to place him on a ship waiting to sail for England. The marshal's men returned from Salem to Boston without any cargo from London. Williams was ill, they said, and they believed an attempt to take him might prove fatal. A frustrated Puritan court demanded obedience, and its agents were again dispatched to Salem. By this time, not surprisingly, Roger Williams was gone, and "whither they could not learn."

Dressed in Pilgrim hat and long coat, Williams trudged alone through the New England winter to evade the pursuing Puritans—at least, so runs the legend that Williams himself encouraged. Like all good legends, it contains some embellishment.

The banishment orders for Williams, for example, were given and immediately extended, first for six weeks, then for six months. Surprisingly, John Winthrop may even have given Williams advance warning of the impending deportation order. All the while, the renegade preacher prepared to lead a spring exodus from Salem with his followers. Williams was likely caught off guard when the marshals arrived in January.

For fourteen weeks, Williams wandered without "bread or bed." He followed the suggestion of friends in Plymouth who urged him toward Narragansett Bay, where there were not yet any English settlements. In April 1636 Williams founded Providence on land he purchased from the local natives. The government he and his followers established was more democratic than any other in New England and allowed for religious freedom and civil liberties previously unthinkable.

The tolerance Williams practiced toward other religions comes as a surprise if one considers his occasionally bizarre behavior toward his own congregation. Williams frequently combined a dangerous measure of radicalism with a large dose of unrepentant Calvinism. He once insisted that women be veiled when attending church, according to Paul's first epistle to the Corinthians. Thoroughly determined to break with the established religion of Massachusetts Bay, Williams also declared those who did not profess likewise were not allowed to pray in his church.

Nevertheless, Roger Williams helped to define religious freedom in the American model. By welcoming Quakers, Anabaptists, and other dissenters to Rhode Island, Williams denied the primacy of any single faith and introduced the notion of a nonsectarian society.

The General Court establishes a "schoale or colledge," later named for benefactor John Harvard (1636).

ON OCTOBER 25, 1636, the same day it passed legislation forbidding the sale of lace for garments except for "binding or small edging laces," the Massachusetts General Court also "agreed to give £400 towards a schoale or colledge, whearof £200 to bee paid the next yeare, and £200 when the worke is finished, and the next Court to appoint wheare and what building."

The Puritans' commitment to higher education was hardly trifling, since £400 represented almost one quarter of the Massachusetts Bay Colony's total tax levy in 1636.

In November 1637 the legislators chose "Newetowne," later renamed Cambridge, as the school's site. According to Samuel Eliot Morison, who wrote the definitive *History of Harvard University*, the English-born founders were very likely thinking of Oxford and the original Cambridge when they fixed on "Newetowne." They would have believed a college required a river and that its campus should be located well enough inland. They rejected without comment a proposal to locate it on a three-hundred-acre farm between Salem and Marblehead. By contrast with the future Harvard Yard, the Salem land abutted the rough sea.

This act of 1636 directly led to the founding of Harvard College in Cambridge, though its namesake had not even left England. A well-to-do man of gentry background, John Harvard, twenty-nine, was recently graduated from Emmanuel College as an ordained clergyman and was newly married when he arrived in the colony in 1637.

In London the Harvard family owned several homes and a good deal of land. As a devout Puritan, however, Harvard chose to leave all that for the hardships of Massachusetts. Once settled, John Harvard was installed as an assistant to the local minister.

Meanwhile, after three years of planning, the new college at Cambridge opened in the summer of 1638. Throughout that fateful summer, there were "signs and portents." In June an earthquake came with a rumble loud enough to remind John Winthrop of the "rattling of coaches in London." In August a hurricane lashed the Massachusetts shoreline and was felt particularly forcefully in Charlestown, where it toppled a windmill not far from the Harvard house.

No one knows for certain, but a curious John Harvard may have visited the new campus and formed the kernel of a resolution that would earn him enduring fame. When he succumbed to consumption on September 14, 1638, Harvard had made his deathbed wish clear to several witness: He desired "to give one half of his Estate (about £1,700) toward the erecting of a Colledge and all his Library."

The next spring, the General Court resolved to name the first Massachusetts college in his honor.

Little else is known about John Harvard, and no contemporary likeness of him survives. The model for Daniel Chester French's statue in Harvard Yard was not Harvard at all, but a member of the Class of 1882, Sherman Hoar.

♣ ♥ ♠

Stephen Day publishes the *Bay Psalm Book*, the first book printed in the colonies (1640).

THE FIRST AMERICAN PRINTER in the English language was Stephen Day (or Daye), who had no known experience as a printer before he arrived in Cambridge in 1638. Day divided his time among several business interests, including working as a locksmith, prospecting for iron ore, and attempting to make a settlement in Nashaway (now Lancaster, Mass.).

Stephen Day was middle-aged and a successful locksmith and ironworker when he sailed for Boston in 1638. He had contracted for his passage with Jose Glover, a church rector in Sutton, County Surrey. In exchange for Day's labor for two years, Glover agreed to pay transportation costs for the locksmith's family and assistants as well as to purchase him equipment for an ironworks.

On the transatlantic voyage to the New World, Glover was stricken with fever and died. He willed his printing press to his wife, and she apparently entrusted its operation to Day once the emigrating group was settled in Cambridge. The only experienced printer among them was Matthew Day, Stephen's son.

As a result, historians now conjecture that Matthew Day may have done the typesetting work while his father supervised and took all the credit. Indeed, a letter supposedly written in the elder Day's hand shows him to be a poor speller (even for the seventeenth century) as well as barely able to write a coherent sentence. Despite modern doubts about his role, the General Court awarded Stephen Day three hundred acres of land in 1641 as reward for being "the first that set upon printing."

Extant copies of Stephen Day's best-remembered printed work—cited as the first book published in the English colonies—are virtually priceless today. Eleven copies are known to remain of *The Bay Psalm Book,* which appeared in an edition of seventeen hundred copies in 1640. In 1947, a single copy sold for $151,000, then a record price for a published work. No one can say how much a copy would be worth today.

A rather plain collection of verse meant for Puritan church meetings, *The Bay Psalm Book (The Whole Booke of Psalmes Faithfully Translated into English Metre,* reads its title page) comprises a literal translation of the biblical psalms from the original Hebrew by a trio of Massachusetts Bay ministers—Richard Mather, John Eliot, and Thomas Weld. The modest and typically Puritan aim was to render the psalms in a plain, unadorned style. According to Mather, the translators preferred to choose "conscience rather than elegance, fidelity rather than poetry."

The English, of course, were not the only colonists in the New World, and the matter of which really was the first book printed in the Americas remains an open question. The favorite candidate is a translation of a religious work of St. John Climacus, printed in Mexico City in 1535 and now lost. The first printed book of which a copy exists is a religious manual published in 1544, also from Mexico City.

The Massachusetts General Court requires the elementary education of all children (1642).

EVEN FROM THE VERY earliest days, public education in America was infused with social goals. A law passed by the Massachusetts General Court on April 14, 1642, noted "the great neglect of many parents and masters in training their children in learning and labor and other implyments which may be profitable to the common wealth."

The Puritans envisioned public schools as a remedy for ignorance and moral degeneracy. This was a progressive vision, but within limits. The first public school law issued in the English-speaking world mandated coeducation, but required "that boys and girls be not suffered to converse together, so as may occasion any wanton, dishonest or immodest behavior." Puritan schools were also charged to prepare students to "read and understand the principles of religion and the capital lawes of the country."

Five years later, the Massachusetts legislature took further steps toward establishment of a public education system. A 1647 law required towns of fifty families to "appoint a master to teach all such children as shall resort to him to write & reade." In addition, towns of a hundred families were required to establish a "grammar" school to prepare students for college.

The Puritans, for obvious reasons, emphasized ecclesiastical instruction over other subjects. They believed a Christian congregation should be able to read the Scriptures in their own tongue, and primary education naturally emphasized teaching children to read and write English. A preamble to the 1642 school law noted that "ye ould deluder, Satan, [wanted] to keepe men from the knowledge of ye Scriptures by keeping ym in an unknown tongue." Before this, schools in England and elsewhere were usually conducted in Latin and other classical languages.

♣ ❦ ♣

Saugus Ironworks marks the beginning of American industrial history (1646).

THE MATERIALS NECESSARY TO produce iron were easily obtained in the Massachusetts Bay Colony at the middle of the seventeenth century. Seemingly endless forests would provide charcoal for furnaces and lumber for the mills. Surging rivers would deliver energy to turn waterwheels and operate other primitive machinery. There was iron ore in abundance and, most importantly, the first successful miners could expect a monopoly on manufacturing rights for twenty-one years.

Only one problem: No one in Massachusetts knew the first thing about how to run an ironworks.

John Winthrop, the son of the governor, decided to solve the dilemma. The younger Winthrop was a canny businessman with a background in metallurgy gained at Trinity College, Dublin. He understood that English capital was necessary if the colonists were to open an ironworks from scratch. In 1641 he sailed from Boston to England with iron ore samples and the General Court's endorsement.

Winthrop scoured London for investors to join a proposed "Company of Undertakers of the Iron Works in New England." Not surprisingly, he was most successful with the city's Puritans.

Winthrop also hoped to entice skilled and unskilled workers to follow him back to Boston. He managed to sign several skilled workers for the venture, but only a few of these were devout Puritans. Regrettably, they presented a menace to Boston's moral probity.

For his unskilled laborers, Winthrop took home an especially unsavory group. John Becx, a shareholder in the investment company, purchased the freedom of sixty Scotsmen after they were captured by Cromwell's army and imprisoned. The hapless Scots now became the indentured servants of the Massachusetts Puritans, which must have seemed an attractive alternative to rotting in an English prison.

Known as Hammersmith, Winthrop's ironworks was opened at a site on the Saugus River in 1646. Miners collected ore from nearby ponds and swamps. The ore and flux, a substance that separates iron from the raw ore, were dumped with heaps of charcoal into an enormous furnace. Molten iron then collected in crucibles until workers let it run into furrows dug in sand, where the iron formed bars. The bars were shaped into tools and nails. Molten iron was also cast in molds as pots, kettles, and iron "firebacks" for hearths.

Massachusetts court records show that many of the first ironworkers were frequent visitors to Puritan courtrooms. They were usually tried on charges of drunkenness, wife-beating, foul speech, and nonattendance at church. Others married into Puritan families and adopted sober ways.

The ironworks at Saugus operated until 1668, when it was shut down under the burden of mounting debts. The Saugus workers dispersed throughout the English colonies, where their knowledge and experience formed the foundation of American industry.

♣ ♥ ♣

Boston engravers John Hull and Richard Sanderson strike the first American silver coin (1652).

PURITANS ARE SO THOROUGHLY associated with the origins of modern commerce and the "Protestant work ethic" that it comes as a surprise to learn that they were habitually short of cash. In fact, for almost a generation after John Winthrop and his band first landed in Boston, the Puritans had no money at all.

From 1630 until 1652, the Massachusetts Bay Colony practiced a barter economy. Furs, grain, dried fish, and even musket balls were all exchanged for local produce and for merchandise shipped to Boston from England.

In addition, "wampum" was adapted as legal tender following the practice of local Indians, who strung together beads made from shells and calculated their value based on the amount of time taken in making it. The official wampum exchange rate was pegged in 1640 at one farthing for a white bead, one halfpenny for a blue. Over the next ten years, however, that rate fell by half, probably owing to the large supply of counterfeit.

The moneyless Puritans were not intentionally behaving like antimaterialists. The royal authorities in London simply forbade colonists from transacting business with silver, gold, or any internationally circulating currency such as Spanish and Mexican dollars.

In the early seventeenth century, a nation's worth was calculated not according to gross national product but by the amount of gold and silver held within its borders. If an English shilling circulated anywhere outside England—in Massachusetts, for example—the mother country was considered worth one shilling less than it should be. Crown authorities strictly patrolled for any cracks in the national monetary armor. Offenders caught committing *lèse-majesté* by using or making coins faced punishment as traitors.

The "Puritan revolution" that toppled King Charles and saw him beheaded in 1649 provided a convenient pretext to overcome royal objections. They argued that if there was no king, he could not possibly mind if they carried shillings in their pocketbooks rather than musket balls.

On May 26, 1652, the Massachusetts Bay Colony General Court authorized John Hull and Richard Sanderson of "the Great Street" in Boston (at the corner of Washington and Summer streets today) as its mintmasters. The first silver coins minted in what is now the United States were barely more than silver plugs stamped "NE" on one side and XII, VI, or III on the other (with twelve pence equal to one shilling).

In a few short months, the Puritans recognized that these plain coins were susceptible to forgery as well as "clipping" or "shaving," in which a minute amount of the precisely weighed silver was removed. The legislators then decreed a second design, bearing a tree with the inscription

"MASATHVSETS IN" encircling it, and on the reverse side "NEW ENG-
LAND AN DOM" clustered around the year 1652 and the denomination.
Over the next thirty years the tree evolved from first an oak, to a willow,
then finally to a pine.

The last of these coins, the well-known "pine tree shillings," were
minted from 1667 until 1682, though the year "1652" persisted on all
coins. The wily Puritans left it as a cover for their actions. If the king ever
returned to his throne, the "obsessive date" allowed them to claim the
coins were minted harmlessly during the interregnum.

The Puritans were too careful by half. In 1684, following the
Restoration, the Massachusetts Bay Company's charter was revoked for,
among other reasons given, violating the royal right to mint currency.

> Colonial Massachusetts also holds the distinction of
> issuing the first government-backed paper money in the
> Western world. In 1690, war-weary soldiers returned
> from a failed attempt to take Québec from the French
> and demanded payment from an empty Boston treasury.
> They were eventually paid with paper "bills of credit"
> issued per order of the General Court and backed by
> taxes and fees to be collected later.

♣ ♥ ♣

Christmas is banned (1659).

THE MOST NOTORIOUS OF the "blue laws" was written in the painstakingly direct, plain style favored by Puritan legislators:

"Whosoever shall be found observing any such day as Christmas or the like, either by forbearing of labour, feasting or in any other way ... every such person so offending shall pay for every such offence five shillings, as a fine to the county."

In eighteenth-century usage, a "blue law" was one considered especially strict or rigidly moral, generally used in a disparaging sense. Another theory for the term's origins, however, asserts that an account of Sabbath regulations by Samuel Peters for his *General History of Connecticut* was printed in 1691 on blue paper. "Blue" is also a synonym for lewd, lascivious, indecent, and obscene (as in "blue movie"), and it may even be possible that the Puritans meant to ban "blue" behavior with their blue laws.

The blue laws of Massachusetts, Connecticut, and other Puritan-ruled colonies followed prescriptions set out in the Bible for the observance of the Sabbath. Ordinary work was banned as well as buying and selling goods; traveling; public entertainment; and any sports.

In the English colonies of the Puritan era, biblical law allowed the church to govern through the instrument of a secular state. Samuel Peters listed some forty-five blue laws in his history, but historians have dismissed most of these as spurious or false. Those that were indeed on the books in New Haven—and presumably in Boston likewise—included such now unconstitutional rules of justice as "the judges shall determine controversies without a jury" and "a wife shall be good evidence against her husband."

In addition, town selectmen who had determined any children in their community to be "ignorant" were given authority to "take them from their parents and put them into better hands, at the expense of their parents."

Sanctions on Christmas celebrations were lifted as early as 1681, when second-generation Puritans began to assume political control across the commonwealth. Puritan sons and daughters proved not quite so strict as their fathers and mothers in matters of religious observance.

♣ ♥ ♣

Quaker Mary Dyer is hung on Boston Common (1660).

THE PURITANS MAY NOT have allowed theater or other entertainments in their midst, but for sheer spectacle they could always take a stroll through the Boston Common. Passersby might linger there at the stocks and pillory, the whipping post, and the gallows and enjoy thrilling demonstrations of the efficacy of leather straps, hot irons, and the noose when properly used by trained personnel.

Contemporary accounts of public punishments in seventeenth-century Boston can read like the diary entries of the Marquis de Sade. William Brend, described as "a man of years," went to the whipping post and received "One Hundred and Seventeen Blows with a pitch'd rope so that his Flesh was beaten Black and as into a Gelly." Women offenders were "stripped naked [and] beaten with whips of threefold knotted cord until the blood ran down their bare backs and breasts." Luckier convicts were branded, mutilated, or simply shackled and left to starve.

Among crimes deserving of hanging was the offense of being a practicing member of the Society of Friends. Known derisively for their pacifism as "Quakers," the Friends were denounced in 1656 by the Massachusetts General Court as a "cursed sect" who were "open blasphemers, open seducers from the Glorious Trinity...and from the Holy Scriptures as the rule of life, open enemies of government itself."

One of those who successfully pushed for passage of a law banishing any discovered Quakers under penalty of death should they return was

Rev. John Norton, a pastor of Boston's First Church. Barely able to contain himself, Norton vented his righteous anger thus: "I would carry fire in one hand and fagots (kindling wood) in the other to burn all the Quakers in the world," he thundered. "Hang them or else."

Surprisingly, the Puritans and Quakers shared much in common. Both groups sought to restore simplicity to Christian practices. Both also denied the importance of sacraments and formal prayer. Like Anne Hutchinson and the "Antinomians," however, Quakers professed their primary reliance on an "inner light" rather than obedience to law or Scripture. This position put Massachusetts Quakers in open conflict with the reigning Puritan theocracy.

Indeed, Mary Dyer, "a comely and grave matron," first drew the attention of the Puritans when she took Anne Hutchinson's side against them in 1635. Later, rumors circulated that Dyer had delivered a stillborn "monster," with a witch acting as midwife. She finally left Massachusetts with Hutchinson in 1638 and lived quietly in the more tolerant Rhode Island for almost twenty years.

In 1657, Mary Dyer traveled provocatively to Boston and was immediately arrested. The authorities released Dyer into her husband's custody upon his promise not to let her speak while in Massachusetts. Defiantly, Dyer returned to Boston two years later to visit several Quaker prisoners, including an eleven-year-old girl. A Puritan court now formally banished her and made aware its intention to hang Dyer if she dared come back a third time, which the irrepressible Quaker did the following month.

On October 27, 1659, Mary Dyer approached the gallows on Boston Common with Quakers William Robinson and Marmaduke Stephenson at her side. She was bound and made to watch the men die first. With a handkerchief loaned from an attending minister, the executioner covered the woman's face before a reprieve—prepared in advance and given Dyer on account of her sex—was read to dramatic effect. Nevertheless, Mary Dyer could not be denied her martyrdom. She returned to Boston the next year and was hanged June 1, 1660. "I have been in paradise several days" were her last words.

♣ ♥ ♣

John Eliot translates the Bible into the Algonquian Indian language; it is the first Bible to be printed in North America (1663).

WHEN HE GRADUATED IN 1622, eighteen-year-old John Eliot left Jesus College, Cambridge University, thoroughly trained in written and spoken Latin, Greek, and Hebrew as well as the Bible, ancient history, logic, and public declamation. Cambridge dons had provided Eliot, the son of a prosperous yeoman landholder in Hertfordshire and Essex, with the sort of rigorous education common in Europe throughout the Middle Ages. The various skills he acquired—some obviously useful, others less apparently so—served Eliot well in the wilderness of Massachusetts.

In 1625 Eliot was ordained in the official Church of England. Over the next five years, however, the young minister drifted into the Puritan camp, where his piety and intellectual achievements were highly valued. In 1631 he sailed for the Bay Colony just as persecution of "dissenters" like himself was reaching a high pitch in England.

In the early seventeenth century, spreading the gospel was a busy line of work. Many Puritan colonists of Massachusetts Bay were determined to collect for God the souls of the country's native Indians. With unintentional irony, these Puritan preachers also thanked their God for the plague that decimated Massachusetts tribes living around Boston in the years immediately before its settlement. Puritan missionaries may have wanted Indian souls for conversion, but not so many that they couldn't properly handle them all.

As an evangelist, John Eliot took the challenge of preaching to the Indians one step farther than his colleagues. Rather than wait for the natives to learn English, which was the typical practice, the enterprising pastor of the First Church in Roxbury set out to master the native people's own language. To put it mildly, he started from scratch. The Algonquian tongue spoken in Massachusetts had as yet no articulated rules of grammar, no written texts, and no dictionary.

While philosophers and others strenuously sought to prove that Algonquian and all Indian languages were derived from Hebrew (based on a theory that one of the lost tribes of Israel had somehow managed to cross the Atlantic), Eliot brazenly puzzled it all out. He carefully listened to and penetratingly questioned Cockenoe, a young Indian who worked in a Dorchester colonist's home and spoke fluent English. With Cockenoe as his source, Eliot discovered that Algonquian nouns were not divided by gender, as in many European languages, but by a distinction made between animate and inanimate objects. He also cataloged the many inflections possible in Algonquian and decoded multisyllabic word chains.

By 1653 Eliot had published a translation of the Book of Psalms, and in 1658 he told friends that his self-appointed task of translating the whole Bible was complete. From England, the Society for the Propagation of the Gospel provided financial assistance for the ambitious printing job. The New Testament appeared from the press of Samuel Green in Cambridge in 1661, and a complete edition of Old and New Testaments was published in 1663. It was the first Bible published in North America in any language.

Mamusse Wunneetupanatamwe Up-biblum God, begins the title page. *Naneeswe Nukkone Testament kah wonk Wusku Testament.*

During the long work of translation, Eliot found time as well to preach extensively and to establish more than a dozen "Praying Indian" towns. The first of these, Natick, was created in 1650 from a grant of land by Dedham (parts of this original Natick are now the separate towns of Wellesley, Sherborne, and Needham). These settlements usually included a meetinghouse, school, and fort. The assimilated Indians lived in wigwams, farmed their own land, and chose their own leaders. In 1645, Eliot also founded the Roxbury Latin School, now located in West Roxbury.

John Eliot, eighty-six, died in 1690 and is remembered on his tomb as the "Apostle to the Indians."

♣ ☙ ♣

King Philip of the Wampanoag rebels against English colonists (1675).

WAMSUTTA AND METACOM, THE two sons of Chief Massasoit, visited Plymouth together in 1660 following their father's death. Wampanoag royal tradition demanded that the English settlers could not call the brothers by their given names. Accordingly, the colonists gave the pair names of kings from ancient Greek history: Wamsutta, the elder, became Alexander; Metacom, his younger brother, was rechristened Philip.

On their return home, Alexander died and Philip became Wampanoag chief or "sachem." In his case, at least, the son was of an entirely different cast than his peace-loving father. Philip resented the frequent summons he received to come to Plymouth. He greatly aggravated the authorities by selling his land to whomever he pleased without their consent.

King Philip explained his reluctance to negotiate with the colonists as a matter of royal prerogative. "Your governor is but a subject of King Charles. I shall not treat with a subject," he said boldly. "I shall treat of peace only with the king, my brother. When he [Charles II] comes, I am ready."

Moving inexorably toward conflict with the English, King Philip sought to forge an alliance among New England tribes. He was successful, however, only in persuading the Nipmucs and Narragansetts to join him. When he finally went to war in 1675, Philip found himself nearly alone against the colonists, but he was "determined not to live until I have no country."

King Philip's War began ostensibly as a reaction to the trial and execution of three Wampanoag warriors who had murdered a fellow tribesman for informing on King Philip's plans. Wampanoags, Nipmucs, and Narragansetts raided numerous farms and settlements, including Swansea, Rehoboth, and Taunton.

The colonists' response was predictable and harsh. The English even turned against the assimilated tribes of "Praying Indians," whom, they feared, might join with Philip as allies. Native residents of Natick and Wamesit (now Tewksbury) were transported under harsh winter conditions to concentration camps on Long Island and Deer Island in Boston Harbor.

In July 1676 King Philip's wife and son were captured by English soldiers. "Now I am ready to die," the proud sachem declared.

When a fellow tribesman suggested that the Wampanoags should sue for peace, Philip gave his answer by executing the man instantly. He could not bring himself to surrender. This last rash act cost Philip dearly. The dead warrior's brother fled camp and informed the English where the Wampanoag sachem could be found.

Benjamin Church, who had doggedly pursued Philip across Rhode Island and southeastern Massachusetts, prepared for a dawn attack. The advantage of surprise was lost when a nervous colonist's gun discharged unexpectedly. In the confusion, Philip tried to escape but was hit by musket fire and mortally wounded. The chief's body was brutally quartered and the pieces hung in trees. A Pocasset tribesman named Alderman, who had fired the deadly shots, received Philip's hand as a memento. The colonists traveled to Plymouth with Philip's head, where it was left on display as a gruesome symbol of the white man's power.

In all, some twenty-five hundred colonists died in King Philip's War, along with at least an equal number of Indians. The rebellion was the most sustained outburst of native resentment ever seen in New England—and the last.

♣ ♥ ♣

Sir Edmund Andros, governor of the New England Dominion, is overthrown in a bloodless coup (1689).

IN 1643, THE COLONIES of Massachusetts, Plymouth, Hartford, and New Haven formed the New England Confederation. When other confederation members voted to declare war on the Dutch in 1653, Massachusetts refused to send soldiers or provide supplies. There was no war, and the confederation quickly disintegrated.

Massachusetts, the largest and wealthiest of the New England

colonies, next annexed the territories of Maine and New Hampshire. In 1679, royal investigators arrived from London and ordered New Hampshire separated from the commonwealth's control. Five years later, King James II revoked the original Massachusetts Bay charter, which had given the colony a large degree of independence. The British monarch further consolidated royal influence by creating the Dominion of New England out of Massachusetts, Maine, and New Hampshire. In 1686 James II appointed Sir Edmund Andros governor of the territory.

Andros arrived at Boston in the company of a hundred British soldiers and subsequently won several important skirmishes against recalcitrant Indian tribes. The new governor angered colonists, however, when he levied taxes and usurped the power of the still preeminent Congregationalist church.

At the end of 1688, King James II, a Catholic, was overthrown in the "Glorious Revolution." The Protestant William of Orange replaced him on the throne and ruled jointly with Mary, his wife and James's daughter.

News of the "Glorious Revolution" did not reach Massachusetts until the spring of 1689. With James II deposed, Andros now had no clear authority to govern. Puritans surrounded the governor's mansion on April 18, 1689, and persuaded the powerless Andros to accept a carriage ride to the Boston's wharves, where a ship was waiting to return him home.

The euphoria across Massachusetts that attended this bloodless coup against Andros was misplaced. Despite citizens' wishes, the colony would not receive back its original charter. In 1691 King William established a crown colony of Massachusetts, which joined the Bay colony with Plymouth and the islands off Cape Cod.

♠ ♥ ♠

Salem witch trials begin (1692).

EXISTENCE OF DEMONS AND the efficacy of witchcraft were accepted facts throughout the world in 1692. The Puritans of Salem Village (now Danvers) were certain of the devil's hand in every incident of evil they suffered, from petty misfortune to appalling tragedy. Witches and other agents of "the ould deluder" Satan delivered to the people of the commonwealth all manner of torments: deadly epidemics of smallpox; murderous raids by Indians; and ignorant children.

In 1648, Margaret Jones of Charlestown was the first person executed in Massachusetts for witchcraft. A practicing physician, Jones fell under suspicion of having a "malignant touch" after certain of her patients vomited or suffered violent seizures. Prison guards testified that they watched a little child run out of the witch's cell into another room, where the apparition vanished. Trial records described Jones as "very intemperate, lying notoriously and railing upon the jury and witnesses."

The magistrates and good people of Boston were later assured of the propriety of their verdict and sentence. On the same day and time as Margaret Jones went to the gallows, they learned, "there was a very great tempest at Connecticut, which blew down many trees." Puritans required no further proof of the witch's guilt than such "spectral evidence" as this.

A thunderstorm was among the more substantial of the weird signs Beelzebub and his demons gave for their presence. More typical was "spectral evidence," which amounted simply to dreams and hallucinations. In court, testimony of the accused witch's "shape" making an appearance to its victim was the most notorious of such "evidence." Puritan magistrates took as doctrine that the devil could not assume the shape of an innocent person. Thus testimony that one's "shape" had visited the victim's bedroom was considered irrefutable.

In the winter of 1692, Elizabeth Parris, nine-year-old daughter of Rev. Samuel Parris, and Abigail Williams, her eleven-year-old cousin, began to have fits of convulsions. The girls complained of a choking feeling in their throats and that they sometimes could not see or hear properly. An invisible hand was pinching them all over and tiny marks appeared on their skin.

An unpopular minister with a notoriously cranky congregation, Rev. Parris was eaten with fear that he faced termination from his poorly paid position. The children's behavior unnerved him still further. All winter, he insisted the children reveal who or what was afflicting them.

Finally, the girls accused three women of spiritually torturing them: Tituba, a slave in the Parris household who was born in Barbados; Sarah Good, a nearly destitute woman with a reputation for being slovenly; and Sarah Osburne, a woman of property, until recently a widow, who was known for enjoying male company and who did not attend church services regularly. Under pressure, Tituba confessed: She had spoken with cats with wings and red rats who commanded her to serve them.

Now the tinderbox of Salem Village erupted and an inferno spread across the commonwealth. By the end of September 1692, at least 150 people (including many children) were arrested, and 19 were hanged. Rebecca Nurse, aged mother of eight children, was one of five witches hanged on Gallow's Hill in July despite the pleadings of her family. Giles Corey, who had earlier testified against his wife, Martha, was led to a field beside the Salem jail on September 19. To extract a confession, the sheriff laid stones on Corey's chest, and the victim was killed—"pressed to death"—for remaining unrepentant. "More weight, more weight" was all Corey could manage to say.

At last, in October, Massachusetts governor Sir William Phips threw out the validity of spectral evidence and halted further trials. Several magistrates insisted on continuing to hear witchcraft cases, but any convictions were swiftly set aside. Sense slowly returned to those in the commonwealth who, in the words of one judge, "had walked in clouds." January 15, 1697, was designated a day of repentance. The legislature annulled all the convictions, and in 1711 Massachusetts made restitution to the victims' families.

♣ ♥ ♣

During a smallpox epidemic, Rev. Cotton Mather urges Boston physician Zabdiel Boylston to experiment with inoculations (1721).

THE *SEAHORSE* ARRIVED AT Boston Harbor from the British West Indies in April 1721. Along with a cargo of sugar and other goods, the ship carried two slaves ill with contagious smallpox. In short order, a devastating epidemic began to spread throughout the city. Among a population of 11,000, nearly 6,000 people became infected with the disease, and 844 died.

At the height of the smallpox terror, Boston's wharves were all but deserted. Funeral bells rang continuously from church towers, and weary citizens complained about the depressing din. In Charlestown, the sexton was restricted to three funeral tolls daily so that the sick and their families might not be overly discouraged.

The epidemic of 1721 proved to be the worst of its kind to hit Boston in the eighteenth century, yet remarkably, it might have been even worse.

Before 1721, Boston's authorities relied on various methods of quarantine to isolate smallpox victims from the general population. A quarantine hospital was built on Spectacle Island in 1717. However, in an era when most physicians believed that disease was spread by bad air or "miasms," smallpox was only slightly checked by what were, undoubtedly, loosely observed quarantines. The infected slaves aboard *Seahorse*, for example, were brought to shore and confined, yet the smallpox spread all the same.

Cotton Mather watched the mounting epidemic with urgency. A respected if not especially well-liked minister of Boston's largest Puritan congregation, he somberly conducted funeral masses for the dead. Mather also sought to calm his son, Samuel, who returned from Harvard in June with terrifying news: His roommate had come down with the disease and died. Samuel himself showed no sign yet of having smallpox, though it was perhaps only a matter of time.

With his congregation and his own family in mind, Cotton Mather now gathered his courage. He feared the consequences of what he would say, but he feared more the consequences of silence. Boldly, Mather exhorted Boston physicians to begin a course of inoculation against small-pox, something never before tried in the colonies. In theory, inoculation initiated a mild form of smallpox, one to which the body was capable of resisting and that would leave an individual immune against other, more virulent strains.

The minister, author of *The Wonders of the Invisible World,* a catalog of witchcraft and demonry, had learned of inoculation in British scientific and medical literature. In addition, Mather had the fascinating testimony of an African slave, Onesimus, who told him how a tribal operation had miraculously left him immune to smallpox. Onesimus showed the curious Puritan a telltale scar on his arm. The Puritans had often noted that their African-born slaves rarely fell ill with smallpox.

Less obvious now than in 1721 is the great fear physicians felt over attempting inoculation without any assurance of success. If the inocula-tions backfired, they would inadvertently be helping to spread smallpox rather than providing immunity against it. The Boston physicians chose to hedge their bets. They stubbornly refused to follow Mather's advice. After all, most people recognized that the minister was something of a crank.

One physician broke ranks: Zabdiel Boylston of Muddy River (now Brookline). A survivor of smallpox in his infancy, Boylston inoculated his six-year-old son and two slaves with pus from a smallpox patient. He used a sharp toothpick and quill as his surgical instruments. All three patients subsequently had mild infections and became immune.

For a time, Dr. Boylston became a prisoner in his own home, unwill-ing to face the wrath of fearful neighbors and enraged colleagues. The brave physician managed despite the dangers to inoculate nearly 250 peo-ple, and only 6 of these died from smallpox. In Roxbury and Cambridge, two doctors inoculated 36 others. Resistance to the procedure persisted, nevertheless. In November, a bomb broke through a window in Mather's house but failed to explode. "I'll inoculate you with this with a pox to you," read an attached note.

The vicious smallpox epidemic finally subsided in Boston the following spring.

♣ ♥ ♣

Benjamin Franklin leaves Boston for Philadelphia (1723).

IN 1721, JAMES FRANKLIN, a Boston printer, began to publish his own newspaper with a press he brought from London. Franklin's journal, the *New England Courant,* became the second ever to appear in America; the first was the *Boston News-Letter,* which Boston postmaster John Campbell began printing in 1704.

The tiny *News-Letter* was printed on both sides of a single sheet of paper $6^1/_2$ by $10^1/_2$ inches, and even in its own day was considered a poor excuse for a newspaper. It carried mostly foreign news that was often as much as one year out of date. The paper's coverage of events in New England was typically dismal. Not surprisingly, the *News-Letter* had fewer than three hundred regular subscribers throughout the colonies.

James Franklin's friends at first advised him against his unusual publishing venture. One newspaper, they said, no matter how dull the *News-Letter,* was enough for America. To his paper's credit, Franklin assembled a noteworthy cast of contributors from among the literary and political acquaintances who frequented his printing shop. Their entertaining essays on local subjects quickly made the *Courant* popular with Bostonians.

As the *Courant's* contributors gathered in Franklin's printing shop to admire their published work and discuss the issues of the day, Benjamin Franklin, younger brother of James, watched with envy from his apprentice's corner. The adolescent Ben was a voracious reader who longed to write himself. His only role permitted with the *Courant,* however, was to hawk the paper through Boston's streets.

Unable to contain himself and certain that his brother would not knowingly accept his work, Benjamin Franklin finally submitted an anonymous article to the *Courant* by slipping it under the printing house door at night. The paper's clique of writers appeared as usual the following morning and examined the unsigned essay.

"They read it, commented on it in my hearing, and I had the exquisite pleasure of finding it met with their pleasure," Franklin recalled in his *Autobiography*. Several further submissions, also made anonymously, were equally well received.

When his identity was eventually revealed, it did not surprise Ben Franklin that his brother took offense. The pair fought frequently, and James Franklin never hesitated to beat his young apprentice. In the *Autobiography*, Ben Franklin observed with keen psychological insight that his brother's "harsh and tyrannical treatment of me might be a means of impressing me with that aversion to arbitrary power that has stuck to me through my whole life."

Nevertheless, when James Franklin was imprisoned for offending the authorities, Benjamin Franklin willingly took up his brother's defense in print and became temporary publisher of the *Courant*. As condition of his release from prison, James Franklin was ordered to cease publishing his newspaper, but the *Courant* carried on boldly under the name of Benjamin Franklin, publisher. "A flimsy scheme it was," he admitted, but it worked until Ben and his brother were again at odds.

In 1723, seventeen-year-old Benjamin Franklin departed Boston for Philadelphia, where he had found employment with a printer. His abandonment of restrictive Puritan Boston for more tolerant Quaker Philadelphia raises intriguing questions of how Franklin's native city might have greeted his presence in later years. The inventive freethinker he became in adulthood would likely have found himself often at odds with the commonwealth's staid establishment. By the force of his will, intellect, and *joie de vivre*, Benjamin Franklin might have single-handedly set Boston on a more enlightened course.

♣ ♥ ♣

Jonathan Edwards delivers a hellfire sermon, "Sinners in the Hands of an Angry God," which ignites the "Great Awakening" (1741).

FOR OBVIOUS REASONS, MASSACHUSETTS minister Jonathan Edwards had a speaking style known as "the preaching of terror."

"The God that holds you over the pit of hell, much as one holds a spider, or some loathsome insect, over the fire, abhors you, and is dreadfully provoked!" he roared to a presumably sweating Enfield congregation on July 8, 1741. "His wrath towards you burns like fire!"

That memorable image from "Sinners in the Hands of an Angry God" serves to condemn Jonathan Edwards as the quintessential preacher of "hellfire and brimstone." Rather than fit the accompanying image of a narrow-minded zealot, Edwards was a keen intellectual who was scrupulously well read in contemporary philosophy as well as the latest scientific discoveries. For all that knowledge, he firmly believed in the Puritan doctrine of predestination and the eternal torment of lost souls.

Jonathan Edwards was born in Windsor, Connecticut, in 1703. At thirteen, he entered Yale College, where he studied divinity and taught for most of the next seven years. Influenced by Locke and Newton as much as by contemporary religious figures, Edwards gradually developed what he called a "rational account" of Christianity. In 1729 the twenty-six-year-old was appointed to the pulpit at Northampton, considered then the most important such post in New England outside of Boston.

In his sermons, Edwards deplored the colonists for what he saw as lax religious behavior. He condemned them for their increasing distance from God and for the growing belief of free will.

Owing much to Edwards's effort, a revivalist movement known as the "Great Awakening" swept through New England and spread soon into other English colonies. Hundreds were routinely converted by making public professions of faith, which the Northampton minister firmly insisted was the only path to salvation. Edwards delivered a series of sermons in November 1734 that caused more than three hundred people to make professions of conversion, but it was not until 1740 when other preachers, specializing in "pathetical" or "emotional" sermons, set off a nearly hysterical round of mass conversions.

Hell, for Jonathan Edwards, was as real as anything could be. He did not make idle threats. Edwards spoke as plainly and convincingly as a journalist reporting from the scene of the latest famine or war.

"Imagine yourself to be cast into a fiery oven, all of a glowing heat, or into the midst of a glowing brick-kiln, or of a great furnace, where your pain would be as much greater than that occasioned by accidentally touching a coal of fire, as the heat is greater," Edwards said suggestively to his audience. Lying there in that oven, he added, there would be no end to the pain even "after millions of millions of ages."

Not everyone in the commonwealth found reason to admire Edwards and his ilk. A century after Winthrop and the first Puritans arrived to establish the Massachusetts Bay Colony, the majority of people had become at least partly secularized. They slowly grew weary of hellfire sermons and conversions. Their attention was diverted by war and by the daily concerns of business.

In 1750 Edwards was dismissed from his pulpit at Northampton. He became pastor of a frontier church in Stockbridge, where he tried with difficulty to convert the Indians. Edwards continued to publish philosophical essays and was appointed president of the well-respected College of New Jersey (now Princeton University) in 1757. In January 1758, shortly after he arrived in Princeton, Edwards contracted smallpox and died.

♣ ♣ ♣

James Otis declares "Taxation without representation is tyranny" (1761).

JUST AS THE FRENCH Revolution was known for the rallying call of "Liberty, equality, fraternity," so the American Revolution had its own slogan, "Taxation without representation is tyranny." These few words summed up directly the dilemma of colonists from Massachusetts to Georgia.

After nearly a century and a half of separate development, Great Britain expected much from the colonists and gave little in return. The colonists chafed under the rule of a distant mother country, but they dared not challenge royal authority.

When King George III, then recently installed on the British throne, issued a "writ of assistance," the colonists could withhold their anger no longer. Intended to enforce long-neglected customs laws, this writ was an open-ended warrant for British officials to search homes, warehouses, and ships for smuggled goods. Neither the goods nor the homes to be searched needed be named on the writ of assistance for it to be enforceable.

Following the end of the French and Indian War, Boston Harbor was crowded with peacetime commercial shipping traffic. Shipowners had grown accustomed during the war to avoid paying the proper duty for molasses imported for local rum distillers from the French and Dutch West Indies. The new writ of assistance, and the British determination to enforce it, threatened their livelihood.

In February 1761, several Boston merchants chose to challenge the writ of assistance in court. They hired for their lawyer James Otis, thirty-six, son of his politically powerful namesake who was Speaker of the Massachusetts House of Representatives. Highly regarded for legal erudition and for an easily provoked temper, the younger Otis refused to accept any fee for the privilege of challenging royal power in the person of Thomas Hutchinson, the commonwealth's chief justice. A notable Tory sympathizer without any legal experience, Hutchinson had received his appointment to the bench over Otis's father.

In his court argument, Otis applied several basic principles of common law and natural law. Citizens have a right to protection against forced entry as long as they behave peacefully in their own homes—in other words, a man's home is his castle. Parliament could not legally write a law that nullified any rule of common sense, which was, after all, the very basis of the unwritten English constitution. Otis further reminded the court that arbitrary acts by Charles I had cost him his throne and his head.

In an address lasting four hours, Otis enunciated many a tenet of natural law, those unchanging principles common to all human beings. One of these may have been that "Taxation without representation is tyranny," but no contemporary transcript exists to verify it. For the now legendary attribution to Otis of "Taxation without representation is tyranny," we have the word of John Adams, who in 1761 was a young lawyer from Quincy listening intently to Otis's arguments along with many others. Adams did not publish his notes until twelve years later.

In the meantime, "Taxation without representation is tyranny" became the watchwords of a growing antiroyalist faction.

♣ ♥ ♣

The Sugar Act and the Stamp Act arouse antiroyalist sentiments (1764–65).

THE FRENCH AND INDIAN War, fought from 1754 to 1763, diverted American colonists from any festering quarrels they might have with British authorities. Redcoats and their colonial allies ultimately proved victorious over the French, who had received assistance from various Native American tribes. In 1760, several hundred Massachusetts soldiers were part of a British force that successfully attacked the French outpost in Québec. The Treaty of Paris in 1763 consolidated these and other British victories. Any remaining French colonists were subsequently driven out of Canada.

Rather than reinforcing British rule in the colonies, the British triumph in the French and Indian War eventually served to undermine it. The thirteen English colonies, led by men such as Benjamin Franklin, began to see a need to unite for their common defense. In addition, George Washington and other American military leaders had received considerable battle experience; they would put such lessons to use later against their former allies.

When peace came at last in the French and Indian War, profit-minded Bostonians were ready to resume the businesses that hostilities had interrupted. The British, likewise, saw an opportunity to replenish a treasury drained by eleven years of war. In 1764 King George III signed the first of a series of tax acts that severely provoked his colonial subjects. The Sugar Act decreed a tax on refined sugar and molasses purchased from non-British sources in the French and Dutch West Indies.

In 1765 the Stamp Act sought to raise additional revenue for the British from a tax—signified with an affixed stamp—to be imposed on all colonial newspapers, legal papers, and other printed matter. Boston merchants now joined with anti-British agitators known as "the Sons of Liberty" to practice an early form of civil disobedience. The Bostonians refused to purchase or sell any tax stamps, as British law required of them. They also organized a boycott of all imported British goods. A "Stamp Act Congress" composed of outraged representatives from nine American colonies, including Massachusetts, later met in New York in October 1765.

Parliament reluctantly repealed the Stamp Act in March 1766, though the legislators insisted on reaffirming London's right to tax the colonies. The point was obviously crucial if Great Britain were to maintain effective control of its overseas territories. A year later, a stubborn Parliament passed the Townshend Acts, taxing paper, paint, tea, and other goods imported to the colonies; again, Bostonians organized a boycott.

The Sons of Liberty, with Samuel Adams as their leader, controlled an increasingly rebellious Massachusetts legislature. The General Court sent a "Circular Letter" to other colonial assemblies successfully asking them to join in the Massachusetts boycott of British goods and ships. In turn, the

Crown ordered customs agent sent to Boston to enforce its will. By the end of 1768, British redcoats of the 29th Regiment were stationed in Boston.

♠ ♥ ♣

John Singleton Copley of Boston anonymously submits a portrait for exhibition at the Royal Academy in London (1765).

THE UNSIGNED SUBMISSION TO the Society of Artists in London carried two unmistakable clues to its exotic origin.

First, a portrait in oils, *Boy with a Squirrel,* was executed on pine board of a kind found only in North America. Second, the tiny animal was a species native to the same American forests. The obvious conclusion for the society's judges flew in the face of the most powerful evidence of all: the painting's masterful style. In 1765 no untutored American could possibly have used a brush with such sublime grace.

Among those who viewed the mysterious painting was Sir Joshua Reynolds. London's greatest portrait painter hailed the maker as "a genius" and advised that the unnamed artist should come to Europe and study the masters. Benjamin West, a Philadelphia native who had immigrated to London and was a founder-member of the Royal Academy, raved, too. "What delicious coloring," he gushed, "worthy of Titian himself."

The society's rules, nevertheless, prevented exhibition of any anonymous work. At last, the artist was revealed as John Singleton Copley, twenty-seven, of Boston.

He may have been unknown to London, but Copley was already a wealthy man as a result of his great success in Boston as a portraitist. Elegant renderings of ladies wearing elbow-high satin gloves and gentlemen snugly buttoned in their waistcoats earned him a following among the city's elite and a constant stream of commissions. He also painted memorable portraits of such revolutionaries as Samuel Adams, John Hancock, and Paul Revere (the silversmith pensively regards a Revere bowl).

John Singleton Copley was born in Boston in 1738 of parents who recently had emigrated from Ireland. Richard Copley, his father, owned a tobacco shop on Long Wharf, but he died when his son was not yet ten years old. Fatefully for the boy, Mary Copley was soon remarried to Peter Pelham, an engraver, portrait painter, and schoolmaster. Pelham taught his trade to his precocious stepson. Copley accepted his first commissions when he was only fifteen.

According to those subjects who patiently sat for him, Copley was no hack painter. For a portrait, he required from fifteen to as many as twenty-five sittings, each of six hours' duration. Copley spent most of that time simply looking, and he was said to have the sharpest eye of any painter in the colonies. He made few preparative drawings; when he was ready, Copley painted directly, mixing his own colors as he worked.

Copley submitted *Boy with a Squirrel* anonymously, as a matter of pride. He held back his identity to have his peers in London judge his work by their standards, which presumably were far higher than in the colonies. The warm critical reception for the portrait (showing Peter Pelham, the artist's handsome young stepbrother) came as something of a vindication. At the same time, the businessman in Copley questioned whether he would prosper, or even survive, in London.

Copley remained in Boston and watched in confusion as the city was engulfed in political turmoil. Samuel Adams, who had posed long hours in the artist's studio, led the infamous Boston Tea Party. The tea dumped into Boston Harbor was consigned to Copley's father-in-law, an ominous note for the painter. In 1774 John Singleton Copley left his native city for London and never returned.

♠ ♥ ♣

British troops stationed in Boston fire on a rock-throwing mob, killing five men (1770).

AN ENGRAVING BY PAUL Revere that depicts "the bloody Massacre perpetrated in King Street" may be the best-loved piece of propaganda in American history. It shows a neat line of redcoats firing on a signal from their captain into a horrified crowd.

Very little about the image stands up to what is known of the events of March 5, 1770.

That late winter's evening in Boston, dozens of young men gathered to taunt a lone sentry. Snow and ice were packed on the ground along King Street (now State Street) and made convenient material for snowballs and other boyhood weapons. The pressure in the city had slowly been building since the "damned rascally scoundrel lobsters" had arrived nearly eighteen months earlier.

As tensions mounted, anxious British soldiers left a nearby barracks to aid their solitary comrade. In response, church bells pealed an alarm, and angry townspeople poured through surrounding streets and alleys. Crispus Attucks left a waterfront tavern and rounded up a group of men who wielded clubs and other weapons. Six feet tall and powerfully built, Attucks (also known as Michael Johnson) was a person of color, though historians today are uncertain whether he was a former slave, a full-blooded member of the Natick tribe, or someone of mixed blood.

Seven British grenadiers, armed with bayoneted muskets, valiantly fought the urge to defend themselves against the mob that faced them. Standing not far from the Old State House, Capt. Thomas Preston instructed his men to load their rifles, though he withheld the order to fire.

The besieged men could no longer withstand the snowballs, the stones, and the taunts. At last they began firing into the crowd. Before the first shots rang out, the Bostonians believed the British had loaded their weapons only with powder. Now several of their fellow citizens had fallen to the ground wounded, dead, or dying. Eleven men were eventually hit by the soldiers' bullets; three were killed instantly and another two lay mortally wounded. Among the dead was Attucks, the first person of color to fall in the American cause of freedom.

In the immediate aftermath of the "Boston Massacre," two Adams men figured prominently. Samuel Adams, firebrand and leader of the Sons of Liberty, organized a rally the following day at Faneuil Hall to take full advantage of the opportunity to press his demands that British soldiers withdraw from Boston. Later, John Adams, his cousin, agreed to defend Captain Preston and his soldiers, who were charged with murder. John Adams was also a member of the Sons of Liberty, but unlike Sam, he refused to see men unjustly sent to the gallows.

For his defense, John Adams relied on the testimony of several witnesses who rebutted the allegation that Preston had ordered his men to fire. The young lawyer also painted the Boston mob as provocateurs. After two and a half hours' deliberation, the jury in the Boston Massacre trial returned with its verdict: Captain Preston and five of his men were "not guilty," they declared. Two others in the dock, however, were convicted of manslaughter, and as punishment the men were branded on their thumbs.

♣ ♥ ♣

Phillis Wheatley is the first published African-American poet (1773).

IN 1761, A YOUNG African girl arrived in Boston aboard the slave ship *Phillis* and was sold to Mrs. Susannah Wheatley. Her new owner noticed that the girl was losing her front baby teeth and concluded she was about eight years old.

Over the next six years, Phillis Wheatley divided her days as a domestic servant while accepting tutoring from Mary Wheatley, the family's teenage daughter.

Phillis soon spoke English and later learned Latin. She also mastered the Bible and classical mythology.

The Wheatley family apparently treated their slave like an adopted daughter, and she was a frequent guest in the homes of many wealthy Bostonians. The Wheatleys also warmly encouraged the girl's gift for self-expression, and Phillis's first published poem appeared in the *Newport Mercury* on December 21, 1767, when she was thirteen years old. Her poem on the death of evangelist minister George Whitefield, published three years later, helped gain considerable fame for its author.

When a proposal appeared in the *Boston Censor* on February 29, 1772, "for Printing By Subscription, A Collection of POEMS, wrote at several times, and upon various occasions, by PHILLIS, a Negro Girl, from the strength of own Genius," well-read Bostonians would have discerned the author's identity quickly, but response to the subscription appeal was tepid. The notice ran again on March 14 and April 11, but the necessary three hundred subscribers—that is, people who pledged to purchase Wheatley's book when published—did not come forward.

A determined Susannah Wheatley next pursued printers in London. When one was found willing, Wheatley was obliged to overcome an unusual objection: The skeptical Englishman demanded proof that the author truly was what the manuscript represented—an African-born slave.

Eventually, the Massachusetts governor, lieutenant governor, and more than a dozen other prominent citizens of the commonwealth, including John Hancock, signed a statement attesting that the poet was "a young Negro Girl, who was but a few Years since, brought an uncultivated Barbarian from Africa, and has ever since been, and now is, under the Disadvantage of serving as a Slave in a Family in this Town." The printer was satisfied, and the author's notoriety was ensured.

In 1773 Wheatley traveled to London and was received as a celebrity by the earl of Dartmouth and other nobility. Her book *Poems on Various Subjects, Religious and Moral* was later published in Boston. At the request of influential Englishmen, Wheatley was freed soon after she returned to Boston.

In March 1776, days before the British Army evacuated Boston,

George Washington invited Wheatley to his Cambridge headquarters. A refugee of war, the poet was living in Providence at the time and there had composed a poem in Washington's honor. Ironically, the freed Boston slave and the Virginia slave owner discussed the subject of American liberty.

♣ ♥ ♠

Bostonians protest a three-pence tax on tea by throwing a shipment overboard into Boston Harbor (1773).

AFTER SEVERAL ATTEMPTS TO impose taxes on the colonists, most of which were unsuccessful, Parliament approved the Tea Act in April 1773. This new legislation was primarily meant to shore up the all-but-bankrupt East India Company.

In the bill, probusiness legislators provided the giant mercantile firm, which owed the government £1 million in back taxes, with a £1.5 million loan written on generous terms. Parliament also allowed the company a virtual monopoly on the tea trade in the colonies. Lastly, it reaffirmed an existing three-pence tax on East India's tea.

Boston merchants received word of the Tea Act with anger not only because it revived the prickly issue of Parliament's right to tax the colonies but also because its monopolistic provisions restricted a profitable trade in importing tea. John Hancock, one of the wealthiest men in the colonies, faced a considerable loss of income, and he was not alone. Urged on by Samuel Adams, the Sons of Liberty called for a boycott on East India tea. They threatened to name any violators as traitors.

On November 28, 1773, the *Dartmouth* landed in Boston Harbor at Griffin's Wharf (near today's Rowe's Wharf). The ship carried a cargo of East India Company tea as well as other commodities. Its arrival stirred the Sons of Liberty to action. Adams called a series of meetings at Faneuil Hall and organized a committee to watch the ship so that none of its tea would be unloaded.

According to customs law, the owner of the *Dartmouth* had twenty days to pay the necessary tax on its tea cargo or risk the tea being seized and destroyed. The *Dartmouth's* owner bounded over the following three weeks between near-riotous town meetings of patriots and heated discussions with the ham-fisted governor, Thomas Hutchinson. The harried merchant simply hoped to save his cargo and his ship, one way or another. It became clear, however, that the patriots would not allow anything to be unloaded from the *Dartmouth* or to leave the port.

On December 16, with time all but gone, Sam Adams gave a signal, and a crowd at Old South Meeting House began to whoop and make other warlike cries. Throughout the day, Bostonians had fanned the flames of their emotions with flagons of ale at the Green Dragon tavern. Patriots poured into the streets and headed for the wharf where the *Dartmouth* was tied beside two other tea ships, the *Beaver* and the *Eleanor*.

In a not entirely original tactic for American rebels, many of those who approached Griffin's Wharf that night were dressed as "Indians." They wore blankets wrapped around their shoulders and feathers in their hair; their white faces were darkened with charcoal.

The raiders of the Boston Tea Party behaved methodically. In three hours they dumped overboard about forty-five tons of tea but had touched nothing else. Before they left for shore, the "Indians" swept the ships' decks clean and submitted to inspections to guard against unsanctioned smuggling.

Tea from the Boston Tea Party so thoroughly polluted Boston Harbor that it clogged shipping lanes. As punishment, Parliament quickly passed legislation that closed the city's port to all but ships delivering food and fuel.

♠ ♥ ♠

Paul Revere warns colonists from Boston to Lexington of suspicious British troop movements (1775).

THE PAUL REVERE WHO rode toward Lexington on the night of April 18, 1775, was not the Paul Revere as portrayed in Longfellow's famous poem. As everyone knows, Revere did not even finish the famous ride (many Americans recount this with the sort of glee traditionally reserved for exposing frauds and cheats). Neither did Paul Revere ride alone to every Middlesex village and farm; William Dawes, Dr. Samuel Prescott, and perhaps as many as sixty other riders were involved.

Nevertheless, Paul Revere remains today an exemplary figure of early American history, a man of great artistic skill who combined personal courage with public audacity. Before he hopped astride "Brown Beauty" in Charlestown, Revere already stood in the first rank of Boston patriots.

A silversmith and metallurgist by trade, Paul Revere had published an engraving of the Boston Massacre that proved pivotal to the patriots' cause. Admittedly fanciful in its depiction of the event, the engraving was yet a persuasive tool in galvanizing public opinion against the British. In 1773 Revere joined with Sam Adams and his band for the Boston Tea Party. He served, too, as a principal rider for Boston's Committee of Safety—a paramilitary group and predecessors of the Minutemen—and had traveled to New York and Philadelphia as its representative.

On Saturday, April 15, 1775, Revere and others in Boston observed an alarming trend in British troop movements. Routine patrols were canceled, and work was begun to ready troop boats for action. The patriots surmised that the British were preparing either to arrest John Hancock and Sam Adams, who were in Lexington for a meeting of the Massachusetts Provincial Congress, or else to seize a cache of arms hidden in nearby Concord. Early on the following morning, April 18, Revere rode to Lexington to warn Adams and Hancock. The militia in Concord was similarly advised of possible trouble.

Back in Boston later that day, Revere and the Charlestown Committee of Safety established the well-known signal to be hung in the North Church tower: one lantern if the British went by land, two if they moved on the water. The signal was intended for other patriots and was useless to Revere as long as he remained in Boston.

On the night of April 18, British troop action reached a fever pitch. Revere was rowed by friends across the mouth of the Charles River to Charlestown, where he received a horse and galloped off.

According to depositions given years later, Revere reached Lexington at midnight, and William Dawes followed him a half hour later. They rode together to Concord, where Dr. Prescott joined them. Somewhere on the road, British troops halted and tried to arrest the trio. Prescott dismounted and escaped; Dawes rode back in the direction of Lexington and likewise eluded capture; Revere, on the other hand, looked down at raised pistols and wisely yielded.

The British soldiers and their prisoners returned to Lexington, where Revere was immediately released. He went once again to where Adams and Hancock were staying and was able to see them off before British troops arrived at Lexington Green for a fateful confrontation with the Minutemen.

♣ ♥ ♣

The Revolutionary War begins in Lexington and Concord (1775).

THE MINUTEMEN OF LEXINGTON assembled haphazardly on the town green in the early morning of April 19, 1775, not quite sure what they should do. They knew only of Paul Revere's warning that British redcoats in military formation were approaching the town. Several of those under Capt. John Parker's command had not even bothered to bring ammunition for their muskets.

Fate—history by another name—would eventually determine the course of the day. British major John Pitcairn called on the Americans to

lay down their arms and disperse. The Minutemen replied by falling out of ranks, but they resolutely held on to their weapons. British officers repeated the call to disarm, without success. A shot was fired, though from which side will never be clear. The American Revolutionary War had begun.

The well-trained British let fly with one volley, then another. Eight Massachusetts men soon lay dead on Lexington Green; ten writhed in pain from their wounds. Struck by a British ball, Captain Parker was finished off with a redcoat bayonet thrust. The Minutemen had returned the fire unconvincingly: One British soldier received only a flesh wound in his leg.

Quickly, Major Pitcairn led his men away to Concord, where they hoped to seize a hidden store of weapons. The British, who were swaggering now, marched to the music of fife and drum. Traveling in the opposite direction were Sam Adams and John Hancock, who had earlier received Revere's warning to flee. Adams remarked about the glorious morning, and Hancock apparently thought his carriage companion referred to the weather. "I mean," said Adams, "what a glorious morning for America."

At North Bridge, the British crossed the Concord River to take the house of Col. James Barrett, where Minutemen arms were supposedly stockpiled. When fires began in the town courthouse and elsewhere, Concord's defenders—who were outnumbered and, up to this point, had held their fire—now descended on the British companies at North Bridge. The element of surprise was in the Massachusetts men's favor, and the redcoats took their first serious casualties, including three dead (two British soldiers remain buried at North Bridge).

In short order, the British began a disorderly retreat back to Boston under intermittent fire throughout the afternoon from local militia. After nearly forty miles of marching, the redcoats ended the day where it began, though they arrived in Charlestown not half as confident as when they had departed. From there to Concord lay a bloody chain of dead and wounded redcoats side by side with American civilian casualties. At least fifty Massachusetts men were killed as well as more than seventy-five British soldiers. Several hundred altogether were wounded on both sides, with the British bearing the greater losses.

From headquarters hastily set up at Cambridge, Dr. Joseph Warren immediately sounded a general call to arms. The young general soon had twenty thousand volunteers milling about in Harvard Yard. The men were prepared to enlist in the army of a nation as yet without a name.

♣ ♥ ♣

Dr. Joseph Warren dies in the Battle of Bunker Hill (1775).

FROM OPPOSITE ENDS OF the Charles River basin in 1775, the peninsulas of Boston and Charlestown would have seemed like the pincers of a lobster poised to snap shut. Three hills in Charlestown—Breed's, Bunker, and Moulton's—afforded fine views of the North End and other parts of the nearby town center. Likewise, Dorchester Heights—a hammer-shaped peninsula farther south of Boston—commanded a clear view of Boston's flank as well as the harbor's entrance.

In June, Gen. Thomas Gage, commanding the British forces in Boston, and Gen. Artemus Ward, commanding the newborn American army from Cambridge, looked with equal longing on these positions. Any army wishing either to hold or to take Boston would find the Charlestown hills and Dorchester desirable outposts.

Responding to a call from the Committee of Safety (an influential citizens' group acting as a revolutionary government for Massachusetts), General Ward sent Col. William Prescott to a nearly deserted Charlestown on June 16. Ordered to fortify Bunker Hill, Prescott and his American troops instead began to dig their defenses at Breed's Hill. The choice was probably not accidental, for while Breed's Hill was shorter than Bunker, it was closer to Boston.

At dawn, British ships in the harbor began shelling the still-unfinished American position, but with little effect. Far worse damage was to come in the early afternoon, when a force of fifteen hundred British under Gen. William Howe landed at the Charlestown waterfront for an attack on Breed's Hill. An incendiary shell landed inland, and Charlestown began to burn.

On Breed's Hill, the American forces included Dr. Joseph Warren, recently commissioned a major general. The Yankees held their fire until the advancing redcoats came within fifty yards of their positions. The delaying tactic was prompted by a need to conserve ammunition, but it has since given rise to the legend that Colonel Prescott ordered his men, "Don't fire till you see the whites of their eyes." In fact, the remark was something of a military cliché; it was probably first made at least thirty years earlier, by a Prussian prince.

Withering musket fire slaughtered the British forces as they made their first charge up Breed's Hill. A second assault met the same fierce welcome. When their ammunition was gone, the Americans began a retreat, with British fusiliers hot on their heels. The redcoats turned their muskets and their bayonets on anyone still inside the fort.

June 17 took a bloody toll on both sides. All the British officers who accompanied General Howe to Breed's Hill lay dead or wounded. In addition, 226 British infantry were dead, 828 wounded. For the Americans, 140 had died, 271 were wounded. Dr. Warren was among the last to flee; he died from a bullet in the back that killed him instantly. Warren was buried in unmarked grave later that day on Breed's Hill, and General Howe remarked that his opponent's death was worth five hundred men to him.

♣ ♥ ♣

The *Hannah* receives its letter of marque from Gen. George Washington (1775).

IN 1775, GEN. GEORGE WASHINGTON, in command of the Continental Army at Cambridge, gave orders for the military conversion of the *Hannah,* a fifty-two-foot, seventy-eight-ton Grand Banks schooner. The *Hannah* was registered in Marblehead and had a Marblehead crew, but its owner, John Glover, chose to launch the retrofitted vessel from a Beverly wharf. As a result, both towns claim to be the "birthplace of the American Navy."

The first settlers of rocky Marblehead were probably regarded by their pious Puritan neighbors in Salem as destined to writhe for eternity in the fires of hell. Descendants of Cornish fishermen, the early Marbleheaders were likewise disdainful of their faithful fellow citizens. They had come to America for the good fishing, after all, not for the church services. And the fishing in waters off Marblehead made very good eating, indeed—which was more than could be said for most ministers' sermons.

When British forces closed the port of Boston in 1774 as punishment for the city's revolutionary behavior, Marbleheaders eagerly seized a business opportunity. The town's port was opened to all vessels previously destined for Boston's wharves. Marblehead also became a refuge for privateers who went to sea in search of profit and a bit of old-fashioned hell-raising. Local Tory merchants and British merchant marine captains were terrorized equally.

When General Washington called for creation of an American navy, John Glover, a Marblehead sailor who held the rank of general in the Continental Army, responded dutifully. He quickly pressed into patriotic service the *Hannah* and its crew. When the *Hannah* received its wartime commission in August 1775, Marblehead skipper Nicholson Broughton was commander.

The *Hannah* was not intended to take on British naval vessels but to strike at cargo ships carrying vital foodstuffs, arms, and other goods. Rather than take on the British merchant marine, which might have risked the wrath of His Majesty's navy, however, Captain Broughton preferred to commandeer American vessels. When he returned to port, he easily could claim that the confiscated goods were those of the enemy.

With another Marblehead fishing captain, John Selman, Broughton also sailed the *Hannah* to Nova Scotia, where the pair of privateers raided a village and kidnapped several people. When Captain Broughton returned with his loot and prisoners to General Washington in Cambridge, he was disappointed to find his commanding officer embarrassed rather than pleased. On Washington's orders, Broughton's prisoners were released, and the Marbleheader's navy commission expired without renewal.

On Christmas Day 1776, General Glover's "amphibious regiment" cunningly used muffled oars to row General Washington and his men across the Delaware River for a sneak attack against British and Hessian troops.

British redcoats evacuate Boston (1776).

WISE MILITARY MEN PREFER not to repeat the mistakes of their defeated predecessors. In July 1775, only a few weeks after the Battle of Bunker Hill, Gen. George Washington arrived in Cambridge to take command of the Continental Army. He studied intently the bloody lessons taught on June 17 but was not ready to show off his conclusions for eight months.

From the start, Washington faced severe obstacles in his ambition to drive the British army from Boston. The men under his command behaved not like soldiers but like the undisciplined farmers they mostly were. The Virginian patrician was appalled to find, for example, that Massachusetts militiamen elected their own officers.

In addition, Washington lacked the heavy guns necessary to threaten convincingly General Howe's and his redcoats. Ethan Allen and the Green Mountain Boys of Vermont had captured British cannons at Ticonderoga in May 1775. If those powerful guns could be brought to Boston, Washington would have his arsenal.

Accordingly, Gen. Henry Knox of Boston, formerly a bookseller, was dispatched to handle the formidable task. He chose to wait for winter snows and then transported the more than fifty pieces of heavy artillery on sleds hauled by teams of oxen. In three months, Knox—a large man who resembled something of an ox himself—had successfully completed the journey of more than two hundred miles from Ticonderoga.

While he waited for Knox, Washington felt the sting of public criticism for his inaction. At last, in February 1776, he was prepared to strike at his enemy across the Charles River. Washington's study of the Battle of Bunker Hill told him that Colonel Prescott might have fared better if his partially constructed fortifications hadn't failed to hold back the full brunt of the British attack. With the help of Col. Rufus Putnam, Washington ordered a kind of ready-made fort to be prepared for transportation to Dorchester Heights in easy-to-assemble sections.

American forces presented an astonishing sight to General Howe on the morning of March 5. The British commander found himself staring at a line of well-made fortifications completed seemingly overnight on Dorchester Heights. Rear Adm. Molyneaux Shuldham, commanding the Royal Navy in Boston Harbor, warned Howe that his ships could not remain long as sitting targets of any heavy guns placed on the heights. A frustrated General Howe chose to abandon his positions at Boston.

On March 17, 1776, the last British ship loaded with men and supplies pulled away from Boston's docks to positions elsewhere in the colonies. A tacit agreement was reached with the American forces to allow the redcoats to evacuate the town without disruption as long as they would not burn it.

Across the colonies, George Washington was hailed for achieving a bloodless victory that freed forever the seat of the American rebellion. Among other honors, the Virginian received an honorary doctorate of laws from Harvard College.

♣ ♣ ♣

John Adams drafts the Constitution of the Commonwealth of Massachusetts (1780).

 "ALL MEN ARE BORN free and equal," declares the first article of the Constitution of the commonwealth of Massachusetts. That simple statement—drawn up by John Adams under the influence of Locke and Rousseau and amplified since by the experience of two centuries—has proven immensely powerful. With seven words, its author shifted forever the balance of political power from a few who ruled by divine right to the many who ruled themselves by human right.

In a true revolution, nothing remains of the past. The American Revolution—in which a group of colonies for the first time had removed themselves from the power of a distant monarch—theoretically left the new country without laws or government. Perhaps not surprisingly, men such as Adams, Franklin, Jefferson, and others in the new country's ruling class showed reverence toward the past. They greatly admired the Roman republic and Athenian democracy, too.

These men of British descent also cherished the mother country's unwritten constitution and its common law. As the Declaration of Independence makes clear, any argument with England was not with its people or its traditions but with the king ("He has refused his Assent to Laws...He has obstructed the Administration of Justice... He has plundered our Seas...").

Those appointed with the responsibility to make laws for the new country realized that if the British system had any flaw, it was that the constitution was unwritten. By setting out on paper the limits of a government's power, they would address this problem.

Massachusetts became the first colony to wrestle with creating a suitable written constitution. In 1778 the legislature prepared a document, which was then submitted to the public for approval. Voters defeated this first constitution by a substantial five-to-one margin. They rejected it not so much for what it said but for what was left unsaid. Newburyport's

Why a Commonwealth?

Blame John Adams. The state constitution, as he wrote it in 1780, was specifically a "declaration of rights and frame of government [for] the commonwealth of Massachusetts." Adams owed the term to Thomas Hobbes and John Locke, English political philosophers who described the body politic as the "commonwealth" or "commonweal" (in Old English, the common "weal" was the common good or common welfare). "Commonwealth" was also the name given to the antiroyalist republican regime led by Oliver Cromwell that ruled Great Britain from the execution of King Charles I in 1649 until the restoration of Charles II in 1660. In English politics, "a commonwealth" came to evoke the notion of a government by the people rather than an aristocracy.

In 1789 the framers of the U.S. Constitution modeled their document extensively on the Massachusetts Constitution. It specifically charges the federal government, for example, with a responsibility to "promote the general welfare," or in other words, "the common weal." The first ten constitutional amendments, collectively the Bill of Rights, echo Massachusetts's own Bill of Rights.

Among the fifty states, Massachusetts, along with Kentucky, Pennsylvania, and Virginia, are officially "commonwealths," though the title confers no legal distinction from the others.

Theophilus Parsons published a pamphlet listing the most important omissions, including a Bill of Rights, separation of powers, and religious freedom.

In addition, the constitution-writing process was seen as less than the ideal. Rather than allow an ordinary legislature to draft a constitution for their vote, the people preferred to choose a special body for that purpose. A group of 293 delegates to a constitutional convention were chosen in a vote by all Massachusetts men over twenty-one years (the first time those without property had received the franchise).

The Massachusetts Constitutional Convention gathered for the first time in Cambridge on September 1, 1779. Among their number were Samuel Adams, Robert Treat Paine, and James Boudoin as well as John Adams and Theophilus Parsons. A vote by committee gave John Adams much of the editorial responsibility. He submitted a draft in time to leave for Holland, where he was sent as his country's ambassador. Throughout the spring of 1780, at town meetings across Massachusetts, voters examined the document clause by clause and ultimately gave their approval.

The inclusion in the Massachusetts constitution of a Bill of Rights substantially influenced the drafting of the first ten amendments to the U.S. Constitution seven years later. The United States, however, would take far longer to follow the commonwealth's lead in abolishing slavery. Those opening words, "All men are born free and equal," were quickly interpreted to include slaves. Several lawsuits successfully challenged the constitutionality of slavery in Massachusetts. By 1790 a census found no slaves living anywhere in the commonwealth.

♣ ♥ ♠

The *Empress of China* leaves Boston port, beginning China trade (1784).

A PROUD DANIEL PARKER and his business partners touted their new boat in heroic terms in a report to their insurance agents: "She was Built in Boston under the direction of the Celebrated Mr. Peck on a Model that is universally acknowledged in this Country to be greatly superior to any other." Such a boast might help keep down the premium costs, but the

Empress of China needed to prove Parker and the others right if they were going to reap any profit from their investments.

For the great ship's durability, the owners banked not on their own publicity but on the design skill of "the celebrated" John Peck. Boston's master shipwright, who had no formal training in this area, relied not on formally drafted plans but on his practical experience and the craftsman's intimate knowledge of form and function. The ship's owners proclaimed the results: "She is entirely New, Stout, Staunch & Strong," they declared, "her Bottom was Coppered in Boston with great attention & Care & her Hull is as fully Strongly & Compleately finished as this country is capable of doing it."

In November 1783 the *Empress of China* left its shipyard dock for New York to meet captain, crew, and cargo. When the boat finally sailed past Fort George, New York, in February 1784, it already enjoyed a reputation as "an exceeding swift sailor."

The first time out, the *Empress of China* would be well tested. Capt. John Green planned to take the 400-ton vessel and crew of 42 sailors on a southeasterly course past the Cape of Good Hope in South Africa, north through the Indian Ocean, and finally into port at Canton, at the South China Sea. Altogether, Green anticipated a grueling 180-day, 18,000-mile voyage.

Deep in the enormous boat's hold lay a precious cargo of ginseng root, fifteen tons in all. The supposedly medicinal plant was one of the few products from the Western world that interested Chinese merchants. The Chinese believed that ginseng root soothed nerves, lengthened life, and cleared up acne. In May 1785, fifteen months after departing New York, the *Empress of China* returned laden with what Americans and Europeans treasured even more than a long life and a good complexion: silk and jade. And China was open for business.

"The China trade" was conducted from the commonwealth's busy wharves at Boston, Salem, and Newburyport. Merchants' attention slowly began to shift from Europe and the West Indies to Africa and the Far East. Massachusetts's boats became frequent visitors to Cape Town,

Zanzibar, and Burma. As the eighteenth century ended, Salem's captains briefly cornered the world market in black pepper. In contemporary terms, such a trading coup was as valuable as holding an international franchise on silicon chips.

By terms of a 1638 treaty with the Japanese, the Dutch enjoyed exclusive right to trade with that otherwise impenetrable island nation. An ongoing conflict with the British, though, stymied this commerce until the Dutch decided to contract with neutral country boats to avoid King George's wrath. In 1797 the Dutch hired the *Eliza,* a New York vessel, to sail to Nagasaki under the U.S flag. When it was partially sunk in a storm, the American ship became trapped in the Japanese port. The crew refloated the ship, but anxious Dutch merchants, who went for a long period without any news of the *Eliza's* fate, decided to hire a second boat, the *Franklin,* of Salem. The *Franklin's* officers agreed to make the risky voyage for a $30,000 fee to be paid them in coffee, black pepper, cloves, indigo, tin, cinnamon, and nutmeg.

On July 18, 1799, the *Franklin* was escorted into Nagasaki according to strict ceremonial dicta. The American flag was lowered and a Dutch flag raised in its place on the Salem boat's mast. Various gun salutes were exchanged before Japanese officials finally boarded the *Franklin* and presented gifts of fish to the crew.

The Japanese soon got down to business. They instructed the captain to collect from his sailors all their money, and the Americans were prohibited from buying anything while in Japan. In addition, all books on board were gathered up and locked away safely in a trunk until the boat's departure. The Japanese feared that the written word of foreigners might escape and invade their country with the same effect as a conquering army.

♣ ♧ ♣

Daniel Shays leads a revolt against the state and federal governments (1786).

MASSACHUSETTS RELIED INCREASINGLY ON merchant trade for its wealth as the eighteenth century ended, but subsistence agriculture remained the bedrock of its economy. In the years just after the Revolution, "yeomen" farmers made up 70 percent of the rural population. When those farmers faced financial ruin and foreclosure in the depression that followed the signing of a peace treaty with England in 1783, everyone in the commonwealth felt the shock.

Peasant rebellions appear regularly in medieval and modern European history and usually are bellwethers of economic hardship. When deprived farmers have seen enough of their families and friends starve or be driven off their land, insurrection becomes a means to achieve justice or, at least, a measure of revenge.

In 1785 the commonwealth's legislators toed a line drawn by Boston merchants and revoked the legal tender of Massachusetts's paper money. As a result, all debts, including those for taxes, were to be paid only in silver or gold coin. Farmers, who usually paid debts in produce and could not easily come up with the required "specie," found themselves hauled into court by creditors.

At the hands of unsympathetic judges, hundreds of farmers suffered the indignities of foreclosure and property loss. Desperate yeomen in five counties near Springfield took arms in the summer of 1786 and marched to prevent several courthouses from opening. Among those leading the insurgents was Thomas Shays, who had served with distinction in the Revolution, fighting at Lexington and in the Battle of Bunker Hill as well as at Ticonderoga, Stony Point, and Saratoga. Many in his ranks, who were called "Shaysites," were war veterans aware that power flows from the barrel of a gun.

In January 1787 Shays approached the Springfield federal arsenal with twelve hundred men. The farmers' goal was to overthrow the

Massachusetts state government, and the arsenal's cache of muskets, powder, shot, and shell made a logical target. As the rebels charged, loyal militiamen fired their cannons. Four farmers fell dead; another twenty were wounded. The survivors quickly broke ranks.

For another month, the yeoman insurgents moved like a guerrilla army. They raided the stores of hated shopkeepers and played cat and mouse with the state militia. After defeat in a clash with troops in Petersham, Shays escaped across the border to Vermont, which was then an independent republic. The rebellion disappeared with him. Shays was later condemned to death along with thirteen other rebel leaders, but he and the others were eventually pardoned and returned to their farms.

♣ ♥ ♣

Charles Bulfinch supervises construction of the Massachusetts State House (1795).

WHEN JOHN WINTHROP FAMOUSLY declared that New England should be "as a city upon a hill," he envisioned that Puritan Boston would serve as a moral beacon for the world. Beacon Hill was named in a more literal sense, however, for a torch left blazing at its summit that guided ships safely into Boston Harbor. For the past two centuries, the promontory's only true beacon, moral or otherwise, has been the spectacular dome of the Massachusetts State House.

At a ceremony on July 4, 1795, fifteen white horses (representing the fifteen states in the Union that year) drew a cart that carried the new State House cornerstone to the top of Beacon Hill. Massachusetts governor Samuel Adams and fellow patriot Paul Revere laid the stone in place as Charles Bulfinch watched. The young architect had waited eight years to see the work begin.

Bulfinch, a Boston native and son of one of the city's wealthiest families, studied at Harvard College during the Revolutionary War period and graduated in 1781. Dr. Thomas Bulfinch dissuaded his son from taking up the practice of medicine, and at least until 1789, Charles Bulfinch's occupation appears in the town directory only as "gentleman."

From 1785 to 1787 Bulfinch traveled through Europe on an inheritance. At the suggestion of Thomas Jefferson, he toured the major architectural sites of France and Italy and was especially impressed by late Georgian London.

In November 1787, not long after returning to Boston, Bulfinch, then barely twenty-four years old, boldly submitted "a plan for a new Statehouse" to a legislative committee that was charged "to consider a more convenient Place for holding the General Court." The architect's inspiration for the State House design was likely Somerset House in London, a government building designed by Sir William Chambers in 1778 in a symmetrical style Bulfinch greatly admired. Bulfinch's plan languished until the commonwealth's legislature finally gathered enough courage to approve it in February 1795. In the meantime, Bulfinch successfully designed the Connecticut State House (now Hartford City Hall) and was becoming well regarded for his elegant, neoclassical work.

When he designed the Massachusetts State House, Bulfinch did not have Beacon Hill specifically in mind as the site. Boston was not even guaranteed to remain the Massachusetts state capital, certainly not if Worcester or Plymouth could persuade legislators otherwise. Before 1790, Beacon Hill was a wilderness at the city's edge. That year, Charles Bulfinch designed and erected on its summit an attractive "Memorial Column" commemorating the Revolution, and in 1791 Dr. John Joy commissioned him to design the first of many Beacon Hill homes.

The direction of the city's growth shifted enough even for the Massachusetts General Court to take notice. In 1795, Boston purchased John Hancock's pasture on the south face of Beacon Hill and designated it as the site of the new capitol building. The General Court appropriated £8,000 for the building's construction, but Bulfinch knew better. "My own experience," he warned, "has convinced me of the fallacy of estimates in general, and especially in buildings of a public nature." His concern was justified when the final bill came to more than four times the original estimate.

In January 1798 a ceremonial procession marched from the old State House up Beacon Street, with Bulfinch prominently at the front. The seat of government was officially transferred, and the commonwealth had closed one chapter of its history only to open another.

Charles Bulfinch is today recognized America's first full-time architect. From 1817 to 1830 he served as fourth in a line of architects of the U.S. Capitol.

♣ ♣ ♣

John Adams is elected second president of the United States (1796).

IN 1796 JOHN ADAMS prepared to vacate a government post he had grown to despise. The vice presidency, he wrote his wife, Abigail, was "the most insignificant office that ever the invention of man contrived or his imagination conceived." With General Washington unwilling to run for a third term, the nation's first vice president was chosen to serve as its second president, a decidedly significant office. Circumstances ensured, however, that John Adams enjoyed the power of his new position even less than the inconsequence of his last. As his vice president, John Adams was saddled with Thomas Jefferson, a former friend turned hated enemy who dogged the president's every political step. His party, the Federalists, eventually turned on Adams, too. The unpleasant experience of finding opponents on all sides made it a foregone conclusion that John Adams would be the first incumbent president turned out of office. In 1800 Jefferson swept into the White House on a landslide vote, and a dour Adams retired to Massachusetts.

John Adams was a difficult to man to like. He was variously considered rude and overbearing, jealous and spiteful, vain and self-important. Doubtless the man had some attractive qualities; after all, few husbands are as beloved of their wives as John was of Abigail.

The peripatetic John Adams was often away from home, sometimes for years at a time (he was a commissioner of the revolutionary government to France; he negotiated peace terms with the British in Ghent; and he served as America's first ambassador to the Court of St. James's in London). Remaining behind with their four children, Abigail Adams managed the family farm in Braintree and maintained a correspondence with her absent mate that forms the Ur text of American feminism. In 1776, when John Adams was a delegate to the Continental Congress in Philadelphia, his wife famously asked him to consider the cause of liberty from a previously neglected angle.

"Remember the ladies," Abigail Adams pleaded. "Be more generous and favorable to them than your ancestors. Do not put such unlimited power in the hands of the husbands. If particular care and attention is not paid to the ladies, we are determined to foment a rebellion, and will not hold ourselves bound by any laws in which we have no voice or representation."

Women's rights were not Abigail Adams's only concerns; she also expressed abhorrence of slavery and a great admiration for public education. As First Lady, she helped move the young American government to its permanent home in Washington. In 1800 the Adams family was the first to live in the still-unfinished White House.

John and Abigail's eldest son, John Quincy Adams, grew up at his father's side and traveled widely throughout Europe. President Washington appointed the young Adams ambassador to the Netherlands in 1794 when he was not yet twenty-seven years old. Later, as ambassador to Prussia, Russia, and the United Kingdom, he earned a reputation as America's greatest diplomat.

In 1817 John Quincy Adams returned to America to become President James Monroe's secretary of state. Despite the name, the Monroe Doctrine of 1823 was principally Adams's work. In 1824, like his father before him, John Quincy Adams went to the White House with lackadaisical public support. Like his father, too, he was sent packing from the capital after serving a single four-year term.

In the political world of the commonwealth, however, the Adams name still carried weight. Two years after leaving Washington, John Quincy Adams returned there, not as resident of the White House, but as a member of Congress from the district of Quincy, Mass. He shrugged off suggestions that the action was demeaning to the presidency and he set about becoming a constant thorn in the side of congressional proponents of slavery.

For the next dozen years, John Quincy Adams fought the various gag rules preventing citizens' petitions from being heard in the House of Representatives. In 1837 he daringly presented an abolitionist petition from twenty-two slaves and was threatened with censure. In 1841 a group of Africans mutinied on a Spanish slave ship and brought the vessel to New York; instead of receiving the freedom they expected, the Africans were arrested and threatened with return to their masters. Adams successfully defended their case in the U.S. Supreme Court.

As he delivered a speech against the injustices of the Mexican-American War, John Quincy Adams collapsed on the House floor and died in a congressional office two days later, February 23, 1848.

Other distinguished members of the Adams family include John Quincy's son, Charles Francis Adams, who as President Lincoln's ambassador to the United Kingdom won the important struggle to maintain that nation's neutrality in the Civil War (three generations of Adams men served their country at the Court of St. James's—John Adams, John Quincy Adams, and Charles Francis Adams); also Charles's son, Brooks Adams, a historian who accurately predicted that the world would one day be divided between the superpowers of Russia and the United States; and Henry Adams, another son of Charles Francis Adams, who admitted in his autobiography that as a child he expected to become president of the United States one day as a matter of birthright. For the failure of this to occur, Henry Adams appropriately blamed democracy.

♣ ♥ ♠

The "gerrymander" appears in a political cartoon condemning a legislature redistricting plan (1812).

OF ALL THE STRANGE politic animals to roam the commonwealth, few have ever made a more enduring mark than the "gerrymander."

The sighting of this editorial cartoon appeared in 1812, when the Republican-controlled Massachusetts state legislature voted to rearrange the commonwealth's voting districts. To suit their political ends, Gov. Elbridge Gerry and his fellow Republicans (a party then in its progressive, Jeffersonian incarnation) carved out an inelegantly shaped district of a dozen North Shore towns. In the new district, voters of Republican-dominated Marblehead made a majority over Federalists in Chelsea, Lynn, Danvers, Lynnfield, Andover, Methuen, Haverhill, Amesbury, and Salisbury.

It took little enough imagination to realize that the contorted new district was a bald attempt by Republicans to shape the next election's outcome. It was left to Elkanah Tisdale, an engraver, however, to see in the curious arrangement of towns on a map a creature resembling a salamander. Tisdale drew this beast, "the Gerry-Mander," and gave it clawed feet, wings, and fangs. He published his drawing as a political cartoon in the *Boston Weekly Messenger,* an act that forever after changed the American political lexicon.

To "gerrymander" is to manipulate the boundaries of a constituency to give undue influence to some party or class. Gerrymandering essentially attacks two fundamental principles of democratic rule applied to electoral districts: compactness and equality of size. Wherever any legislature gathers to create voting districts, the gerrymander rears on its clawed feet and bares its fangs. The temptation to ignore local boundaries and even the principle of "contiguity" in favor of partisan interests is, and always will be, too great to resist.

Moreover, gerrymandering works. In 1812, only eleven Federalist state senators were elected in the commonwealth against twenty-nine Republicans, even though the Federalists outpolled the Republicans statewide. The infamy of his association with the gerrymander, however, forced Governor Gerry from the state house. He was not idle for long; later that same year, former governor Gerry, who was a signer of the Declaration of Independence for Massachusetts, was elected vice president on the winning Republican ticket with John Madison.

♣ ♥ ♠

U.S. frigate *Constitution* earns its nickname "Old Ironsides" (1812).

IN OCTOBER 1797 THE young American Navy's newest frigate, the *Constitution,* was ready for launching at the Hartt Brothers Shipyard in Boston.

The great boat was the largest American warship yet built and was designed to carry 44 massive guns, though it typically had more than 50. At 204 feet long and with a displacement of 2,200 tons, the *Constitution* was longer and heavier than any other ship of its kind. Paul Revere had cast the bolts fastening its timbers as well as the copper sheathing for the boat's bottom.

The freshly painted *Constitution* descended the long launching cradle leading into the harbor on greased wooden planks that smoked from the tremendous friction. Suddenly the ship squealed to a stop only halfway to the water. Three more tries were required before the *Constitution* was safely afloat.

According to sailing superstition, a launching mishap portended bad luck for the boat. Nevertheless, the *Constitution* gallantly survived several wars and narrowly escaped more menacing threats of dismantling. Today it is the oldest commissioned warship in the world.

The beginning of the nineteenth century saw American merchant ships become the hapless prey of pirates, particularly from the Barbary states on the northern coast of Africa. Bandits from Tripoli regularly seized American ships and held the crews for ransom. In 1802 Congress finally declared a state of war with the Tripolitans and ordered their ports blockaded.

A still young *Constitution*, as yet untried in battle, arrived at Gibraltar in September 1803. There the frigate joined a growing fleet of navy warships patrolling in the Mediterranean.

With Commo. Edward Preble commanding, the *Constitution* proceeded to blockade Tripoli. Its cannons sent several punishing bombardments into the city and helped to wear down Barbar resistance. In June 1805 officials signed a treaty of peace directly on the decks of the *Constitution*.

When Congress again declared war, in 1812, this time against the British, the *Constitution* was to gain immortal fame in a contest with the *Guerrière*, a Royal Navy frigate.

On August 19, the *Guerrière* was eager for a duel and approached the Constitution at pistol firing range. An American sailor watched a British cannonball bounce off the *Constitution* and exclaimed, "Good God, her sides are made of iron!" Then the *Constitution* let loose with a ruthless broadside. The British boat continued to wrestle with the American ship but never fully recovered. In an hour's time the *Guerrière* surrendered.

The reputation of "Old Ironsides" grew with each passing victory. In three major engagements during the War of 1812, the *Constitution* captured four British ships. The Royal Navy finally capitulated to the Americans in 1815.

Even before the age of planned obsolescence, the thirty-one-year-old *Constitution* faced possible scrapping in 1828. A Department of the Navy survey had compared costs for extensive repairs necessary on the frigate with those for construction of an entirely new ship and found the *Constitution* an expensive floating monument. The report was leaked to the press and an outcry ensued.

In a poem first published in the *Boston Advertiser,* Oliver Wendell Holmes summed up public sentiment. "The meteor of the ocean air/Shall sweep the clouds no more," despaired the poet. "The harpies of the shore shall pluck/The eagle of the sea!" The navy relented and the *Constitution* continued its useful life, first on diplomatic duty and later as a training ship.

In 1927, following a public fundraising campaign that was abetted by a Hollywood feature, *Old Ironsides,* starring Wallace Beery, the great old frigate was entirely restored. The *Constitution* now approaches its two hundredth birthday in a permanent berth at Charlestown.

♣ ♛ ♣

The American Industrial Revolution begins with steam-powered looms in Waltham (1814).

NINE MILES WEST OF Boston, Waltham in 1813 was still an obscure village on the banks of the Charles River. What transformed Waltham in just a few short years would eventually transform the United States and the world: the technology of the power loom, which made possible the Industrial Revolution.

It may be said with some truth that Robert Cabot Lowell carried the battle plans for the American campaign of the Industrial Revolution in his head. In 1810 the prosperous Massachusetts merchant traveled to Great Britain with his family. He toured Manchester, a river city whose mills hummed with activity by workers who produced vast quantities of quality textiles for markets around the world and generated sumptuous profits for the mill owners. His hosts little suspected that Lowell was too interested an observer by half.

When Lowell returned home after two years, the sharp-eyed Yankee had memorized the intricate workings of Manchester's great power looms.

He and a group of investors, including his brother-in-law Patrick Jackson and Nathan Appleton, formed the Boston Manufacturing Company. English law forbade the export of manufacturing equipment or the emigration of anyone trained to operate it. To build a mill complex in Waltham, the Boston Manufacturing Company hired Paul Moody, a local mechanic who could construct what Lowell had seen and could describe.

In 1814, the country's first power loom became operational under the single roof of a fully integrated mill. The "Waltham-Lowell" system proved wildly successful. A second mill opened in 1819. A bleachery and an iron foundry; a research laboratory and even a crayon factory soon followed.

Almost as quickly as Waltham grew, however, the limitations of the Charles River as a power source became apparent. The officers of the Boston Manufacturing Company looked elsewhere for an appropriate development site for still more mills. They settled on East Chelmsford, where the Merrimack and Concord rivers met at Pawtucket Falls.

In 1796, Newburyport merchants interested in shipping timber downriver for their shipbuilding enterprises had underwritten construction of the Middlesex Canal at East Chelmsford. The canal's system of locks and aqueducts led twenty-seven miles to the Mystic River; along it, horse-drawn barges hauled goods to market. A sawmill, glassworks, and woolen mill were opened at East Chelmsford to take advantage of the convenience the new waterway afforded their businesses. In 1821 the Boston Manufacturing Company purchased the Middlesex Canal and surrounding farmland between the canal and the river. A factory town, each element precisely planned and laid out, quickly rose up.

Mills, canals, stores, and housing were built as well as a church (Episcopalian) and a company cemetery. The workday began at five in the morning and ended fourteen hours later. Men received up to $8 a week for their labor. Women, newly entered into the workforce, were paid half the men's wages.

On March 1, 1826, East Chelmsford was renamed Lowell in honor of the Boston Manufacturing Company's founder. The Waltham Watch

Company, manufacturers of the first machine-made watches in the United States, opened in 1854, and by century's end, Waltham was known as "Watch City." The Boston Manufacturing Company went into receivership in 1929 at the start of the Great Depression. Today the no. 1 mill (built in 1813) is site of the Charles River Museum of Industry.

♣ ❦ ♣

The Handel & Haydn Society presents its first concert on Christmas Day (1815).

AN END TO WAR is always a fitting occasion for a celebration. In 1815 Bostonians welcomed conclusion of a three-year war against Great Britain with a festive concert from the fledgling Handel & Haydn Society.

In the early nineteenth century, the commonwealth had limited musical resources. Choirs and singing groups were organized beginning in 1786, with the Stoughton Musical Society, but these performed mostly in churches. Boston boasted only two professional musicians in 1815: Gottlieb Graupner, a German-born piano teacher, and Dr. George K. Jackson, British-born organist of Trinity Church. Graupner had played oboe in London at performances of Haydn symphonies conducted by the composer. In Boston he taught piano, sold music from a shop on Franklin Street, and operated a small concert room. Jackson was educated at St. Andrews' College and held a doctoral degree in music.

On Christmas Day 1814, U.S. and British negotiators at Ghent agreed to terms of peace and ended what was known as the War of 1812. The news did not reach America, however, for another seven weeks. On

February 13, 1815, thirty-two hours after messengers left New York, Boston finally learned of the treaty.

The city responded wildly, with spontaneous parades and fireworks displays. In churches and public halls, people gathered to pray and celebrate. A previously scheduled concert of sacred music by the Second Baptist Singing Society for February 16 included the "Hallelujah!" Chorus from Handel's *Messiah* and the first part of Haydn's *The Creation*. A "peace jubilee" concert was then quickly arranged for Washington's birthday, February 22, with a similar program.

The critical and public success of both these performances spurred Gottlieb Graupner to call a meeting in his music room of amateur players, among whom were the consuls of the United Kingdom and Russia. The name "Handel & Haydn Society" was settled on, and the group's constitution declared their high-minded "purpose of improving the style of performing sacred music and introducing into general use the works of Handel and Haydn and other eminent composers."

The original H&H membership were mostly from choirs at Old South, Trinity, Park Street, and other Boston churches. The rehearsals were lively affairs, judging at least by the provisions carefully itemized on accountant's vouchers: "8 lbs. Smoaked Beef; 1 Gall. Brandy and 1 Gall. Spirit."

On Christmas Day 1815, the Handel & Haydn Society, conducted by Col. Thomas Webb, gave its premiere concert at King's Chapel with a program of familiar works including, again, the "Hallelujah!" Chorus and the first part of *The Creation*. A perhaps easily impressed journalist for the *Boston Centinel* raved, "We have no language to do justice to the feelings experienced in attending to the inimitable execution of a most judicious selection of pieces from the fathers of sacred song."

"H&H" is now the nation's oldest continuously performing arts organization. The society presented the first complete performance of Handel's *Messiah* in 1818 and has played the work annually since 1854.

♣ ❦ ♣

Capt. Henry Hall of Cape Cod is first to cultivate cranberries (1816).

IN SUMMER AND FALL, ripening wild cranberries can transform an ordinary bog into a blazing red sea. The spreading vermilion stain gives the landscape a haunting and unearthly quality.

For all its natural beauty, however, the cranberry was mostly ignored throughout the first two centuries of European settlement in Massachusetts. Not before a ship's captain in North Dennis noticed a peculiar effect of shifting sand on the cranberry plant did the commonwealth's farmers show any serious interest in the sour little fruit. Today Cape Cod cooperatives produce half of the world's crop on 12,500 acres of cranberry beds.

Only three commonly eaten fruits are native to North America: the blueberry, the Concord grape, and the cranberry. To grow properly, cranberries require an acid, peat soil; an adequate supply of fresh water; sand; and a growing season lasting from April to November. All those conditions occur naturally on large stretches of Cape Cod, where receding glacial ice created impermeable, clay-lined "kettle hole" bogs.

According to Native American mythology, a dove carried the first cranberry from heaven to earth in its beak (the legend later inspired the now well-recognized trademark of the Ocean Spray cranberry growers' cooperative). In 1647, Indians at John Eliot's praying villages harvested wild cranberries and sold them to settlers. Throughout the eighteenth century, these wild cranberries were harvested by hand in Massachusetts and shipped to England and elsewhere in Europe, where they competed with those imported from Russia.

When the Crimean War started in 1853, the flow of the Russian crop halted, and American cranberry growers prospered by default, especially in the English market. By then, the commonwealth's farmers were ready to meet the sharply increasing demand.

The man Massachusetts cranberry growers had to thank was Henry Hall, a native of North Dennis. Born in 1760 and directly descended from an English settler who arrived on Cape Cod in 1630, Henry Hall served briefly and with no great distinction in the Revolutionary War. Town records from 1778 list "Captain" Henry Hall as owner of a sixty-nine-foot schooner, the *Viana,* which he skippered regularly between the cape and Boston.

In 1800 Captain Hall and two partners opened a saltworks on public land near a pond where wild cranberries had long been harvested. This swampy area, Hall observed, was submerged in winter and dry in summer. The keen-eyed captain also noticed that when sand blew over the cranberry vines, the plants were not killed but grew even more strongly.

Ignoring ridicule from his neighbors, Hall began to test his theories in 1816 by transplanting and maintaining cranberry vines in protected fields, which he flooded in winter and then covered over with sand. Soon Hall was clearing and draining more land to create what he called "cranberry yards."

The clever Yankee had stumbled on the keys to the natural success of cranberry vines. According to agricultural scientists, freezing water protects delicate plants from winter damage caused by wind and snow even as a layer of windblown sand slowly collects over the thin crust. As the ice thaws in spring, the settling sand controls insect populations and stimulates the vines to put down roots. By 1820 Hall was successful enough with his cultivated cranberries to ship thirty barrels to New York for sale at produce markets. His annual yield eventually rose to unheard-of heights— seventy to a hundred bushels per acre.

Cranberries may have a naturally sour taste, but they treat farmers quite sweetly. Vines require relatively little care once they are planted, and they will spread quickly to cover available ground. Cranberry plants are virtually indestructible: Some vines on Cape Cod are more than 150 years old.

Captain Hall's discovery may have inadvertently helped preserve Cape Cod wetlands by tens of thousands of acres. In the early nineteenth century, government officials were pushing landowners to convert marshes, bogs, and meadows into productive farmland. Cranberry cultivation, however, cannot be sustained without an extensive wetlands system and healthy aquifers. As a result, "useless" bogs were not drained to become fields. Today, for every one acre of cranberry beds, farmers maintain four acres of open wetlands.

♣ ♥ ♣

Maine is separated from Massachusetts in the Missouri Compromise (1820).

IN 1819, MISSOURI APPLIED for admission to the Union as the twenty-third state. The move, which threatened to shift the balance of power in favor of those states where slavery was practiced, precipitated a crisis that foreshadowed the Civil War.

The United States at the time of James Monroe's administration resembled a complex chemical equation: a great many volatile elements were delicately balanced to prevent a catastrophic explosion. In the Senate, eleven northern "free states" offset the presence of an equal number of southern "slave states" (the more populous North already controlled the House).

From the very beginning of the country's history, however, slavery had proven a corrosive political element in the United States. Slaveholders, who feared that their opponents' zeal might one day rob them of their chattels, repeatedly sought and won protection for what was called the South's "peculiar institution." The rights of slaveholders were duly enshrined, first in the Constitution and, later, in legislation of Congress.

In 1787 the Northwest Territory Ordinance barred slavery from all new states north of the Ohio River. The territory of Missouri, a portion of the vast Louisiana Purchase that Thomas Jefferson made in 1803, lay above that line between the Mississippi and Missouri rivers. In the territory's first decade in American hands, Missouri's sprawling, rich farmlands were rapidly settled by slaveholders from neighboring southern states. Missouri's proposed state constitution, not surprisingly, made slavery legal and permanent.

Abolitionists were not about to allow a new slave state into the Union without a fight. In the House, Rep. James Tallmadge of New York proposed legislation to abolish slavery in Missouri. A debate raged over whether Congress had the authority to make such a law. Eventually Tallmadge's bill passed the House but died in the Senate.

In Massachusetts, the growing influence of abolitionists helped push forward a key element in what became known the Missouri Compromise. The territory of Maine, which had been part of the commonwealth since early settlement days, applied for admission to the Union. In an arrangement backed by Speaker of the House Henry Clay of Kentucky, Maine and Missouri would both be admitted, thus preserving the prevailing balance of senatorial votes and allaying southern fears. Slavery would be banned from the rest of the Louisiana Territory above what is now the northern boundary of Arkansas.

The intense argument that preceded passage of the Missouri Compromise fanned passions on both sides. Thomas Jefferson, a slaveholder himself, wrote that "this momentous question, like a fire-bell in the night, awakened and filled me with terror. I considered it at once as the knell of the Union. It is hushed, indeed, for the moment. But this is a reprieve only, not a final sentence."

♣ ♥ ♣

The *Essex,* a Nantucket whaleship, is struck by a large sperm whale and sunk, inspiring sailor Herman Melville later to write *Moby Dick* (1820).

TO ACCOUNT FOR THE climactic conceit in Herman Melville's masterpiece, literary detectives point to the bizarre cause of the wreck of the *Essex,* a

Nantucket whaleship under the command of Capt. George Pollard. At the time of the incident, Melville was a fifteen-month-old infant living in New York City.

On November 20, 1820, after sailing from Nantucket more than a year earlier, the *Essex* lay in the Pacific Ocean just below the equator, one thousand miles due west of Ecuador. With the usual shouts of "There she blows!" sailors sighted a shoal of whales, and two boats were sent into the water. First Mate Owen Chase pursued in one boat, Captain Pollard in the other. Chase harpooned a whale but was forced to cut his line after the injured creature opened a hole in the boat with its tail.

Chase and his men managed to return to their ship, where they immediately began repairs to the boat in the hope of resuming the chase for the injured leviathan. Suddenly, a sperm whale, which Chase estimated at eighty-five feet long, appeared near the *Essex*. It bore down on the ship at three knots and struck near the bow with its head.

"The ship brought up as suddenly and violently as if she had struck a rock," Chase wrote later. "We looked at each other with perfect amazement, deprived almost of the power of speech." The whale vanished beneath the waves, only to return for a second, even more vicious attack.

Like the smaller boat before it, the *Essex* now began to fill with water from the force of the beast's powerful blows. Pollard and Chase realized quickly enough that pumping was futile. Gathering up bread and water as well as compasses, map books, and other navigation aids, they divided the sailors among three boats.

For three months, the *Essex* sailors drifted in the open sea. They were forced to turn to cannibalism to survive. On Captain Pollard's boat, which was separated from the others, the men chose lots to determine who should die so that his colleagues might live. In late February the remaining survivors of all three boats were recovered by several passing ships.

Herman Melville did not cross paths with the strange tale of the Essex wreck until 1841. As a sailor aboard the *Acushnet* out of New

Bedford, he met Owen Chase's son, William Henry Chase. The pair must have enjoyed swapping stories of whaling adventures, and presumably the younger Chase lent Melville a published copy of his father's *Narrative of the Most Extraordinary and Distressing Shipwreck of the Whale-Ship* Essex.

Ten years later, Melville referred to a copy of the *Narrative* when completing his whaling novel. In writing *Moby Dick,* Melville artfully transformed the Essex disaster. No Ahab and no Ishmael figured in Chase's *Narrative* nor ever could have. "Thus, I give up the spear!" is a cry worthy only for literature.

♣ ♥ ♣

Boston is granted a city charter and elects its first mayor, John Phillips (1822).

THE TOWN MEETING MAY be a hallowed tradition of New England democracy, but even a time-honored system breaks down under certain conditions. By 1820, the national census indicated that Boston's population was 43,298, with the number of qualified voters well over 7,000. "When a town meeting was held on any exciting subject in Faneuil Hall, only those who obtained places near the moderator could even hear the discussion," wrote one weary citizen of the day.

"A few busy or interested individuals easily obtained the management of the most important affairs in an assembly in which the greater number could have neither voice nor hearing," he added ruefully.

Finally, a consensus gathered that Boston should adopt a city government with elected officials representing various districts. In 1821 the commonwealth's voters approved an amendment to the constitution permitting Boston to remake itself as a city, the first ever to be so approved for Massachusetts. City government was less rare elsewhere. New York became a city as early as 1665, and in Connecticut, city charters were freely granted even to what were condescendingly referred to as "a little clump of Indians."

In January 1822 attorney Lemuel Shaw presented at one of the last town meetings held in Faneuil Hall a city charter for Boston voters' approval. A prominent lawyer who would later serve as chief justice of the Massachusetts Supreme Judicial Court (he was also father-in-law and principal financial supporter of author Herman Melville), Lemuel Shaw drafted the charter document almost entirely without precedent to guide him. A special committee initially approved his plan for the new city government, which consisted of a seven-member board of "selectmen" who would elect a chief executive to be called "the intendant."

True to town meeting form, however, the debate in Faneuil Hall was contentious, and eventually it took three days to work out the details. Voters attending these sessions decided, among other points, to rename "the intendant." Even to famously humorless nineteenth-century ears, "intendant" must have seemed a title better suited for an employee of the city's stables. They wisely gave the chief executive the dignified and ancient title of "mayor." The "selectmen" were likewise renamed "aldermen."

Almost immediately, the new "City of Boston" was divided by a cantankerous race for mayor. Prominent citizen Josiah Quincy dared to face Harrison Gray Otis, an eminent Federalist politician. Quincy would likely have won in a two-way contest, but when Democrats nominated Thomas Winthrop as a last-minute spoiler, Quincy did not receive the necessary majority of aldermen's votes. Quincy and Otis then withdrew their names and a compromise candidate, John Phillips, was put forward. Inaugurated on May 1, 1822, Phillips is remembered as a man of integrity and good judgment but not especially as a charismatic figure.

A year later, Josiah Quincy became Boston's second mayor, and he set the style of flamboyant city executive. "The great duty of the mayor of such a city as this," Quincy declared in his first inaugural address, "is to identify himself, absolutely and exclusively, with its character and interests."

Known as "the great mayor," Quincy rose at dawn each workday to survey Boston by horseback, and he personally confronted owners of double-parked wagons outside Faneuil Hall. In April 1825 Quincy laid the cornerstone at the new city market, subsequently renamed Quincy Market in his honor.

Unitarianism, first organized in Boston, becomes the unofficial religion of Boston Brahmins (1825).

STRICT PURITAN MORALISM DISSIPATED in the commonwealth throughout the eighteenth century as a rising merchant class amassed ever greater wealth. Increasingly, Calvinism proved inconvenient and even unreliable as a philosophical underpinning for international commerce. God's will could not be counted on to provide consistently for substantial profits on all business transactions. Of far greater importance to the bottom line was the human will.

Crafty though they became, Boston merchants were not entirely unethical types. They gradually lost interest in restrictive religious dogma and theological debates, only to replace them with concerns over conduct and behavior. They often acted out of self-interest, yet they also showed themselves committed to compassion, philanthropy, and social reform. The commonwealth's new merchant class, unlike the Puritans before them, did not seek converts to their religious faith but instead conformists to their moral principles.

In Massachusetts, the drift away from Calvinism accelerated immediately following the end of the Revolutionary War. First to emerge from the fatalistic darkness of Puritanism was Universalism, a new creed transplanted from Europe that optimistically affirmed the ultimate salvation of all. According to Universalism, guilt and punishment for sins were the burden accepted by Jesus Christ on the cross; God would eventually forgive everyone, even Satan and his fallen angels.

In 1780 English immigrant John Murray became minister of the first Universalist congregation in America at Gloucester. The movement eventually coalesced twenty years later around Hosea Ballou, a New Hampshire native. As author of *Treatise on Atonement* in 1805 and later as pastor of Boston's Second Universalist Church, Ballou influenced a generation of Boston intellectuals, including Ralph Waldo Emerson and the

Transcendentalists, with his then-radical view of a benevolent God inca-
pable of condemning humanity to eternal punishment.

Congregationalists, the direct theological descendants of the Puritans,
faced an internal challenge from liberals within the church at the beginning of the nineteenth century. Leading the attack on Calvinist orthodoxy
was William Ellery Channing, minister at Boston's Federal Street Church,
who defined a new strain of religious thinking in an 1819 sermon,
"Unitarian Christianity." Similar to Universalism, Unitarianism proposed a
view of humanity that was positive and affirming and encouraged moral
responsibility. In addition, Unitarianism, as the name implies, rejected the
doctrine of the Holy Trinity as well as the divinity of Christ.

The American Unitarian Association was formed in Boston in 1825 as
an association of individuals, not churches, with Channing, Theodore
Parker, and others as charter members. Unitarians played a large role in
making Boston a center of abolitionism as well as supporting the city's
development as a literary center. "Moral philosophy" classes taught by
Harvard College Unitarians also provided the Brahmins with sufficiently
enlightened self-justification.

In the garden cultivated by humanistic Unitarian clergy grew the
Boston now remembered as "the Athens of America." Its citizens were
serious, prosperous, and thoroughly patrician, yet they managed to be progressive owing to a consistent promotion of public education and private
scholarship. "Nothing quieted doubt so completely as the mental calm of
the Unitarian clergy," Henry Adams later remembered. "Doubts were a
waste of thought ... Boston had solved the universe."

♣ ❦ ♣

First commercial railroad hauls granite blocks from Quincy to Charlestown for the Bunker Hill Monument (1827).

OVERLOOKING BOSTON HARBOR IN Charlestown, the Bunker Hill
Monument rises 221 feet and 294 muscle-numbing steps. Like the battle it

commemorates, the monument is misnamed; it actually stands on Breed's Hill (Bunker Hill lies not far away and is surmounted by St. Francis Church).

The obelisk of Quincy granite blocks was designed by Solomon Willard, a Boston carpenter-carver turned architect, who apparently had assistance from Alexander Parris, the architect of Quincy Market and St. Paul's Cathedral. Both men were committed practitioners of the Greek Revival movement, then quite popular with the Boston Brahmins.

The Bunker Hill Monument Association was founded in 1824 in anticipation of the battle's fiftieth anniversary. Prominent citizens, including Col. Thomas Handasyd Perkins, a wealthy shipping merchant in the China trade (for whom the Perkins School for the Blind was later named), began a public subscription campaign for the monument's construction. On June 17, 1825, General Lafayette came from France to lay the cornerstone. Another seventeen years would pass, however, before the ambitious building project was completed.

Transporting stone quarried in West Quincy to Charlestown via the Neponset River proved a daunting commercial and technical challenge. Someone suggested that the granite be carried in winter on enormous sledges. A Boston engineer, Gridley Bryant, had a perhaps more practical solution: He proposed construction of a railway for horse-drawn carts.

Until this time, single-purpose railways were common enough, but these were never intended as permanent operations. Bryant urged Colonel Perkins and other members of the association to investigate the potential of a permanent commercial railway. On January 5, 1826, the legislature received a petition for the incorporation of the Granite Railway Company.

Construction of such a railway, however, raised many new and provocative questions over such points as right-of-way, safety and liability, and abutters' rights. The legislature very nearly balked at the legal and social tangle involved, but on March 4, 1826, by the thinnest of majorities, they issued the railway a forty-year charter.

Like Francis Cabot Lowell, Bryant was inspired by the example of the

English, who had constructed commercial railways for carrying coal from mines, when designing the first such American system. He was compelled to make improvements, nevertheless, particularly in the construction of rails strong enough to accommodate the heavy loads of granite. By 1830 Bryant became frustrated with pine rails and chose to replace them with what was particularly handy for him: granite rails.

On March 27, 1827, the Bunker Hill Monument Association signed a one-year contract for transportation of stone, the first written in the United States for carriage of freight by rail. That spring, the work of hauling granite to Charlestown began. The contract was not renewed, but the railway was profitable enough with its other business. Wisely, the railway had purchased its own quarry so it would not have to rely on the monument for all its business.

In 1870 the Granite Railway Company was purchased by the Old Colony and Newport Railroad Company. Only then did the new owners replace Bryant's sturdy Quincy granite rails with those made of iron.

♣ ♥ ♣

Edgar Allan Poe is stationed at Fort Independence (1827).

EMOTIONAL AND FINANCIAL DISASTER forced Edgar Allan Poe, eighteen, to leave the University of Virginia. His fiancée, Sara Elmira Royster of Richmond, had been forced into a marriage with another man. To make matters worse, the young man's stepfather refused to pay his burdensome gambling debts.

Seeking a fresh start, Poe traveled to Boston, where he had been born on January 19, 1809. His parents, David Poe, Jr., and Eliza Arnold Hopkins Poe, were both actors at the Boston Theatre. When his mother died, Edgar was taken to Richmond, where he was raised by foster parents John and

Frances Allan. While in Boston, Poe privately published his first book, *Tamerlane and Other Poems.*

The young writer next sought adventure in the army. With a characteristic flair for mystery, he enlisted as "Edgar Allan Perry" and was stationed at Fort Independence on Castle Island in Boston Harbor.

From fellow soldiers, Poe heard the tale of a Fort Independence duel between two officers ten years before. A much-disliked senior officer accused a young lieutenant of cheating at cards. In a duel on Christmas morning the lieutenant was run through with a sword. Seeking vengeance, the dead man's friends conspired to ply the winning duelist with drink. They led their man to the fort's deepest dungeon and sealed him within a stone wall.

Poe was sworn to secrecy by his fellow soldiers, but the macabre tale eventually proved too rich for the author to resist. In his classic short story "The Cask of Amontillado," an Italian lord seeks to avenge himself on an enemy. Through a dank catacomb, he leads his unsuspecting victim:

"A moment more and I had fettered him to the granite. In its surface were two iron staples, distant from each other about two feet, horizontally. From one of these depended a short chain, from the other a padlock. Throwing the links about his waist, it was but the work of a few seconds to secure it. He was too much astounded to resist."

Throughout his life, Poe published and lectured intermittently in Boston, but he was never reconciled to the city's conservative literary establishment. After public acclaim followed publication of "The Raven" in 1845, Poe was invited to lecture at Boston's Odeon Theatre. His improvised remarks for an October evening included a ringing denunciation of the commonwealth's most respected writers. Poe condemned Longfellow and other locals as "the most servile imitators of the English it is possible to conceive." Not surprisingly, the hall began to empty of Bostonians. Poe recovered somewhat with a "Raven" recital. At dinner later with his hosts, the well-oiled poet mocked Boston further and dismissed his own lecture as "a hoax."

The Boston press roundly censured Poe for these offenses. In a reply mailed from New York, he neatly silenced the critics by characterizing provincial Boston as "Frogpondium."

In 1905, workers renovating the decommissioned Fort Independence haphazardly broke through a stone wall. They discovered inside a skeleton dressed in the tattered rags of an ancient military uniform. The bones and rags they found and later buried at the fort's cemetery bore a fascinating relationship to American literary history.

"I hastened to make an end of my labour. I forced the last stone into its position; I plastered it up. Against the new masonry I re-erected the old rampart of bones. For the half of a century no mortal has disturbed them. *In pace requiescat!*"

♣ ♥ ♣

Dr. Samuel Gridley Howe opens the New England Asylum for the Blind, the first school of its kind in the United States (1829).

BLINDNESS WAS A COMMON condition in early nineteenth-century Massachusetts. Diseases, particularly childhood illnesses, frequently robbed people of their sight as well as other senses. Formal education for blind and deaf children and adults did not exist. As a result, the disabled faced limited opportunities for personal development.

In 1784 the first school ever organized exclusively for blind children opened in Paris. Founded by Valentin Hauy, "L'Institut National pour Jeunes Aveugles" (The National Institute for Blind Youth) pioneered a movement to establish similar schools in Vienna, London, St. Petersburg, Dublin, and elsewhere throughout Europe. For nearly fifty years, however, that effort did not cross the Atlantic.

Traveling as a medical student, John Fisher of Boston visited Paris in 1826 and toured the National Institute. The blind students he met there learned reading, writing, mathematics, geography, and languages from specially trained teachers. Programs at the French school also included music instruction (specifically, training the blind students to become church organists) as well as an in-school publishing house where students printed their own embossed books.

After Fisher returned home to practice medicine, he found the commonwealth's citizens engaged in the first rounds of a vigorous debate over the nature of public education. The young doctor spoke passionately among friends and colleagues on the need for opening up education to the blind.

Finally, in February 1829 at a meeting in Boston's Exchange Coffee House, Fisher organized a group to apply for a private school charter. A year later, the trustees of the New England Asylum for the Blind ("asylum" referring to a "haven" or "retreat") sent another Boston physician, Samuel Gridley Howe, to tour several European schools for the blind and report on what he saw.

Contrary to Fisher's evangelical enthusiasm following his own tour, Howe returned highly critical of the Continent's schools. Raised-type books were in short supply, and other instructional tools were poorly designed. In Howe's view, the students were poorly prepared for life as independent adults. In summary, the European schools were "beacons to warn rather than lights to guide."

The school Howe prepared to open would not be a "retreat" but a stimulating balance of academics, crafts, games, and music. In July 1832 Howe began teaching his first pupils in his father's house; within a month enrollment tripled to six students ages six to twenty. In 1833 Boston merchant Thomas Handasyd Perkins provided his home on Pearl Street for the school's use. Supporters held a fundraising bazaar in Faneuil Hall.

Even as he led the Perkins School through its early days, Samuel Gridley Howe served as coeditor of the abolitionist newspaper *The Commonwealth* with his wife, the author and women's rights advocate Julia Ward Howe. (In 1862 Julia Ward Howe's poem "The Battle Hymn of the Republic" became a rallying song for Union supporters.)

The Perkins School's most famous student was Helen Keller, an Alabama native who enrolled in 1887. The blind and deaf seven-year-old was patiently taught by Anne Sullivan, herself a Perkins graduate. "We had scarcely arrived at the Perkins School...when I began to make friends," Keller wrote in *The Story of My Life*. "I was in my own country." In 1904 Helen Keller graduated *cum laude* from Radcliffe College, where Sullivan used a manual alphabet to "spell" the lectures into Helen's hand.

♣ ♥ ♣

William Lloyd Garrison begins publishing the abolitionist journal *The Liberator* (1831).

SON OF A NEWBURYPORT seaman who abandoned his family, William Lloyd Garrison began adult life as an activist journalist working in Boston and Bennington, Vt. He gravitated to the emerging abolitionist movement as a convert from the American Colonization Society, which urged the peaceful repatriation of slaves to Africa. Instead, Garrison and others favored "immediatism," the immediate emancipation and assimilation of former slaves into American life.

In 1830, 2 million slaves lived in the territory of the United States, and their contribution to the young country's growing wealth was perhaps incalculable, but auctioneers were expected to do their best. A field hand in his prime who could pick 150 pounds of cotton in a single day fetched about $1,300 on the block in New Orleans's busy slave market.

The South's "peculiar institution," from its secure place in the U.S. Constitution, demanded and received a surprising degree of respect. Few dared to challenge slavery or slaveholders with any vehemence. This accepting attitude changed dramatically in 1831: In Virginia, Nat Turner led a rebellion of slaves, and in Boston, William Lloyd Garrison published *The Liberator,* the first abolitionist newspaper.

Several weeks after Turner's rebellion was put down, Garrison warned prophetically that worse was to come: "The first drops of blood, which are but the prelude to a deluge from the gathering clouds, have fallen," he declared in an editorial. He termed the U.S. Constitution "an agreement with hell" and set a copy alight at a Framingham rally. Garrison relished the uproar his words and actions caused among southern slaveholders and northern sympathizers. "If those who deserve the lash feel it and wince at it," he wrote, "I shall be assured I am striking the right persons in the right place."

Until the Civil War's end, Garrison agitated for abolition as fervently as anyone in the United States. Garrison saw a parallel in the slaves' fight with freedom with another uprising against tyranny.

"Rather than see men wear their chains in a cowardly and servile spirit, I would, as an advocate of peace, much rather see them breaking the head of the tyrant with their chains," Garrison told a Boston audience in December 1859. "Give me, as a nonresistant, Bunker Hill, and Lexington, and Concord, rather than the cowardice and servility of a southern slave plantation."

♣ ♥ ♣

Mount Auburn Cemetery, the nation's first "garden cemetery," opens in Cambridge (1831).

AS A REFORM MOVEMENT among many then thriving in Boston, burial reform was hardly as incendiary as calls for abolition of slavery; as ponderous as the recently concluded drive to establish a municipal form of government; or as fundamental to existence as the possible construction of a public water reservoir.

Nevertheless, burial reform managed to capture the public's attention throughout the 1820s. Debate raged in Boston over how best to address the bizarre urban dilemma of rapidly diminishing burial space.

This housing crisis for the dead was a direct result of the tripling of Boston's population in the generation since the end of the Revolutionary

War. Ensuring proper sanitation and healthful living conditions for all citizens became a new concern. Civic leaders faulted Boston's narrow, winding streets for encouraging disease, while they encouraged development of the Back Bay, an odoriferous swamp.

Overcrowding in the city's cemeteries was not entirely a new concern. The King's Chapel, Copp's Hill, and Old Granary burying grounds were already reaching capacity as early as 1730. A fourth burying ground was opened in 1756 with another added in 1810, for a total burial space of fewer than five acres. A new interment was likely to unearth remains of coffins and bones from previous burials. Grave robbers (called "resurrection men") harvested cadavers for local physicians from the bumper crop of corpses. Health concerns eventually led to calls for a ban on cattle grazing in cemeteries.

Remarkably, the lot fell to a man named Coffin to set burial reform in motion. On July 4, 1823, Dr. John Gorham Coffin, a highly regarded physician, published a pamphlet opposing urban burying grounds on the grounds that putrefaction fostered disease. In their place he called for creation of a sprawling suburban cemetery where bodies might decompose quickly and without exposing city inhabitants to danger from unhealthful air. This new graveyard would not be located near a church; instead, nature would substitute its grace and repose for a respectful setting.

Another physician, Dr. Jacob Bigelow, took up Dr. Coffin's argument with great enthusiasm. A professor of medicine at Harvard as well as a botanist, Dr. Bigelow eventually persuaded George Brimmer, who had assembled a seventy-two-acre lot in rural Cambridge and Watertown, to sell his large holding at cost to the Massachusetts Horticultural Society. As proprietors of the first rural cemetery in the United States, the Society began selling family burial lots in June 1831. For the cemetery's name, Dr. Bigelow recast a common nickname for the area given by Harvard students. "Sweet Auburn" thus became "Mount Auburn."

Within a relatively brief time after its opening, Mount Auburn Cemetery was well known as the final resting place for some of Boston and Cambridge's most famous names (Longfellow, Bulfinch, Otis, Gardner, and Homer, to name only a few, are among its more than eighty-six thousand permanent residents). A thoughtful landscaping plan of shady trees and flowering plants also attracted many visitors simply for the sake of taking a stroll in a relaxing atmosphere. Mount Auburn thus played an important inspirational role in the nineteenth-century movement to create urban public parks.

♣ ♟ ♣

During an anti-Catholic riot in Charlestown, an Ursuline convent is set afire (1834).

WHEN CONSIDERING WHETHER TO send their daughters to the convent school in Charlestown, parents read the school's prospectus carefully.

The Ursuline sisters of the Mount Benedict School for Girls, promised the leaflet, would "spare no pains to adorn their [students'] minds with useful knowledge and to form their hearts to virtue." Accordingly, reading, writing, and grammar were taught as well as "plain and fancy needlework." The prospectus further noted that "particular attention is paid to Orthography." In other words, the nuns wished to make it absolutely plain that spelling always counted.

Operated as a boarding school by Irish-born sisters who were themselves educated in exacting French convents, the Mount Benedict School for Girls was opened in 1824 at a time when Charlestown was a predominantly working class town of ten thousand. Well-to-do "young ladies" from Protestant families on Beacon Hill were enrolled along with students from as far north as Canada (who came for the benefit of Boston's warmer climate) and as far south as New Orleans (because it was cooler and more comfortable in Boston).

Set on a hill two miles from Boston, the convent, school, and grounds of the Mount Benedict School for Girls overlooked the Mystic River. A contemporary woodcut illustrating the prospectus showed the main school building in a practically bucolic setting. In and outside the classroom, the students would probably have known few distractions from their duties.

That is, unless parents doubted the school's meticulously worded prospectus and chose rather to believe the author of an incendiary pamphlet, *Six Months in a Convent*. Published in 1834, *Six Months in a Convent* purported to be an account by a former Mount Benedict student relating the constant pressure applied by the Catholic sisters to make her convert against her will. The author also described in lurid detail the bizarre behavior and eventual disappearance of a wayward nun, "Sister Mary John." In that xenophobic era, teamsters, bricklayers, and other hardworking, God-fearing Protestants were ready to believe the worst about Catholics. *Six Months in a Convent* scandalized the good citizens of Charlestown. Rabble-rousers demanded the release of Sister Mary John and the destruction of the convent.

On August 11, a crowd gathered at sunset outside the Mount Benedict school grounds. The mother superior appeared and told them that a group of town officials had visited the convent earlier in the day and found all the rumors to be baseless, but her words fell on deaf ears.

At eleven o'clock, the mob tore down a fence on school property and set a large bonfire as a signal. Still more people congregated in a crowd later estimated at four thousand. They threw stones through windows and finally charged the convent building. In the confusion, the nuns and the "young ladies" inside managed to escape to a neighbor's house, only to watch helplessly as the convent collapsed in a fiery heap.

A day later, Boston mayor Theodore Lyman called a public meeting in Faneuil Hall to condemn the riot. "The Protestant citizens of Boston," according to the resolution, "do pledge ourselves...to unite with their Catholic brethren in protecting their persons, their property, and their civil and religious rights."

♣ ☙ ♣

President of the Massachusetts Senate Horace Mann oversees creation of the first state board of education (1837).

IN THE EARLY NINETEENTH century, Massachusetts could boast of a long-standing tradition of support for public education: State laws mandating publicly funded education as well as the public Boston Latin School were already two centuries old. Yet Horace Mann was not impressed. The brilliant president of the Massachusetts Senate was a determined social reformer with an incisive legal mind and great oratorical skill. In 1833 he helped establish a state hospital in Worcester for the mentally ill, the first of its kind in the United States, and that was later referred to with honor as "Mann's Monument."

Next, Mann turned to the commonwealth's schools. "Men are cast-iron, but children are wax," he wrote with a view to the tremendous power of education to shape the future. The crusading Mann found the prevailing conditions in public schools to be a public disgrace.

Bare walls, no maps, a few books, and a switch to keep some semblance of discipline were the typical schoolmaster's only materials. A class of fifteen students might be crammed into a space fourteen by eighteen feet. An outhouse was a luxury that students and schoolmaster alike lived without. Public school teachers such as Henry David Thoreau in Concord and Henry Melville in a rural school near Pittsfield gave up the profession rather than continue in what they considered a form of servitude.

Massachusetts parents showed little concern for improving the schools, and town officials showed even less desire to pay for any improvements. The state government, Mann and others realized, must step into the breach.

In 1837, Mann, acting as the president of the Senate, was at the head of the push to establish a state board of education, the first of its kind in the nation. Supporters believed that the new agency, although advisory in nature, would spur a movement for much-needed reforms. The board's first members, including the governor, convinced Mann that only he was qualified to serve as its first secretary. He knew his acceptance meant relinquishing, or at least suspending indefinitely, a promising political career.

In eleven years as secretary of the board, Mann gained national prominence and exerted a lasting influence on the public conception of education. Among the principles he firmly established were that public education must be sectarian and free of religious dogma; that all children, regardless of their background, must be educated equally; and that only a professional cadre of teachers can deliver a worthy education.

Such tenets hardly seem debatable today, yet they upset many Massachusetts residents in the 1840s. Clergymen thought sectarian schools would promote atheism. Local officials were offended that Mann and the state government should try to usurp their authority. Mann, a progressive knight, was undeterred from his crusade for educational reform. He later became the first president of Antioch College, in Yellow Springs, Ohio, which was dedicated to providing a university education regardless of race, creed, or sex.

♠ ❦ ♠

Mary Lyon founds Mount Holyoke College, the nation's first college for women (1837).

WHEN MARY LYON, FIFTY-TWO, died in 1849, she had seen more than sixteen hundred young women pass through the doors of the Mount Holyoke Female Seminary in the dozen years since she helped to found the school. Along with teachers and foreign missionaries (occupations that nineteenth-century women often found themselves confined to), Mount Holyoke's early graduates included some of the nation's first women doctors.

Mary Lyon was born in 1797 on a country farm in Buckland, Mass. At the time, the western portion of the commonwealth was already becoming a popular retreat for American and European travelers who leisurely followed a well-worn stagecoach route from Boston to New York via Springfield, Hartford, and New Haven. These mostly urban visitors enjoyed the gentle landscapes of the Connecticut River valley and appreciated the quiet charms of rural New England.

At seventeen, Mary Lyon began her first teaching job in Buckland's one-room schoolhouse. In 1821 she received important training at Rev. Joseph Emerson's school for teachers in Byfield, north of Boston near Newburyport. Lyon was quickly recognized for her teaching abilities and her commitment to education. She was soon appointed "preceptress" at Sanderson Academy, Ashfield, nearer her childhood home.

The region north of Springfield had changed dramatically since Mary Lyon was a girl. By the 1830s, "Canal Village" at South Hadley Falls was a booming factory town with two woolen mills, three paper mills, two pearl button factories, and a linseed oil processing plant, which together employed hundreds of men and women. Local landowners, mill bosses, and merchants were determined to see their young daughters receive what was then called a "seminary" education. In 1834 seven such men gathered in Mary Lyon's home after she circulated a plan for such a school, "The New England Seminary for Teachers."

In January 1835 South Hadley's citizens voted to support the new school with an $8,000 "subscription," helping to lure Lyon and her colleagues away from establishing it in either Sunderland or South Deerfield. By all accounts, Mary Lyon was an especially capable fundraiser, even in the face of a national economic depression. She traveled frequently and could persuade equally wealthy businessmen and ladies' sewing circles to support the school. Individual donations given toward the endowment ranged from six cents to $1,000.

A four-story school building accommodating eighty students was ready at last on November 8, 1837. According to a schedule prepared by Mary Lyon, the first school bells rang at 4:00 A.M. and the last at 10:00 P.M. For health reasons, there was a daily walk requirement of one mile.

"Go where no one else will go," Lyon urged her students, "do what no one else will do."

In addition to classroom education, the founder of Mount Holyoke emphasized a "domestic plan" of study that required students to do much of the school's housekeeping. The effort involved, she believed, would help to build young characters (and save money on administrative costs). Well respected for her thrift, Lyon was notorious for paying teachers poorly. She defended herself by calling the school "a family." To her credit, Lyon maintained a policy of keeping tuition and boarding costs as low as possible in order to admit the daughters of middle-class families.

♣ ♥ ♣

Margaret Fuller is appointed editor of *The Dial*, a new journal of Transcendental thought (1840).

EVERYONE IN THE TRANSCENDENTALIST Club wanted to see the group publish a literary journal, but no one wanted to serve as the editor. As the group's founder, Ralph Waldo Emerson must have felt the pressure on him to take up the task, but he instead turned to his friend Margaret Fuller and proposed the idea to her.

As editor of *The Dial*, Margaret Fuller enjoyed the privilege of wresting prose and poetry contributions from Emerson as well as Henry Thoreau, Bronson Alcott, Theodore Parker, and Elizabeth Peabody, among other New England writers and philosophers. When she found herself short of copy, Fuller filled out *The Dial* with her own work. A sentimental article by her, "The Great Composers," is less absorbing today than "The Great Lawsuit: Man vs. Men, Woman vs. Women," a farsighted expression of radical feminism. In it, Fuller dared to declare equality for women as an inalienable right. "We would have every path laid open to women as freely as to man," she wrote firmly.

Few who knew Fuller would have found anything surprising in "The Great Lawsuit." As a child, she received the same rigorous education as her brothers. Timothy Fuller, a stern but loving father, imbued young Margaret with high standards and an ambition for intellectual achievement. Later, he demanded of an awkward teenager that she also learn proper social manners. The combination she acquired of intellectual ability and personal warmth prepared Margaret Fuller for a controversial life as America's first feminist.

Throughout her twenties, Fuller taught at Bronson Alcott's Temple School in Boston and in Providence; she published a translation of *Eckermann's Conversations with Goethe* and began a never-completed biography of the German author. She became a favorite of the Transcendentalists who gathered for conversation at Elizabeth Peabody's bookstore on West Street in Boston.

With encouragement from her friends, Fuller, then twenty-nine, undertook a series of ten "conversations" for women in the winter of 1839 and continued the practice successfully for five years. She charged $20 for the unusual programs, which were a kind of symposium, with Fuller in the part of Socrates. The topics she chose ranged from the fine arts and mythology to prudence and health. Men were forbidden to attend the sessions. Fuller had formed the idea that by leading only women in intellectual conversation, she might spark a feminist revolution. Her goal was nothing less than sexual equality.

Fuller frequently faced accusations common to women who challenge the authority of men. She was vain, they said, or arrogant. Her male friends criticized her as artificial or sentimental. Nevertheless, Fuller was capable of declaring, apparently without irony, that "I now know all the people worth knowing in America, and I find no intellect comparable to my own."

♣ ♥ ♣

George Ripley creates the Brook Farm Institute of Agriculture and Education in West Roxbury (1841).

RALPH WALDO EMERSON WAS perhaps too much an individualist in the first place, but what seems decisively to have prevented the high priest of

Transcendentalism from living at Brook Farm was the community's unorthodox system of delegating work and paying wages.

Under Brook Farm's bylaws, its members were free to choose their tasks and to start and stop work as they pleased, all according to each person's conscience. They were also paid at exactly the same rate—ten cents an hour—for whatever work was performed, menial or intellectual, be it shoveling dirt or writing a poem.

Emerson preferred the discipline and common sense of the Protestant work ethic, which compensated according to skill and effort applied. In this opinion, he was joined by a Concord neighbor, a farmer who told Emerson he thought the Brook Farm methods so impractical that if he followed them, he would wind up very shortly in the poorhouse.

"It was a perpetual picnic," the philosopher observed after one of several Brook Farm visits, "a French Revolution in small; an Age of Reason in a patty-pan."

Certainly, Brook Farm was all those things, though in a way that Emerson could not conceive, that was the whole point. The community's original members lived together in a farmhouse they called "the Hive." They did not intend to start a profitable business, but they did plan to support themselves by running a farm and school. Like revolutionaries, they wanted to overthrow royalty—in this case, the Yankee King Lucre and its consort, Materialism. In their place, the Brook Farm members would establish a new society of love and harmony.

Such an idealistic living experiment is usually called "Utopian," after Sir Thomas More's sixteenth-century essay describing a perfect society, but "Utopian" can describe any idealistic social venture. George and Sophia Ripley, founders of the Brook Farm Institute of Agriculture and Education in April 1841, were aware of the failures of past Utopias. In businesslike fashion, they financed their experimental community by selling shares of stock at $500 each. To augment any farm income, the Ripleys opened several schools at the site. The Brook Farm School was soon well attended and praised for its efforts to "perfect freedom of relations between students and teaching body."

With its communal living arrangements and liberal philosophy of individual freedom, Brook Farm naturally attracted conservative criticism. Despite rumors of promiscuous behavior among residents, Brook Farm was essentially a religious community, founded on a footloose interpretation of New England's own religion, Unitarianism. The community was set apart from the venal world much as the first Puritan settlements had been.

Among the original shareholders was Nathaniel Hawthorne, though the author found communal living not to his liking, and he left Brook Farm after just six months. Brook Farm members organized concerts, poetry readings, and other entertainments for themselves and their guests. Frequent if not always entirely sympathetic visitors included Emerson as well as his Transcendentalist colleague Margaret Fuller; abolitionist Theodore Parker; and the father of Louisa May Alcott, Bronson Alcott, who in 1843 organized a similar community, Fruitlands, at Harvard, Mass.

To the Ripleys' credit, Brook Farm defied its critics and prospered for several years. In 1844 the community had grown to 120 members and had adopted the theories of Charles Fourier, a radical French philosopher and early socialist. Its members decided to build what they called a "phalanstery," an enormous building planned to include suites of living quarters for entire families as well as a dining room seating 300. After two years of work, the almost-completed-but-not-yet-occupied phalanstery burned to the ground on March 3, 1846. The Brook Farm community never fully recovered from the catastrophe.

A further blow came four days after the fire, when Middlesex County Court in Cambridge heard the case of *Nathaniel Hawthorne v. George Ripley et al.* and found in favor of the plaintiff. Hawthorne had sued for return of his $500 investment in Brook Farm and won a judgment of $560.62 including legal expenses. To add insult to civil injury, the writer later published *The Blithedale Romance*, a stinging satire of his Brook Farm days.

♣ ♥ ♣

Frederick Douglass, an escaped slave, gives his first public speech on Nantucket (1841).

IN THE SUMMER OF 1841, Frederick Douglass set out from his adopted home in New Bedford for a sojourn on Nantucket, where abolitionists were gathering for the first Anti-Slavery Convention. "I have had no holiday since establishing myself in New Bedford," he wrote, "and, feeling the need of a little rest, I determined to attend the meeting, though I have no thought of taking any part in the proceedings."

It was not precisely a vacation, but the five days he spent on the island profoundly transformed Douglass in the way we often hope that time spent away from our ordinary occupations may change us for the better. Three years after escaping bondage in his native Maryland, he departed the New Bedford wharves a shipyard laborer and returned to them an inspiring orator in the cause to end slavery.

That Nantucket should be the setting for such a rebirth is little wonder. Influenced by the libertarian values of a large Quaker community, the island was an established sanctuary for escaped slaves. Nantucket's small but proud African-American community was known as "Guiney" or "New Guinea." Prosperous "Guiney" Nantucketers included Absalom Boston, a whaling captain and real-estate investor, and the prominent Godrey and Harris families.

In the Five Corners section of Nantucket Town, Guiney community members gathered at the African Meeting House for church and meetings. Nantucket's Native Americans and Cape Verdean immigrants also were welcomed. The Meeting House, which remains standing, was used as a school for the island's minority children until all Nantucket schools became integrated in 1846.

With forty other white and black abolitionists, Douglass boarded the steamboat *Telegraph* bound for Nantucket, only to learn from its captain that the ship would not leave unless all the black passengers took up quarters separate from the whites. The convention delegates flatly refused, but eventually they reached a compromise: They would all remain exclusively on the boat's upper deck. Once under way, the abolitionists held a protest meeting against the ferry company's segregationist practices.

Waiting to meet Douglass at the Nantucket dock was William Coffin, a New Bedford bookkeeper and abolitionist who had earlier seen the escaped slave speak at a black assembly. The sight of the two men walking together through the streets of Nantucket Town defied unwritten codes maintaining strict racial separation. Undeterred, Coffin planted the suggestion with Douglass that he should speak during the next day's meetings.

In the autobiographical *Narrative of the Life of Frederick Douglass, an American Slave,* published in Boston by the Anti-Slavery Office in 1845, Douglass recalled the emotional moment of his first speech, August 9, 1841.

"The truth was, I felt myself a slave," he wrote, "and the idea of speaking to white people weighed me down. I spoke but a few moments, when I felt a degree of freedom, and said what I desired with considerable ease… I trembled in every limb."

William Lloyd Garrison's recollection of the address his friend gave was considerably less modest.

"In the course of his speech [he] gave utterance to many noble thoughts and thrilling recollections," the publisher of *The Liberator* recounted. "I rose, and declared that Patrick Henry, of revolutionary fame, never made a speech more eloquent in the cause of liberty, than the one we had just listened to." Turning to the audience, Garrison then demanded, "Shall such a man ever be sent back to slavery from the soil of old Massachusetts?"

The replies of "No!" and "Never!" were said to shake the walls and roof of the Nantucket Atheneum.

♣ ♥ ♣

Manjiro, the first Japanese native to live in the United States, is rescued by New Bedford fishermen (1841).

WHEN CAPT. WILLIAM WHITFIELD of the *John Howland,* a New Bedford whaler, sent sailors in several boats to an uncharted island in the Pacific Ocean, he expected them to return with a catch of nutritious turtles for his ship's dwindling food locker. Instead, Whitfield's men found five stranded Japanese fishermen.

The Massachusetts captain wrote in his log that he "could not understand anything from them more than they was hungry." The lack of understanding between American sailors and Japanese fishermen was to be expected. In 1841, Japan remained as closed to foreigners as it had been for centuries. The country's isolation was strictly enforced by its military leaders. Japanese citizens who were unlucky enough to leave their native island—for whatever reason—faced the death penalty if they should ever return.

The youngest of the five Japanese fishermen rescued was Manjiro, a fourteen-year-old who soon became a sort of cabin boy to Captain Whitfield. Manjiro learned English and studied seamanship, with Whitfield as his teacher. When the *John Howland* finally returned to Massachusetts, Manjiro, rechristened "John Mung," accompanied Captain Whitfield to his home in Fairhaven, where he lived as a member of the family.

Like any child in his predicament, Manjiro hoped to see his mother again one day. Shipping out as a cooper aboard a Pacific-bound whaler, Manjiro left Fairhaven in 1847, but he was distracted from his original purpose by news of the discovery of gold in California. He stopped to pan for gold and stayed two years. Much later in Honolulu, Manjiro was reunited with three of his shipwreck companions and they decided to make the return journey together.

When Manjiro arrived home after a decade's absence, he was immediately taken prisoner of the *shogun* on Okinawa, and afterward, at Nagasaki. Japan in 1851 was under tremendous pressure to open its borders, and the country's military officials realized that Manjiro could prove an asset to them. When Commo. Matthew Perry landed in 1853, Manjiro played a crucial role during treaty negotiations as the only person in Japan with first-hand knowledge of America and Americans. Several accounts, in fact, name Manjiro as Perry's own interpreter.

Manjiro returned to America in 1860 as part of an official Japanese delegation. In 1870, while en route to Europe, he took a train from New York to New Bedford and walked the rest of the way to Fairhaven for a reunion with the Whitfield family. Manjiro died in Tokyo in 1898 after serving as a professor at Tokyo University. In 1987 on a tour of America, the Crown prince and princess of Japan toured Fairhaven with the great-grandsons of Manjiro and Captain Whitfield.

♣ ♥ ♣

Henry David Thoreau begins living at Walden Pond (1845).

IN AMERICAN HISTORY, TWO log cabins have figured prominently. The rugged Hardin County, Ky., home where a son was born to Thomas and Nancy Lincoln in 1809 is the first and arguably more famous. The simple Concord shack where an eccentric Harvard graduate purposefully lived a self-sufficient existence beginning in 1845 is the other.

Few writers have ever made more of their own idiosyncratic behavior than Henry David Thoreau. He could shape a point of principle from his smallest quirk. In this way Thoreau achieved a kind of offbeat heroism that owes nothing to achievement or victory and everything to strength of inner character. "The greater part of what my neighbors call good, I believe in my soul to be bad," wrote Thoreau, "and if I repent of anything, it is very likely to be my good behavior."

Throughout his relatively short life (he died in 1862 at not quite forty-five years old), Thoreau irritated his companions and his neighbors in the same damning fashion as Jesus or Socrates. He was an insufferable scold and clearly enjoyed the role. In an age when the burgeoning railroad symbolized a nation's boundless ambition for wealth, territory, and power, Thoreau observed pointedly, "We do not ride on the railroad; it rides upon us."

Shortly after his Harvard College graduation, Thoreau met Ralph Waldo Emerson, a fellow citizen of Concord. Together they celebrated individualism and promoted reform. At Emerson's suggestion, Thoreau began a diary. He also took up writing poetry, a profession that meagerly supported him for most of the 1840s. With his brother John for company, Thoreau made a canoe trip along the Concord and Merrimack rivers in 1838 and soon began turning out essays on his experiences in nature. Among these was "Natural History of Massachusetts," which Margaret Fuller published in *The Dial* in 1842. *A Week on the Concord and Merrimack Rivers* appeared in 1849 but sold only 220 copies.

The decision to build a cabin in 1845 at Emerson's estate at Walden Pond came upon Thoreau after a dozen years of pursuing his intuition. He declared his intention plainly: "I went to the woods because I wished to live deliberately, to front only the essential facts of life, and see if I could not learn what it had to teach, and not, when I came to die, discover that I had not lived."

While living at Walden Pond, Thoreau was arrested by Sam Staples, Concord's constable and tax gatherer. As a protest against slavery and the conduct of the Mexican-American War, Thoreau had persistently refused to pay his poll tax. He was released after a single night in the town jail, however, when an unknown woman, most likely his aunt, paid the tax for him. Thoreau drew on the experience for his most influential essay, "Civil Disobedience," in which he defended the right of the individual to refuse to comply with the unjust rule of a majority.

When he finally abandoned his cabin at Walden on September 6, 1847, Thoreau was a deeply changed man. He spent the remaining fifteen years of his life apparently reconciled with the contradictory nature of his soul. He became a surveyor, and when his father died, he managed the family's pencil-making business in Concord. Thoreau continued to travel and wrote warmly of his trips to Maine, Cape Cod, and Canada. He also became an ardent abolitionist.

Walden was published in 1854, the second and last of his books published in his lifetime. It took him five years to sell the two thousand copies printed.

☙ ❦ ☙

The first operation under general anesthesia is performed at Massachusetts General Hospital (1846).

BEFORE THE NINETEENTH CENTURY, the history of surgery was inextricably linked to the search for a reliable general "anesthetic" (from the Greek for "absence of sensation"). Ever since God caused a deep sleep to fall upon Adam before the legendary chest operation creating Eve, physicians longed for a method to dull their patients' senses in similar fashion. Brandy, opium, laudanum, and the mandrake root could provide some pain relief and even induce unconsciousness, but results varied widely.

Early narcotics were ingested before surgery. Once administered, the drugs could not be controlled. Supposedly senseless patients often felt pain; complications frequently arose during operations; many patients died.

In 1799 English scientist Sir Humphrey Davy noted the pain relief obtainable from inhaling nitrous oxide, which he called "laughing gas." Sir Humphrey also pointed out that only through the lungs may a drug be withdrawn as easily as it is given. He pointedly suggested that laughing gas be used in surgery.

Davy's pupil Michael Faraday carried this line of research further and discovered the pain-relieving qualities of ether, a colorless, volatile, organic liquid. In time, both laughing gas and ether became popular as intoxicants. Surgeons, however, remained uninterested in any potential medical use until a demonstration of the peculiar properties of laughing gas inspired a Connecticut dentist, Horace Wells, to conduct an unusual experiment in 1844. While Dr. Wells inhaled nitrous oxide, his pupil William Thomas Green Morton painlessly extracted one of the dentist's own teeth.

Traveling to Boston and Massachusetts General Hospital, Dr. Morton persuaded Dr. John C. Warren, the hospital's cofounder, to attempt an operation using ether as a general anesthetic.

On October 16, 1846, in the amphitheater of the hospital's main building (designed by Charles Bulfinch, and still standing), Dr. Warren operated on Gilbert Abbott for removal of a tumor on the jaw while Dr. Morton administered the ether with a device he had designed. Afterward Abbott declared, "I have felt no pain," and Dr. Warren endorsed the procedure with the remark, "Gentlemen, this is no humbug."

Within a year of that successful operation, ether was being used worldwide to relieve the pain of surgery. The Massachusetts General amphitheater quickly became known as "the Ether Dome."

Several other physicians claimed to have used ether as a general anesthetic before the sensational Massachusetts General demonstration. Dr. Morton became involved in a lengthy feud with his former housemate, Dr. Charles T. Jackson, a doctor and chemist from whom Morton learned much about ether's characteristics.

Thus, when it came time to dedicate a monument to the discovery on the Public Garden, sculptor John Quincy Adams Ward faced a quandary of whom exactly to honor. He wisely chose to omit names altogether and honor only the discovery itself. At this diplomatic sleight of hand, Oliver Wendell Holmes quipped that the fountain was "a memorial to ether—or to either."

Located near the Public Garden's Commonwealth Avenue entrance, the Ether Monument rises from a base of lion-headed spouts surmounted by arches and columns to support figures of the Good Samaritan comforting a suffering youth.

♣ ♥ ♣

Maria Mitchell, twenty-nine, of Nantucket, discovers a comet (1847).

GROWING UP ON NANTUCKET Island in the early nineteenth century, Maria (pronounced Ma-RYE-a) Mitchell became enamored with the telescope. Her father was an enthusiastic amateur astronomer who built an observatory in his home with instruments loaned by federal and state authorities in return for a promise to supply survey data. Thomas Mitchell eagerly communicated his own love of the stars and planets to his daughter. With wonder and excitement, Maria focused her telescope on Jupiter and Saturn and dreamed of great discoveries.

As Quakers with liberal views, Maria Mitchell's parents believed in equal education for boys and girls. They wanted to guarantee that their daughters could support themselves should they ever marry sailors or ship's captains who might leave Nantucket and never return.

In 1831 Thomas Mitchell and a twelve-year-old Maria worked together on a task critical for Nantucket's world-girding captains—setting their ships' chronometers. During an annular eclipse (a solar eclipse in which the moon's disk does not entirely cover the sun but leaves visible a thin ring of sunlight), Maria counted the seconds while her father recorded his observations. The measurements they gathered allowed Thomas Mitchell to determine the precise latitude and longitude of his home on Vestal Street in Nantucket Town. With the results, he calculated the correct Greenwich Mean Time and was able to set chronometers accurately for some ninety-two whalers. Sometimes Maria would do the demanding work herself.

On October 1, 1847, Maria Mitchell climbed the stairs at the Pacific Bank offices in Nantucket Town where her father, a cashier at the bank, had installed a rooftop observatory. Squinting through her telescope, Maria Mitchell saw a thin cloudy wisp where there should be nothing at all. She dutifully noted the sighting and sent along a report to the proper authorities. Official designation as "discoverer" of a comet brought her international attention. America's first woman astronomer traveled to

Europe and received a gold medal from the king of Denmark, himself an avid amateur astronomer.

In 1848 Mitchell became the first woman elected as a fellow of the American Academy of Arts and Sciences. The academy's reigning patriarchs, however, were uncomfortable with calling Mitchell a "fellow" and chose instead to refer to her as an "honorary member." Later, in 1850, she was also elected a member of the American Association for the Advancement of Science; that organization apparently did not feel it necessary to put Mitchell in a separate category. The point was an important one for Mitchell, who once remarked, "I believe more in women than I believe in astronomy."

When Vassar College was founded in 1865, Maria Mitchell became the country's first woman appointed as a professor of astronomy. She held the post until a year before her death in 1889 and helped train the first generation of American women scientists, including astronomers Mary Whitney and Antonia Maury; Christine Ladd-Franklin, mathematician and psychologist; Ellen Swallow Richards, chemist; and Ellen Churchill Semple, geographer.

♣ ♥ ♠

A pipeline from Lake Cochituate delivers a reliable water supply to Boston (1848).

ON THE SPLENDID AUTUMN day of October 24, 1848, the air resounded with the clang of church bells. Streets leading to Boston Common were impassable from all sides, yet a parade somehow managed to snake through the crowd.

Squads of pompous city officials passed, followed by Harvard College students, mechanics' associations, and numerous other dignitaries. A complete printing shop was installed on one float, and spectators were handed fresh copies of "A Song for the Merry-Making on Water Day."

Mayor Josiah Quincy waited to preside over what the press had built into a historic event on the order of a presidential inauguration. In the usually dull Frog Pond on Boston Common, as many as a hundred thousand Bostonians were congregated around a new fountain. Finally, Mayor Quincy rose purposefully to the center of the stage as dusk fell. "Do you want the water?" he shouted.

"Yes!" came the all too obvious reply from parched lips and dry throats. The obedient civil servant grasped a dangling lanyard and pulled hard. A specially rigged sluice sprang open.

"A geyser now leaped seventy feet into the air," a reporter on the scene wrote. "Beyond the Common on the crest of Beacon Hill, rockets burst into the air, setting off a display of multicolored fireworks....Then in an explosion of light, the thousands of gas lamps on the walls of the buildings on Tremont Street turned into what seemed one uninterrupted blaze."

The stupendous moment was a long time coming, and the delays leading to it must have accounted for some of the giddiness.

Throughout the colonial period, Bostonians drew their water exclusively from springs. In 1795 Massachusetts governor Samuel Adams approved creation of a fifteen-mile pitch pine pipeline from Jamaica Pond to Bowdoin Square; this pipeline later was replaced with ten-inch iron pipe. By 1826 Boston's growing population prompted serious discussion on how best to provide the city with a sufficient and reliable water source for the foreseeable future. Twenty years and several official commissions later, Mayor Quincy announced, "The time of action has come."

An 1846 citywide referendum approved a $3 million bond issue for construction of an aqueduct and pipeline capable of delivering 18 million gallons daily from Long Pond in Natick, into Boston to the east. On July 4 that year, symbolic barrels of Long Pond water were brought to Boston Common, and the pond was renamed Lake Cochituate, restoring its original Indian name.

The excitement in the city rose as the final steps were completed. On October 12, 1848, water flowed into a reservoir at Brookline, and two days later, it traveled the last few miles to Boston. Contractors checked for leaks and pronounced the pipes in sound condition. Families prepared to welcome their relatives and friends for a fabulous celebration.

A Harvard professor is charged with the murder of a Boston banker (1849).

DR. GEORGE PARKMAN LEFT his Beacon Hill home at 8 Walnut Street on the morning of November 23, 1849, for a round of errands. Among his stops were visits to the bank as well as a grocery store. Sometime in the early afternoon, however, Dr. Parkman disappeared. By the following day, a reward of $3,000 was posted for his safe return.

A wealthy merchant among a family of the same, Dr. Parkman had never practiced medicine. His involvement with the profession was significant enough, nevertheless. He had given Harvard land for construction of Harvard Medical School and endowed the Parkman Chair of Anatomy, held by Dr. Oliver Wendell Holmes.

Several days after Dr. Parkman was missing, John White Webster, a Harvard professor of chemistry, called at the Parkman family's house. He revealed that he had met with Parkman shortly before the man vanished. Professor Webster stated further that he had taken the occasion to repay a portion of a debt, nearly $500 (the Harvard professor owed the Boston banker well in excess of $2,000).

But it seemed that Webster had more explaining to do. While cleaning in the Harvard laboratory where the professor worked, a janitor uncovered several pieces of a man's body behind a partially sealed brick wall. Eventually an entire corpse was found and reassembled.

The trial of Prof. John White Webster for the death and dismemberment of Dr. George Parkman proved only that Bostonians were not averse to a morbid fascination with crime and its consequences. On March 19, 1850, Judge Lemuel Shaw gaveled his courtroom to order to hear the case, *Commonwealth of Massachusetts v. John White Webster.* Gossip-hungry spectators fought for the right to hear the expert testimony. A set of false teeth were identified as Parkman's by the dentist who made them. The president of Harvard College appeared as a character witness for the defense.

Altogether, sixty thousand of the curious public came to watch the trial over eleven days. Circumstantial evidence presented in court strongly linked Webster to Parkman through a chain of indebtedness forged over several years.

When at last he confessed to a clergyman before his execution, Professor Webster insisted that the murder was an act of passion and not premeditated. He had struck Parkman in anger, he said, after his creditor had insisted on full payment. The blow had been deadly, and he had seen no choice but to hide the body. According to testimony at his trial, Webster had performed the considerable dissection work necessary to hide Parkman with a mere jackknife.

Esther Howland establishes the New England Valentine Company in Worcester (1850).

HENRY FORD MAY HAVE had a hit with his Model T, but Esther Howland had the assembly line perfected long before Ford ever cranked an engine. And she did it with a little help from Cupid.

In 1850, Howland founded the New England Valentine Company in Worcester, the first mass producer of Valentine's Day cards. Working at first in her father's stationery store and later in her own valentine factory, the enterprising and romantic Yankee directed card production. The company's annual sales eventually reached more than $100,000, and Howland's creations were especially prized by lovesick soldiers during the Civil War.

Valentines sent as expressions of true love first appeared in England in the fifteenth century. These chivalric valentines originally were gifts left secretly at the beloved's door. As the tradition grew more popular, expensive gifts were replaced by notes and cards. The first valentine delivered in America may have been one sent from England to Boston in 1680.

Esther Howland, the daughter of a prosperous Worcester stationer, graduated from Mount Holyoke College in 1847. A Valentine's Day card her father received the following year from a business friend in England inspired Howland to copy it and add her own improvements. Her brothers took these first Howland valentines with them when they toured the countryside drumming up business. On the strength of the samples, they returned with orders for five thousand cards.

Early Howland valentines were of fairly plain design on embossed paper with little decoration. With help from a few local women, she could produce the first year's run out of her home rather easily.

Throughout the 1850s, Valentine's Day cards experienced a boom in popularity, partly owing to improvements in postal service. The cards themselves accumulated rich innovations—prints of idyllic scenes were sandwiched between layers of lace paper and framed by colorful cloth and tissue paper. Printed messages were introduced, too. "Forget me not" was a familiar plea; "Thee and thee only" was a typical promise.

The work involved to make Valentine's Day cards also grew. In response, Esther Howland hit upon an innovative method for card production: an assembly line. Howland gathered several workers at a table, with each one responsible for attaching a different layer in the collage and passing it along to her coworker.

In 1880 Esther Howland sold her card-making business, which by then also manufactured all types of holiday greetings, to George C. Whitney & Co., a local rival. The woman who created the modern Valentine's Day card retired to take care of her ill father and later moved to Quincy, where she lived with her brother. Although she knew all the words that lovers share, Howland never married.

♣ ♥ ♣

The first national Woman's Rights Convention convenes in Worcester (1850).

A NEWSPAPER REPORTER ASSIGNED to cover the two days of speeches and caucuses decided he could see right through the whole affair. "The whole purpose of the convention was too apparent for concealment," he wrote. "It is *but a new form of antislavery agitation*" (italics his).

The journalist for the *Worcester Palladium* had only noted the obvious. In attendance at the first national Woman's Rights Convention, held at Worcester's Brinley Hall on October 23 and 24, 1850, were such abolitionist luminaries as Frederick Douglass and William Lloyd Garrison as well as famed Quaker activist Lucretia Mott and eleven hundred male and female delegates from eleven states. From the basic proposition that the slaves should be freed, the abolitionists reasoned, it followed immediately that women must be liberated, too.

A year earlier in *The Liberator,* an abolitionist publication, William Lloyd Garrison made the point when he called for women's suffrage, a thoroughly radical notion. His abolitionist colleague Wendell Phillips concurred and boldly described the Woman's Rights Convention as "the first organized protest against the injustice which has brooded over the character and destiny of one half the human race."

In the published "call" for the convention, the language was similarly reminiscent of abolitionist tracts. Promoters denounced "the tyranny which degrades and crushes wives and mothers" and noted further, "Woman has been condemned, for greater delicacy of physical organization, to inferiority of intellectual and moral culture and the forfeiture of great social, civil and religious privileges. In the relation of marriage, she has been ideally annihilated, and actually enslaved in all that concerns her personal and pecuniary right."

One delegate even chose to illustrate the parallel of conditions for women and blacks with a harrowing story of the sort abolitionists never tired of telling. While traveling in Europe, the delegate testified, she witnessed a woman and a cow yoked together and dragging a plow while her husband walked behind and drove the team.

Worcester and the surrounding central Massachusetts region had become a hotbed for feminists. Convention delegates Abby Kelley and Stephen Foster (the abolitionist, not the songwriter), for example, had married themselves in Worcester in 1845 with a statement that pointedly left out the traditional mention of obedience. The Fosters scrupulously divided the chores in the household, and when a daughter was born, Stephen remained at home on their farm while Abby went on lecturing.

At the second national Woman's Rights Convention, a year later, Abby Kelley Foster challenged the other delegates "not to go home to complain of the men." A few of them may have muttered under their breath that their men were no Stephen Fosters.

Runaway slave Anthony Burns is captured in Boston under the Fugitive Slave Act (1854).

THE ARREST OF A twenty-year-old African American on a trumped-up burglary charge set Boston on edge in May 1854. Black and white Bostonians alike were united in a common concern for the fate of Anthony Burns, the property of Col. Charles Suttle of Stafford County, Va.

As part of the Compromise of 1850, a bitterly divided Congress had balanced the entry of California to the Union as a free state with the passage of a strict Fugitive Slave Act that made it easier for southern slaveholders to recover runaway blacks. Federal commissioners were authorized to seize and try any suspected escaped slaves without allowing them to testify in a trial and without a jury. The commissioner received a double fee if he ruled the suspect a runaway slave rather than a legally free black.

For four years the new law had quietly terrorized the commonwealth's black community, which included several hundred escaped slaves. Among them was Anthony Burns, who stowed away on a North-bound ship in February 1854 and found work at a Boston clothing store. After locating his slave through a letter Burns wrote home to his brother, Colonel Suttle demanded his rights under the Fugitive Slave Act. Fearful black Bostonians took to carrying weapons to protect themselves against any further attacks by zealous agents. Even the ordinarily pacifistic Frederick Douglass defended the use of violence in an editorial for *The Liberator,* asking rhetorically, "Is It Right and Wise to Kill a Kidnapper?"

At Faneuil Hall, a multiracial protest attracted what was counted as the largest assembly ever in that famous meeting place. If not the largest such crowd, they were easily the most furious. Abolitionist orator Theodore Parker let the sarcasm drip from his lips. "Fellow subjects of Virginia!" he addressed the crowd. Even as the Bostonians listening shouted "No!" Parker applied salt to the verbal wound. "There was a Boston once," he declared. "Now there is a north suburb to the city of Alexandria."

In a short time, the excited audience no longer bothered to listen to Parker. He had greatly provoked them, and when it was proposed that the protest continue the next morning at the courthouse where Burns was being held, the people were clearly not in the mood to wait. "Tonight! Tonight!" they chanted.

Even as the crowd surged out of Faneuil Hall into the night, a volunteer team of blacks and whites assembled by the abolitionist Vigilance Committee hammered at the courthouse door with a battering ram. Guards armed with cutlasses repelled the attack, but not before one guard fell dead. Reinforcements arrived in time to hold back the Faneuil Hall crowd. "It was one of the best plots that ever failed," remembered one of the organizers. Thirteen were arrested, but later freed. No one was ever indicted in the guard's murder.

Legal arguments on Burns's behalf equally failed. On June 2 Burns was led through the streets to a boat waiting at Long Wharf. The parade route was lined with people, but there was no repeat of violence. Buildings were draped in mourning, and American flags were flown upside down. A coffin labeled "Liberty" lay in state outside Old South Church.

After his return to Virginia in 1855, Anthony Burns regained his freedom. Rev. Leonard Grimes, pastor of Boston's Twelfth Baptist Church, where Burns had worshipped, raised $1,300, Colonel Suttle's price for his slave, plus expenses. A year earlier, Grimes had offered Suttle $1,200 for Burns's freedom but was refused, not by the colonel, but by a federal agent who stood to make a handsome fee if the slave was successfully returned.

♣ ♥ ♣

The filling of Back Bay begins (1857).

ENVIRONMENTAL PROTECTION REGULATIONS TODAY make difficult, if not impossible, the draining and filling of wetlands. In the 1850s, however, no such regulations existed to thwart city and state officials, working in a consortium with private landowners, from filling in Back Bay. The massive landfill project was even something of an environmental boon, as it cleaned up a foul-smelling and unsightly 580-acre public dump and gave the city the Commonwealth Avenue mall.

The Shawmut peninsula, which became the site of the first European settlements of Boston, resembled a cut flower lying on its side in Boston Harbor. Its stem, a narrow natural causeway, was known as the Boston neck and roughly followed what is today Washington Street. The Charles River estuary surrounded the roughly circular blossom of the flower to the west and south. In these tidal marshes, Native Americans constructed fishing weirs thousands of years ago. The same marshes ran up to the far edge of Boston Common and presented early Bostonians with a featureless if not unappealing backyard view.

Visionaries, though, could see the development possibilities in Back Bay from as early as the end of the eighteenth century. In the first decades after independence, Boston grew to bursting size as available land was strained to house a burgeoning population.

Boston accommodated its growth with vigorous action. In 1804 the town annexed Dorchester Neck. Mill Pond, an artificial body of water formed by a seventeenth-century landfill scheme at the mouth of the Charles River, was ordered to be filled with land scooped from the side of Beacon Hill.

In 1813 a Boston town meeting approved construction of Mill Dam and Turnpike Road, which followed a line across the northern edge of Back Bay and extended Beacon Street past Boston Common. Mills in South Boston would operate with power from tidal waters rushing through the dam.

As an inevitable consequence of the dam's construction, however, Back Bay was drained every day. The land was exposed to the sun and other elements that promote unhealthy organic decay. In addition, Bostonians were unable to resist the human urge to dump garbage and other waste where they believed no one would notice it. But people did take horrified notice; the odor, the putrefaction, and the rats were appalling.

The first improvement made in Back Bay was development of the Public Garden on land beyond Boston Common, beginning in 1839. The city's attention soon was drawn to the remaining land in Back Bay as a site for real-estate speculation. In 1849 the area was conveniently declared a health hazard, and a committee was appointed to determine a solution. Elected officials, property owners and amateur city planners responded with fantasy-filled designs that included Elysian Fields, Silver Lake, grand boulevards in the French style, and even for circus grounds on an island in the Charles.

In 1857 the commissioners on Back Bay finally approved a grandiose development plan. Commonwealth Avenue, two hundred feet wide, was to run west from Arlington Street at the Public Garden, with Newbury and Marlborough streets lying south and north, respectively. Beacon and Boylston streets were extended west along their existing paths.

Within a year the state contracted for removal of land from Pemberton Hill as well as for the hauling of gravel by railroad from Needham. The commonwealth paid for the ambitious project by the sale of developable lots. In 1859 a journalist described trains up to thirty-five cars long, each one loaded with gravel and other landfill material, arriving in Back Bay every forty-five minutes, day and night.

Among the first of Boston's elite to move into Back Bay were Mrs. and Mrs. John L. Gardner, who were married in 1859. As a wedding gift from her father, Isabella Stewart and her new husband received the lot for 152 Beacon Street, where they built a four-story mansion in 1862. Construction work continued in Back Bay well into the 1880s. Perhaps the musicians playing in Mrs. Gardner's Parisian-style drawing room helped to drown out the trundling sound of gravel trains and the din of pile drivers.

♣ ♥ ♠

Milton Bradley, a Springfield lithographer, publishes a board game, "The Checkered Game of Life" (1860).

IN A SMALL OFFICE opposite Court Square, Springfield, Milton Bradley and his then-business partner William Child installed a used lithographic press in 1860. Lithography was still a recent printing innovation, and the press was the only one of its kind in the state outside Boston.

The Milton Bradley Company, Publishers & Lithographers, had a quick if unlikely enough hit with a full-color print of Abraham Lincoln of Illinois, the popular 1860 Republican presidential candidate. When Lincoln grew a beard following his election, a hapless Bradley was suddenly left with an obsolete product. A more consistent seller over time proved to be a board game, "The Checkered Game of Life," which the printer had invented and which was introduced in 1860.

The rise of Bradley's career as a creator of board games and other home entertainments coincided with the development of a revolutionary new educational philosophy. German educator Friedrich Froebel had recently invented what he called "kindergarten," based on his theories that children learned best through creative play and self-activity. Froebel also started his own publishing firm for play and educational books. Spurred on by Elizabeth Peabody of Massachusetts, a pioneer in child education,

Milton Bradley adopted the Froebelian idea that learning should be fun.

Now based in East Longmeadow, the Milton Bradley Company is the largest and oldest game manufacturer in the world.

♣ ♥ ♣

Gen. Joseph Hooker of Massachusetts takes command of the Army of the Potomac (1863).

IN DECEMBER 1862, GEN. Ambrose Burnside sent Gen. Joseph Hooker of Massachusetts to take Marye's Heights, where Confederate guns and soldiers were massed to protect Fredericksburg, Va. The Emancipation Proclamation, which Lincoln had earlier issued in September, was to take effect in just two weeks' time. Burnside hoped for a battlefield victory to reinforce the message.

Sadly, Hooker's assault provided hope to the rebels at Christmas rather than the anticipated despair. His charge provoked a massacre as horrible as any yet seen in the bloody Civil War. Union men fell dead and dying, said one officer, like snow melting on warm ground. Altogether, the Battle of Fredericksburg cost the Union Army 12,600 men wounded, killed, or deserted. More than 5,300 Confederate soldiers were lost, though many of them had gone home for the holidays.

In November 1862, Lincoln had sent packing Gen. George McClellan. At the command of the Army of the Potomac for the previous fifteen months, "Little Mac" had deliberated too long in the hunt for Robert E. Lee to suit anyone's taste but his own. McClellan reluctantly made way for Gen. Ambrose Burnside, whose exaggerated facial hair, incidentally, gave rise to the expression "sideburns." Lincoln showed his ineffectual new commander little patience; in March 1863 he relieved Burnside in favor of the man everyone called "Fighting Joe."

On paper, Joseph Hooker enjoyed an overwhelming advantage in the spring of 1863. He was at the head of what was then the world's largest army (the Confederates owned the second largest). As his men approached Lee's units at Chancellorsville in late April, they outnumbered the rebel forces two to one. "My plans are perfect," boasted Hooker. "May God have mercy on General Lee."

At Chancellorsville, Lee made a daring escape from Hooker by splitting his army in two in order to slow the Union thrust for the Confederates' main lines. When Hooker's troops met the rebels on May 1, they were stunned by a forceful counterattack. "Stonewall" Jackson then convinced Lee to split his army a second time and went off to attack Hooker's flank. By the time Hooker completed his now inevitable retreat on May 6, the Union Army had lost another 17,000 men. As small consolation, Confederate forces mourned the death of General Jackson, their daring field commander.

For the next two months, Hooker cautiously kept his army between Lee's and the nearby city of Washington. Hooker resigned his command only days before Lee marched on a Pennsylvania hamlet called Gettysburg. He salvaged his reputation in November 1863 at the head of the "Battle Above the Clouds," a decisive Union victory in Tennessee.

Today, streetcar trolley guides invariably pause on Beacon Street by the statue of Hooker at the eastern side of the Massachusetts State House. They tell innumerable versions of a story whose common point usually is that prostitutes followed Hooker's army on the march and so became known as "hookers."

In fact, "hooker" as a term for a female prostitute predated the Civil War considerably and first appeared at least as early as 1845. There are several theories on its origin: that "hooker" referred to "the Hook," a section of New York City with many brothels; that "hooker" derives from the Dutch-American slang *hoeker,* for huckster; and that "hooker" simply described how a trawling streetwalker linked arms with a passing man.

Civil War soldiers familiar with the term "hooker" took to calling the hardworking residents of Washington's red light district "Hooker's division" as an obvious pun. Hooker had a reputation for drinking, talking, and carrying on. Their commander's reputation made the word play irresistible.

Col. Robert Gould Shaw and the 54th Massachusetts Volunteer Infantry, the nation's first African-American regiment, charge Fort Wagner (1863).

IN MARCH 1863, FREDERICK DOUGLASS strongly declared his pride in the example Massachusetts had set for the nation in the cause of liberty and racial equality.

"She was first in the war of Independence; first to break the chains of her slaves; first to make the black man equal before the law; first to admit colored children to her common school," the former slave noted as he exhorted other former slaves to enlist in the Union Army's first black regiment.

"Massachusetts now welcomes you to arms as her soldiers," he continued. "This is our golden opportunity—let us accept it—and forever wipe out the dark reproaches unsparingly hurled against us by our enemies. Win for ourselves the gratitude of our country—and the best blessing of prosperity through all time."

The regiment that marched through downtown Boston on May 28, 1863, toward troop ships waiting at Battery Wharf included Charles and Lewis Douglass, the great orator's own sons, as well as hundreds of free Massachusetts blacks and fugitive slaves who returned from safety in Canada. The soldiers ceremoniously marched passed the spot near the Old State House where Crispus Attucks had fallen dead in the Boston Massacre. For the first time in American history, African-Americans were formally allowed to fight for their country.

As commander of the 54th, Col. Robert Gould Shaw, twenty-five, made a handsome, sword-bearing symbol of the strength of abolitionist sentiment in Massachusetts. Shaw was raised on Beacon Hill in a household where abolition was regarded as seriously as a religion in others. In 1861, the twenty-three-year-old student with a precisely trimmed mustache left

Harvard in his junior year and enlisted in the 2nd Massachusetts Regiment, where he was commissioned a second lieutenant.

Over the next fifteen months, Shaw saw action in several bloody contests, including Ball's Bluff and Antietam, and rose to a post on the staff of his commander, General John Gordon. Observing that the Union needed whatever help it could get, Shaw wrote a friend in July 1862 that the Army ought to allow blacks to enlist and that "they would probably make a fine army after a little drill."

When the Emancipation Proclamation took effect on January 1, 1863, Massachusetts governor John Andrew seized the moment to form the nation's first black regiment. He offered Shaw its command as a colonel; the young Brahmin first declined, then accepted.

Frederick Douglass may have promised African-American volunteers "the same wages, the same rations, the same equipment, the same protection, the same treatment and the same bounty secured to white soldiers," but the U.S. Army had other ideas. At first, white privates received $13 monthly pay, though black recruits of the same rank got only $7 pay. The 54th Regiment refused to accept these discriminatory wages, and its soldiers went without pay until the Army granted them equal wages in 1864.

In its first weeks of action in July 1863, the 54th Regiment were kept busy as the Union prepared to take Charleston, S.C. They fought in several efforts to take strategic islands and helped rescue the 10th Connecticut Regiment from almost certain massacre. After a forty-eight-hour forced march, the regiment was then asked to lead an attack on Fort Wagner in Charleston Harbor. The order came in the form of a cordial invitation, but Colonel Shaw was quick to accept it. A battlefield veteran, he must have known the consequences.

As darkness fell on July 18, Shaw held his sword high and gave the order to charge. Union shells had battered Fort Wagner all day, but the rebels had not tired. When the 54th Regiment clambered up the parapets, they took the full force of Confederate fire. Shaw was among the first to fall; several hundred more would follow him. He and his dead comrades were later buried together in a mass grave.

The Confederates had meant to disgrace Robert Gould Shaw by so disposing of his corpse, but the act was received by his family as an honor. When Union troops finally captured Fort Wagner in September, Francis George Shaw wrote to dissuade the Army from any attempt to recover his son's body and separate it from those of his comrades-in-arms.

Sgt. William Carney, who rescued the regiment's fallen colors and returned to its lines despite four bullet wounds, became the first African–American to receive the Congressional Medal of Honor.

♣ ♥ ♣

W.E.B. Du Bois is born in Great Barrington (1868).

IN NEARLY A CENTURY on this earth, William Edward Burghardt Du Bois traveled from his birthplace in Great Barrington, Mass., to his deathbed in Accra, Ghana. His arrival and departure—the one in America, the other in Africa—neatly symbolize the man's struggle with the two aspects of his self.

"One ever feels his twoness," wrote Du Bois in *The Souls of Black Folk,* a 1903 volume that plumbed the African-American condition. "An American, a Negro; two souls, two thoughts, two unreconciled strivings; two warring ideals in one dark body, whose dogged strength alone keeps it from being torn asunder."

In the busy mill town on the Housatonic, a young Du Bois felt the first twinge of this dualism. Du Bois eventually abandoned the Berkshires for Nashville, where in 1888 he graduated from Fisk University, a black college.

Following a stay at the University of Berlin, Du Bois ventured home to Massachusetts and Harvard University. He now devoted his life to the study of history and the social sciences. His doctoral dissertation, *The Suppression of the African Slave Trade to the United States,* was published in 1896. In it, Du Bois outlined clearly the role slavery had played in the growth of the early American economy. Appointed a professor at Atlanta University, Du Bois began first systematic examinations of the conditions facing African–Americans.

What Du Bois learned as he worked on his sociological investigations led him to challenge the man who had come to represent—for white Americans, at least—the aspirations of all black Americans. A witness to the effects of Jim Crow segregation laws, race riots, and lynchings, Du Bois could not accept Booker T. Washington's policy of accommodation. Instead, Du Bois called for elimination of all forms of racial segregation. In 1905 Du Bois helped organize the militant "Niagara Movement," and in 1909, on the centennial of Abraham Lincoln's birth, he and a group of socialists and radicals, both black and white, founded the National Association for the Advancement of Colored People.

By the time of the Cold War, a new generation of NAACP leadership exiled Du Bois from its ranks. His plan to petition the United Nations regarding human rights violations against African–Americans in the United States was considered too militant. Among those opposed to the Du Bois petition was NAACP board member Eleanor Roosevelt as well as such important figures as Roy Wilkins and Walter White.

During the Korean War, Du Bois, in his eighties, was tried for being an agent of an unnamed foreign power but was acquitted. Nevertheless, he was denied a U.S. passport for many years. When Du Bois finally could travel freely, he taunted American authorities by visiting China and the Soviet bloc. In 1961, the man who advocated Pan-Africanism, an idea that all people of African background shared common concerns, moved to Ghana in West Africa and renounced his American citizenship. He died there in August 1963.

♣ ♥ ♣

Louisa May Alcott of Concord publishes *Little Women* (1868).

LOUISA MAY ALCOTT AND her father, Bronson Alcott, died two days apart in March 1888. They had shared the same birthday and were eulogized at the same funeral. A century later, they rest side by side in the earth and in the encyclopedia, as inextricably joined together as they were in life.

The elder Alcott's esoteric intellectual musings as well as his impecuniousness comprised a great influence on his daughter, the second of his four daughters born to his wife, Abigail May. At an early age, Louisa May Alcott conceived herself both a reformer and as responsible for her family's support. After stints as governess, seamstress, maid, teacher, and nurse, Louisa May Alcott turned at last to writing.

Raised in Concord among a community of radicals and intellectuals who included Emerson, Thoreau, and Fuller, Louisa May Alcott witnessed the rise and fall of Transcendentalism. Bronson Alcott, who fancied himself an educational reformer, opened a series of children's schools in which the goal was not better test scores but to "awaken thought." At the Temple School in Boston, where Margaret Fuller briefly taught, children received an especially gentle form of instruction. Punishment for classroom misbehavior consisted of the children hitting the teacher with a ruler.

In 1839 Bronson reluctantly closed the Temple School, and following a trip to England, he and British philosopher Charles Lane organized what they called "a new Eden" on a Harvard, Mass., hillside. Residents of "Fruitlands," which opened in 1843, were committed to be vegetarians and refused to wear wool (shearing deprived the sheep of its natural covering) or cotton (which was produced by slave labor). They even attempted to haul plows themselves (rather than burden horses with the work). The experiment—impractical even by typical Utopian standards—failed within a few months.

The zeal for reform that characterized the lives of Bronson and Abigail May Alcott was taken up by their daughter, but in more moderate fashion.

Louisa May Alcott served as a volunteer nurse in the Civil War, an experience that formed the basis of the well-received *Hospital Sketches* (1863). Throughout her life, she signed letters, "Yours for reform of all kinds."

Alcott penned novels and short stories in large quantities, including dozens of potboilers (some of these under a pseudonym, A. M. Barnard). No less a critic than Henry James remarked of *Moods,* an early Alcott novel from 1864, that "the two most striking facts with regard to [the book] are the author's ignorance of human nature and her self-confidence in spite of this ignorance."

When Alcott accepted a commission from a Boston publisher to write "a girls' story," the self-confidence remained, though she hardly proved ignorant of the human nature of girls and women. She knew her sisters, after all, and her mother. Most importantly, Alcott was keenly aware of the forces working against her female characters as they sought fulfillment and happiness in a world that severely restricted their choices.

Immediately on publication in 1868, *Little Women* (Part I) was a critical and commercial hit (a second part followed a year later). Spurred by this success, Alcott eventually completed a full chronicle of the lives of the March sisters, Meg, Jo, Beth, and Amy, as they progress to womanhood in *Little Men* (1871) and *Jo's Boys* (1886).

♣ ♥ ♣

Scientist Léopold Trouvelot mistakenly unleashes gypsy moths in North America (1869).

THE FRENCH SCIENTIST LÉOPOLD TROUVELOT was probably dreaming of great riches and the freedom to perform his research before the outcome of a daring private experiment.

In the last years of the Civil War, Trouvelot lived in Medford, Mass., then a rural enclave outside Boston. There he enclosed five acres of woodlands with an eight-foot-high fence. The trees within this area he wrapped in a filmy gauze so that at the night the shapes vaguely reminded him of

 women in enormous hair nets. From his house, he carefully brought out to the trees thousands of caterpillars, which had earlier hatched from eggs kept in jars.

His neighbors understood that Trouvelot hoped to breed hybrid silkworms that would be superior to those thriving in China. They would be the basis of a profitable American silk industry, which he would control.

To this end, the scientist tested a variety of caterpillars, including a species common in his native France, *Porthetria dispar,* the gypsy moth. Two inches long with tan body segments and stiff tufts of hair, gypsy moth caterpillars later grow into harmless and inoffensive adult gypsy moths. The moths, members of the tussock family, are native to Europe and were then unknown in North America.

While its common name—gypsy moth—suggests an insect with an attractive, romantic wanderlust, the creature's scientific name, *Porthetria dispar,* is considerably more revealing of its true dark character. From the ancient Greek, *porthetria* means to "ravage" or "lay waste." In the caterpillar or larval stage, gypsy moths are capable of attacking a forest and laying waste to vegetation like a marauding army invading a defenseless village.

In several weeks of constant feasting, in fact, these beasts can strip oak, willow, and birch trees entirely naked of their succulent green leaves. A single caterpillar may consume as much as a square foot of leaf surface daily. A particularly damaged area will appear as if dreary autumn has suddenly replaced the brightness and promise of late spring. At night, when the nocturnal caterpillars prefer to dine, the distant crackling static in the trees is the sound of a million tiny mouths snacking. Over the centuries, gypsy moth caterpillars regularly attacked French cork trees, German linden trees, and forests throughout the Continent.

By 1869 Trouvelot realized that his netting and his fence had not prevented gypsy moth caterpillars from escaping out of his open-air laboratory. In North America, *Porthetria dispar* had no natural enemies to help control its spread. Trouvelot contacted scientific journals about the problem but soon left Medford and returned to his homeland.

By the spring of 1889, gypsy moth caterpillars in the millions covered trees in Medford and surrounding towns. Caterpillars clung to leaves and bark in such numbers that one resident likened them to cold macaroni stuck together. The commonwealth convened the Gypsy Moth Commission to attempt to control the pests. Poisonous arsenic compounds were sprayed in trees and vast wooded areas were burned, among other desperate measures.

In 1901, however, the caterpillars were sighted in Providence. By 1920 they were well established across all of New England. Today they range from Nova Scotia to North Carolina and as far west as Michigan and Illinois. The quality of their silk is so poor as to be commercially worthless.

♣ ♛ ♣

Fire sweeps through downtown Boston (1872).

THE FIRST ALARM RANG from Box 52, on the corner of Lincoln and Bedford streets, at 7:24 P.M. on November 9, 1872. A general alarm sounded barely more than fifteen minutes later. The Great Boston Fire of 1872 burned out of control until the following afternoon.

From the first flickers in a five-story granite block at Kingston and Summer streets, the fire eventually destroyed 776 buildings with a total assessed value of $13.5 million and contents valued at $60 million. Flames killed thirty-three people and devoured a sixty-five-acre area within Washington Street on the west, Summer Street on the south, Liberty Square on the east, and State Street on the north.

The fire gutted many buildings surviving from Boston's colonial era. The fire leveled with equal force the offices of the *Transcript,* the preferred journal of Boston's Brahmins, along with those of the *Pilot,* a Catholic weekly then edited by John Boyle O'Reilly. Miraculously spared was the Old South Meeting House at Milk and Washington streets. Looking from its clock tower down Milk Street to the harbor, the city was transformed into a wasteland.

Long before the fire, the downtown district had already lost its fashionable status as a residential quarter for Boston's wealthier merchants. Shops and businesses gradually replaced homes throughout the midcentury. On delicately curved Franklin Street, Charles Bulfinch's elegant Tontine Crescent town house block was razed in 1858 to make way for undistinguished offices.

Residences that were still standing ignited like tinder in the great fire's path. Many of these homes were in poor condition. They had constituted a convenient but hazardous slum for the Irish and other immigrants who worked on the nearby waterfront's bustling docks.

In the early stages of the battle, firefighters became frustrated when outdated water pipes delivered insufficient pressure through their hoses. Contributing to the fire's magnitude was an epidemic of distemper among the department's horses. Steam engines and other heavy equipment were hauled by men.

At the Western Union office on State Street, telegraph operators pleaded for help from every fire department within 50 miles of Boston. Altogether, 2,163 firefighters from 31 neighboring cities and towns answered the call. Of the 33 who perished in the blaze, 13 were firefighters.

The nearly spontaneous rebirth of downtown Boston became a testament to the prudence of well-insured property owners. In the decade following the Great Fire of 1872, the city's center filled with buildings of flame-resistant stone and iron.

♣ ♥ ♣

Dr. Susan Dimock opens the first training school for nurses (1872).

BEFORE THE CIVIL WAR, nurses were not required or even expected to have much, if any, medical education.

Clara Barton, a Worcester, Mass., native, became famous as the Civil War's "Angel of the Battlefield" without benefit of any formal training. She later founded the U.S. Red Cross Society, now known as the American Red Cross.

In 1861 Dorothea Lynde Dix of Boston was appointed superintendent of the Female Nurses of the Army despite a similar lack of medical knowledge. Dix had fought for twenty years to improve conditions in the commonwealth's hospitals for the mentally ill. For the army, she helped recruit more than two thousand women to care for the Union's wounded.

The reform of nursing and the general improvement of conditions for women both as patients and as medical practitioners were thoroughly entwined. A significant advance came in 1862, when Dr. Marie Zakrzewska, a German physician, opened the New England Hospital for Women and Children in Boston. The new hospital provided medical care administered by women for women. It quickly became a clinical proving ground for the nation's first generation of women physicians.

In January 1866 Susan Dimock, nineteen, arrived in Boston from western Massachusetts, where she had taught in the local school. Dimock had shown great interest in medicine since she was a child. Growing up in Washington, N.C., the precocious girl read *Materia Medica* in the original Latin. Her family moved north in the last days of the Civil War after Dimock's father died and her mother lost the family property to the conquering Union Army. Upon completing a reading list drawn up by Dr.

Zakrzewska, Susan Dimock was accepted to attend clinical classes at New England Hospital.

In short order, Dimock became the favorite pupil of Dr. Lucy Sewall, the resident physician who frequently put her students in charge of caring for poor women who came to the hospital in childbirth. Dimock responded with enthusiasm to the task and even volunteered to relieve her fellow students at night.

In 1867, after a year's study with Dr. Sewall, Dimock applied for admission to Harvard Medical School but was denied (the school remained male only until 1945). Dr. Zakrzewska subsequently arranged for her students to receive clinical instruction at Massachusetts General Hospital (MGH) and Massachusetts Eye and Ear Infirmary on separate days from Harvard Medical School students.

Exclusion by Boston's medical establishment stalled but did not halt Dimock's ambition to become a fully trained physician. In 1868 she was admitted to the University of Zurich. The dean of the medical faculty insisted in his acceptance note that, at Zurich, "female students enjoy equal advantages with male students." Two generous Bostonians anonymously paid Dimock's tuition and fees. She returned to Boston in 1872 as Susan Dimock, M.D.

With a women's hospital in place and a staff of qualified women physicians operating it, the next logical step was to establish a training school for nurses. The nation's first such program opened in 1872, with Dr. Dimock as its director. The school's first graduate was Judson Richard, who later become the first "superintendent of nurses" at Massachusetts General Hospital, where she introduced reforms that forever changed the nursing profession. At MGH, Richards insisted that the nursing staff wear special uniforms and that they keep records on all their patients. Under Dr. Dimock's supervision and the commitment of her graduates, the nursing profession began to take the shape we recognize today.

♣ ♥ ♣

Harvard and McGill face off in a two-game series of "Boston football," the direct ancestor of today's American football (1874).

A BASIC YET RADICAL innovation distinguished "Boston football" from the other types of American football played elsewhere in the eastern United States, mostly at elite universities. In essence, this was the same distinction that had earlier separated rugby from soccer: rather than simply kick a round leather ball to move it forward on the field and score a goal, players in the "Boston game" were allowed to throw the ball and, later, to run with it.

College football traditionally celebrates its birthday as November 6, 1869. On that fall day, teams from Rutgers and Princeton squared off on a vacant grass lot in New Brunswick, N.J. (Rutgers won, 6–4). The football they played, however, was nothing like contemporary American football. Teams fielded twenty-five players to a side; no running or throwing was permitted; the ball was advanced by foot, head, or shoulder. Scoring was made by kicking a round ball through an opponent's goal, which was 8 yards wide on a field 120 yards long and 75 yards wide.

The "Boston game" had evolved from a rough-and-tumble sport played on Boston Common from before the Civil War. In 1863 the Oneida Football Club was formed by students from English, Latin, and other city high schools as the first organized football club in the United States. Not surprisingly, prominent family names figured on the Oneida roster, including Lawrence, Peabody, and Bowditch.

In three years of play, Oneida never lost a game or permitted an opponent to score. As the "Boston game" was then played, however, scoring a goal amounted to the same thing as winning (thus all games ended as 1–0). In Oneida football, there was no letup except when the ball went out of bounds. The round ball could be tossed as well as kicked.

Presumably, Oneida's blue-blooded players graduated from high school and carried their football rules with them to Harvard. When a group of colleges including Yale, Columbia, Rutgers, and Princeton gathered in New York City in October 1873, they sought to establish a uniform set of football rules. Harvard was invited to join them, but declined. The Crimson did not wish to give up the Boston version of the game.

On May 14 and 15, 1874, a football team from Montréal's McGill University visited Cambridge for a two-game series with Harvard. McGill's game strongly emphasized running and tackling and was even more like rugby than the Boston game. Harvard football rules permitted throwing and even dribbling the ball, but the game remained like soccer in its heavy reliance on kicking.

Harvard won the first game, 3–0; the second game was a scoreless tie. The Crimson boys were nevertheless impressed with the game McGill played, and they quickly adopted the Montréal style of running with the ball and tackling opponents. Harvard's first football game against an American team came in 1875, when the team played Tufts twice, once in the spring and again in the fall. On November 13, 1875, Harvard played its first football game against Yale, establishing a legendary rivalry.

Later that month, Harvard, Yale, Princeton, and Columbia gathered in Springfield to form the Intercollegiate Football Association. The rules they adopted were Harvard's. Within five years, the "Boston game," as revised, became the dominant form of football played in America.

♣ ♥ ♣

Mary Baker Eddy begins Christian Science (1875).

LIVING ALONE IN LYNN, Mary Baker felt hopeless. She had endured various maladies in her life and, for a time at least, a charismatic spiritual healer had helped to cure her condition. The healer, Phineas Quimby, died in

1866, and Baker's illness—a kind of spinal ailment—returned shortly afterward. An accident, apparently a fall on ice, compounded the pain.

Baker, forty-five, turned to the Bible for solace. In the New Testament she read an account of healing by Jesus and was miraculously cured. The experience led her to believe that all disease was a product of the mind.

In *Science and Health,* which Baker published in 1875 and which appeared in 382 revised editions throughout the rest of her life, Baker outlined her new philosophy. "Christian Science," as she called it, sought to restore "primitive Christianity and its lost element of healing."

Christian Science urged followers to throw off the limitations of flesh by accepting "the mind of Christ." Prayer, ordinarily necessary for spiritual redemption in the next world, acquired curative powers in this one. Christian Science required men and women to look beyond material appearances to find the true spiritual order.

The Church of Christ, Scientist was formally established in Boston in 1872; twenty years later, the church was reorganized as the First Church of Christ, Scientist. The Mother Church in Boston, which opened in 1894, was made responsible for the various branches around the world. The Christian Science Publishing Society began publishing *The Christian Science Monitor* newspaper in 1908.

Mary Baker married one of her followers, Asa Gilbert Eddy, in 1877. Her third husband, Eddy died in 1882, and Baker ended her long life enduring alone the pain that had plagued her since childhood. She became something of a recluse and feared what she called "malicious animal magnetism" directed at her by Christian Science's detractors. Baker died in Chestnut Hill of pneumonia at eighty-nine.

♣ ❦ ♣

Alexander Graham Bell, working in a Boston garret, invents the telephone (1876).

ON MARCH 3, 1876, the applicant's twenty-ninth birthday, the U.S. Patent Office in Washington granted Patent No. 174,465 for "the method of, and apparatus for, transmitting vocal or other sounds telegraphically...by causing electrical undulations, similar in form to the vibrations of the air accompanying the said vocal or other sounds."

At least that was the principle. Alexander Graham Bell, a man overworked to the point of confusion, had not demonstrated that any such improvement in the telegraph would actually transmit human *conversation*. For nearly a year, he and his assistant Thomas Watson had only transmitted recognizable vocal sounds—shouts, mostly, and those were heard but faintly at the receiving end. Their device could not yet carry a single intelligible sentence from one room of a Boston garret to another.

The Scots-born inventor first came to the commonwealth in 1871 on a lecture tour demonstrating his father's system for teaching the hearing-impaired to speak. "Visible Speech for the Deaf" was essentially a written code indicating how one should position the lips, tongue, and palate to make the usual sounds of speech. His success with the program soon led Bell to open his own school for the deaf. In 1873 he was appointed a distinguished professor of "vocal physiology" at Boston University.

All the while, A. Graham Bell (as he preferred to be known) worked nights seeking to perfect what he called a "harmonic telegraph" capable of transmitting sound rather than merely dots and dashes. He was convinced the idea could lead to sending human conversation over wire, but he lacked the mechanical and electrical expertise to realize his dream.

In the shop where he sometimes brought his devices for repairs, Bell found Thomas Watson. The self-taught electrician seemed capable of translating the professor's vision and enthusiasm into reality. At an improvised laboratory on Court Street, the pair struggled to perfect the harmonic telegraph, which transmitted its first sounds in June 1875. When success appeared near, a secretive Bell chose to move the lab, himself, and Watson to a nearby boardinghouse. For a rent of $4 a week, they conducted experiments in one attic room and slept in the other.

March 10, 1876, saw Watson experimenting with raising the volume of transmitted vocal sounds. He rigged a wire from a cup of sulfuric acid to generate an electrical current (much like a typical battery circuit). Watson connected one end of the device and left Bell to go to the other room for a test. As he later recorded in a memoir, Watson next bent to the receiver and was surprised to hear Bell exclaim, "Mr. Watson, come here, I want you!" The clumsy professor had spilled dangerous sulfuric acid on his clothes. "The tone of his voice indicated he needed help," his assistant remembered.

On October 9, Bell and Watson gave a demonstration of the invention to a group of Boston journalists. They carried on what is recorded as the first "long-distance" telephone conversation—from the downtown laboratory to the Walworth Manufacturing Company offices in Cambridgeport, two miles away, using a borrowed telegraph line.

In May 1877, the first telephone for business use on a private line was installed from the State Street offices of Stone & Downer, bankers, to the home of its president, Roswell C. Downer, on Central Street, Somerville. That month there were six telephones in commercial use in Greater Boston. By November the number had jumped to three thousand, and in 1878 the first telephone directory was published in Boston.

♣ ♥ ♣

Trinity Church in Copley Square, Boston, is consecrated (1877).

JUST AS PEOPLE SEEM to resemble their pets, so the architect and his masterpiece shared important character traits in common. Henry Hobson

Richardson was an affable bon vivant whose size grew to almost architectural proportions. His taste in food and friends was exquisitely refined. At his sprawling Brookline estate, Richardson welcomed such distinguished guests as sculptor Augustus Saint-Gaudens. Together they enjoyed Chesapeake Bay oysters freshly shipped from Baltimore, and the best French champagne.

Trinity Church in Copley Square, designed in 1872 and completed more than four years later, in 1877, recalls a sybaritic Romanesque king seated in his throne at court. The tremendous bulk of its granite foundation supports a broad, imposing tower with a simple crown. The building's heavy robes of stone are richly embroidered with statuary and flecked with the baubles of John LaFarge's stained glass. Inside, the church is a feast of painting and decoration.

The triumph Richardson enjoyed with Trinity Church may be best appreciated by first noting what the architect rejected. Not entirely obvious today is that he settled on a very personal style out of keeping with then prevailing fashion. The late Victorian period saw the elevation of an elaborate Italianate Gothic architecture inspired by the critical principles of John Ruskin, an English writer on the history of architecture. In Ruskin's view, certain Gothic styles attained a pitch of perfection that demanded their imitation.

A prominent surviving example in Boston of Ruskinian Gothic stands conveniently opposite Trinity: the "New Old South Church," designed by Cummings and Sears and dedicated in 1875. Old South's Italian cookie wafer terra-cotta facade has admirers, yet it decidedly lacks the powerful magnetism of Trinity's rough-faced granite. If the two buildings could hold a conversation, Old South would speak in the mannered tone of a European diplomat, and Trinity would roar like an indelicate American businessman.

What Richardson found in the Romanesque was an architecture capable of reflecting American confidence and might at the end of the nineteenth century. In Western Europe, the Romanesque directly preceded the Gothic. The Romanesque is characterized by the round arch and a clear arrangement of elements and forms. Like the essential American character, the Romanesque is unpretentious and direct.

Henry Hobson Richardson, the great-grandson of Joseph Priestley, the discover of oxygen, was born in Louisiana in 1838. He came to Massachusetts to attend Harvard in 1855 and never returned to the South. Throughout the Civil War he lived in Paris, where he attended the École des Beaux-Arts and worked in the office of architect Théodore Labrouste. Among only a handful of professionally trained American architects, Richardson was certain of a livelihood when he went home to America in 1865.

The success of Trinity Church helped justify for Richardson a move from New York to Boston in 1874. Until he died in 1886, he worked on numerous New England area commissions, including houses, libraries, suburban railroad stations, and commercial buildings. In Quincy, the Crane Memorial Library from 1880 ranks among his finest work.

The planning for Back Bay never explicitly called for open space, aside from the green strip of the Commonwealth Avenue Mall. Copley Square, which grew organically (the city purchased the land in two triangular chunks in 1883 and 1885), is an unexpected and delightful relief from the analytical grid of streets surrounding it. Quite accidentally, Trinity Church, one of the nation's architectural gems, has acquired a handsome setting worthy of it.

♣ ♥ ♣

The New England Society for the Suppression of Vice, later renamed the New England Watch and Ward Society, is established (1878).

WHEN THE NEW ENGLAND Society for the Suppression of Vice was established on May 28, 1878, it joined the august company of other such groups in London, New York, Philadelphia, Chicago, and Cincinnati. Their mutual goal was the "suppression of all agencies tending to corrupt the morals of youth." Characteristically for the descendants of Puritan witch-hunters, only the Boston group achieved a kind of sublime level of moral fussiness.

Keeping the Puritans pure, to paraphrase H. L. Mencken's *American Mercury,* required more than the ordinary censor's diligence. In one notable year, volunteer members of the captious New England Watch and Ward Society (adopted in 1891, the name referred to Boston's original police force) reviewed a weighty reading list of novels by H. G. Wells, Sinclair Lewis, Ernest Hemingway, Sherwood Anderson, and John Dos Passos. All were properly examined and subsequently "banned in Boston." Typically, the charges leveled were that a work was "pernicious," "filthy," or "Frenchy."

Among publishers, "banned in Boston" became a mark of disgrace that they eagerly sought. Influential booksellers were occasionally offered bribes to augment the list of forbidden tomes, but such underhand tactics were rare. Publishers simply preferred to select another volume of obviously "immoral literature" from the slush pile rather than engage in any hard bargaining.

In late Victorian America, urban crime was rampant, and city police forces were hostage to corruption and political influence. Much to their credit, volunteer watchdog groups of the period were able to force a reluctant government to perform its neglected duties and to enforce the law. Rigged lotteries and suspicious gambling halls were shut down, and notorious prostitution rings were broken as the direct result of efforts by genuinely concerned citizens.

Emboldened by early successes, however, the Brahmins went further than petty crime in their vendetta against "evils that require correction." Boston storekeepers were accordingly cited for displaying "immodest advertising" in their shop windows; all manner of immoral literature was forbidden to be sold; and allegedly obscene motion pictures were heavily edited. Thackeray's *Catherine,* in one instance of fairly typical Puritan zealousness, was put down by a well-placed Watch and Ward Society critic as a "horrid story of a lot of criminals."

In 1925 Clarence Darrow, the usually brilliant defense lawyer, met his match in the New England Watch and Ward Society. The attorney's pleas on behalf of Theodore Dreiser's masterpiece *An American Tragedy* fell on the deaf ears of a Massachusetts Supreme Court justice, and the book's New York publisher was duly convicted on obscenity charges.

At the society's Boston offices, shelves sagged with pernicious books, and files bulged with Frenchy photographs, all of which could be reviewed only by paid-up board members. Private exhibitions were given of film scenes recovered from the censor's cutting room floor. Puritanism, in Mencken's definition, may be "the haunting fear that someone, some-where, may be happy," yet membership in the New England Watch and Ward Society had its moments.

♣ ♥ ♣

Helen Hunt Jackson becomes a national advocate for Native American rights (1879).

THE FOUR MEMBERS OF the unusual lecture tour came east from Omaha in the fall of 1879. Thomas Henry Tibbles was editor of the *Omaha Herald*. His companions were all from the Ponca Indian tribe: Chief Standing Bear; Susette LaFlesche, called Bright Eyes; and Frank, her brother. Asked by a hotel receptionist to give his residence, Standing Bear replied, "homeless."

In Boston, Standing Bear told a reception for the Omaha Indian Committee of the betrayal and indignities his people had suffered at the hands of the federal government. Among the attentive crowd was Helen Hunt Jackson, a Massachusetts native and well-regarded author then living in Colorado. Indifferent to the abolition movement before the Civil War, and later an outspoken opponent of women's suffrage, Jackson was in town visiting with her sister-in-law on Beacon Hill.

The Indian chief's lecture likely appeared to Jackson at first as a diverting entertainment. Nevertheless, she listened closely while Standing

Bear painfully described how his people were driven from their homes in the Black Hills after gold was discovered there. Federal agents promised the Ponca that if the land where they were being displaced was unsuitable for them, the tribe could take their case to the president in Washington.

Indignation rose in Jackson's heart with Standing Bear's every word.

The new land provided for the Ponca proved as worthless as the white man's word, said the chief. Refused any meeting with the president, Standing Bear led a march back to the Ponca's former territory, only for the Army to turn him back again. Trapped on a desperate, circular trek, many of the Ponca tribe, including two of the chief's children, died from starvation and disease.

For his refusal to obey soldiers and federal agents, Standing Bear was arrested. He was subsequently released on a writ of *habeas corpus* after a Nebraska court found the Ponca were not wards of the state "but persons and free." A breakthrough of sorts for Indian civil rights, this decision ironically left the tribe without government protection.

The Ponca finally chose to settle on a small portion of Indian territory land overlooked by federal surveyors, though they required considerable help with planting crops and building new homes. *Omaha Herald* editor Tibbles took up the cause and organized Standing Bear's lecture tour as an attention-grabbing fundraising campaign.

Jackson was immediately enlisted. The woman whom Emerson had called "America's greatest living poet" now wrote a series of fiery newspaper articles about the case. In Boston, Jackson organized the Boston Indian Citizenship Association, and she soon became a national leader in the Indian reform movement.

Two years of research on Indian treaties led to publication of *A Century of Dishonor,* a four-hundred-page tome enumerating the federal government's conduct toward native peoples. The author sent a copy to every member of Congress at her own expense. She wrote a second tract, *California and the Missions,* reporting on the wretched condition of Indian reservations in that state, but her most popular work on the subject was *Ramona,* a romantic novel about a white woman who marries an Indian.

From a century's distance, Helen Hunt Jackson appears a quaint figure. She devoutly believed that if only public officials could learn the truth about the country's past treatment of the Indians, they would take action. Her last letter, written on her deathbed in 1885, went to President Grover Cleveland. The indefatigable author urged him "to strike the first steady blow toward lifting the burden of infamy from our country and righting the wrongs of the Indian race."

♣ ♥ ♣

Frederick Law Olmsted begins work on the "Emerald Necklace" park system of Boston (1881).

THE IMPULSE, ADMITTEDLY HACKNEYED, is to call them Boston's crown jewels. The arrangement of parks and ponds that makes up the "Emerald Necklace" certainly merits high tribute, yet the city wears its green and open spaces as casually and comfortably as if they were only costume jewelry.

Stretching for five miles from the urban confines of Boston Common to the open country of Franklin Park, the Emerald Necklace takes in an astounding variety of landscapes. Thickets and open glades; brackish marshes and freshwater ponds; wild forests and manicured flower beds; these and other elements unfold along the system's route like a nineteenth-century novel dense with subplots and richly populated by idiosyncratic characters.

An author first and later a landscape architect, Frederick Law Olmsted suffered from poor eyesight as a young man, and he trained himself to be a thorough and thoughtful observer. As a reporter for *The New York Times* from 1852 to 1855, the pro-abolitionist Olmsted sent weekly dispatches from the South detailing the degrading character of slavery. He also wrote several incisive travelogues, including *Walks and Talks of an American Farmer in England* (1850) and *A Journey Through Texas* (1857).

In 1857 Olmsted became first superintendent of New York City's Central Park. He was thirty-five, and in a peripatetic youth had acquired wide experience. He had served as a seaman in the China trade and as a farmer in his native Connecticut; he had variously studied engineering, science, and agriculture; and he had endured financial failure in business. Whether these amount to ideal qualifications for a landscape architect is debatable, but Olmsted was perhaps as well prepared as anyone in pre-Civil War America to imagine a new form for the wasteland at the New York City limits. A year later, he and collaborator Calvert Vaux won an open design competition for Central Park with a plan they called "Greensward."

From Yosemite Park to the U.S. Capitol grounds, Frederick Law Olmsted imposed over the next half century a wholly personal vision for landscape design and the preservation of open space. His six principles of landscape design included scenery, suitability, sanitation, subordination, separation, and spaciousness.

Above all, Olmsted held a powerful faith in the ability of landscape architecture to promote a sense of community and to have a positive impact on society. He was deeply aware that the development of public parks in America—once a place of boundless open spaces—coincided with an unprecedented growth of the nation's cities. "Is it not reasonable to regard it as a self-preserving instinct of civilization?" he asked pointedly in 1881.

That same year, while on a winter visit to Henry Hobson Richardson's Brookline estate, Olmsted woke to behold a snow-blanketed suburban landscape and a snowplow clearing the street. "This is a civilized community," he reportedly told the architect of Trinity Church. "I'm going to live here." In 1883 Olmsted moved his family and business practice from New York to a renovated farmhouse at the corner of Dudley and Warren streets.

Olmsted had already begun work in 1878 to create a Back Bay park for the area known as the Fens, a swamp at the confluence of the Muddy River, Stony Creek, and the Charles. Gradually his plan for the Fens grew into a revolutionary treatment for a continuous city park system. The design scheme for what we know today as the Emerald Necklace was first presented to the Boston Parks Commission in 1881. Of one prominent jewel in the necklace, Jamaica Pond, Olmsted wrote seductively that it should be "for the most part shaded by a fine natural forest growth to be brought out overhangingly [sic], darkening the water's edge and favoring great beauty in reflections and flickering half-lights."

The effect today is as the author imagined more than a century ago.

♣ ♥ ♣

Frederick Childe Hassam paints *Boston Common at Twilight* (1885).

ALTHOUGH THE CITY IS richly evoked in several centuries' worth of poetry and prose, Boston, unlike New York or Paris, has rarely served as the subject of any serious painting. On reflection, contributing factors to this lack may include the basic Puritan disdain of the decorative arts and a Brahmin distrust of the unsubstantial nature of an artist's livelihood (a writer, by contrast, is at least considered to be an educated person). To that add a fairly dull quality of light and a climate that is neither resplendent nor vaporous. The Bostonian artist has seemingly little choice but to move on.

It was no surprise that Dorchester-born Frederick Childe Hassam should attach himself at a young age to Europe, particularly Paris, and, later in his life, to New York City. Throughout the late nineteenth and early twentieth centuries, those regions offered the artist an overflowing banquet of subject matter.

The young Childe Hassam spent a Civil War-era childhood developing his painter's eye and acquiring a taste for fine art. When he was still in high school, he began working for a Boston engraver, from whom he learned the techniques of etching and lithography. He was well acquainted with Impressionism long before he ever ventured overseas. From early on in the movement's development, Boston collectors had greatly prized Renoir, Monet, and their compatriots.

On his first European tour, in 1883, the twenty-four-year-old Childe Hassam tramped his easel and watercolors through Britain, Belgium, the Netherlands, Spain, and Italy. An exhibit that same year displayed many of these works in a Boston gallery and won wide acclaim for the hometown artist.

By the time of Childe Hassam's 1883 "grand tour," Impressionism was already a decade-old phenomenon. In 1874 French artists held the first of a series of independent exhibitions in Paris. The movement was, in fact, all but played out when the Bostonian landed in Europe. Impressionism, which emphasized a free play of color and light, had at first shocked and disgusted critics and the public. Nevertheless, it quickly found acceptance, and a generation of artists across Europe and America adopted the easily mimicked style. Childe Hassam was no less susceptible to the romance of Impressionism than his contemporaries.

From his studio on Tremont Street overlooking Boston Common, the painter must have sensed something of the city's European flavor as he made sketches for a street scene in the winter of 1885. The flickering gaslights, the rushing horse-drawn trolleys, the dusty air from a thousand coal fires became an essential part of the work. For a human element, he included a woman and two children feeding seeds or crumbs to gathering sparrows.

Over the next decade, Childe Hassam painted other evocative cityscapes—among them *April Showers, Champs Élysées* and *Fifth Avenue in Winter*—yet the tender scene he captured in *Boston Common at Twilight* was never duplicated. His Impressionistic vision had, for once, elevated Boston above Paris and New York.

♣ ♥ ♣

Henry James publishes *The Bostonians* (1886).

IN *THE BOSTONIANS*, HENRY JAMES intended "to write a very American tale, a tale very characteristic of our social conditions." When planning the

novel in 1883, James wrote in a notebook, "I asked myself what was the most salient and peculiar point in our social life. The answer was the situation of women, the decline of the sentiment of sex, the agitation on their behalf."

The book's fairly flimsy plot hangs on an unusual love triangle: Basil Ransom, lawyer and native southerner, must compete with Olive Chancellor, Beacon Hill doyen and high-strung reformer, for the attentions of young Verena Tarrant, who is beginning a career as a charismatic speaker on women's rights. A conservative and chivalric southerner, Ransom finds much to scorn in Boston, particularly the do-gooders. His infatuation with Verena is less a romantic attraction than a reactionary's desire "to reform the reformer."

Throughout the novel, James dissects Ransom's patronizing attitude toward women even as he ridicules Olive Chancellor's disdain for men. Their contest for Verena ends in a Boston lecture hall when she abandons Olive and her speaking career and flees under Basil's wing. In the book's final lines Verena says with a sigh, "I am glad," but discovers she is in tears. James concludes, "It is to be feared that with the union, so far from brilliant, into which she was about to enter, these were not the last she was destined to shed."

The "city of reform" comes in for a large degree of satire in *The Bostonians*. Critics dispute whether the novel should be considered harshly as an indictment of reform or more lightly as an ironic portrait of a reform movement in its last stages of decay.

The peripatetic James family, originally of New York City, had moved to Boston after sojourns in Geneva, Paris, and London while Henry was still a teenager. Even after years of adult exile in Paris and London, the novelist could thoroughly recall the details of Boston and its society. Of his literary Bostonians, the most recognizable is Miss Birdseye, an aging philanthropist. James describes her as "heroic, she was sublime, the whole moral history of Boston was reflected in her displaced spectacles."

A little of this sort of thing went a long way with characteristically humorless Bostonians. They recognized in Miss Birdseye a great deal of Elizabeth Peabody, Nathaniel Hawthorne's crusading sister-in-law, and they were not amused to find her between the covers of a novel. Even William James accused his brother of poor judgment in drawing such a portrait. The author protested that Miss Birdseye is "the best figure in the book; she is treated with respect throughout the book."

James may have respected the reformer, but he had obvious disdain for the reform movement. "Miss Birdseye wore a short skirt, James writes, "to suggest that she was a woman of business, that she wished to be free for action. She belonged to the Short-Skirt League, as a matter of course; for she belonged to any and every league that had been founded for almost any purpose whatever."

♣ ♥ ♣

Emily Dickinson dies at the family home in Amherst (1886).

SOME DRAMATIC INCIDENT EARLY in her life, which we may never know and will never entirely understand, drove Emily Dickinson of Amherst to spin a lush cocoon of silken words to shield herself from further injury. Unhappily, the butterfly she became never emerged while she was alive.

Today, the remarkable volume of poetry Dickinson composed is judged among the best written in English in the nineteenth century.

The vindicating judgment of history would likely have surprised Dickinson's own contemporaries. To a close friend, she was a "partially cracked poetess." The unkind remark had some basis in her strange habits. For many years until her death, Dickinson dressed only in white, like a nun in a habit. She scrupulously avoided visitors, and for the last twenty years of her life she did not even set her foot outside the family property in Amherst.

In her correspondence and whatever poetry she shared with friends and family, Dickinson trimmed her language so severely that she often baffled her readers. Beside the voluminous spreading oak of typical Victorian verse and prose, her intentionally diminished work appears like a bonsai tree.

Emily Dickinson was born December 10, 1830, at a time when Amherst, Mass., was nearly a frontier village. She attended Mount Holyoke, but left after the first year, apparently because of homesickness. While her father, Edward, served a term in Congress in 1855, Emily traveled once to Washington with her sister, the longest time Emily ever spent away from home.

On the return leg of that trip, Dickinson heard Rev. Charles Wadsworth preach in Philadelphia. The darkly attractive minister became her mentor and "dearest earthly friend" and even visited her in Amherst in 1860. His departure for a church in California in 1862 precipitated the first of Dickinson's several bouts with serious depression.

The great love of Dickinson's life was undoubtedly her father. Edward Dickinson was a puritanical figure—"he steps like Cromwell," his daughter wrote. Through her father, Emily Dickinson acquired a Puritan's characteristic fascination with death and the fate of the soul. With her deep love of nature, quick wit, and skeptical eye, Emily Dickinson transformed this morbid obsession into literature.

Dickinson wrote nearly eighteen hundred poems, but she published only seven during her lifetime, five of those in the *Springfield Republican.* Her surviving sister, Lavinia, published a first Dickinson collection in 1890. Not until 1955 did all her poems finally appear in print.

♣ ❦ ♣

Great Barrington becomes first city to have homes and streets lit with ac electricity (1886).

WILLIAM STANLEY, A BROOKLYN native who spent boyhood summers with his grandparents in Great Barrington, was fascinated by the flood of new

technology made possible by harnessing the power of electricity. In 1879 twenty-one-year-old Stanley dropped out of Yale University and, with money borrowed from his father, invested in a New York electroplating business and made a quick profit. That same year, Thomas Edison perfected the incandescent electric lamp.

In 1880 Stanley jumped at the chance to work in the United States Electric Company, a fledgling electric lamp manufacturer. By 1885 he had worked for several other electrical firms, including Westinghouse, as well as in a private laboratory, and held ten patents of his own on electrical light bulb manufacturing.

William Stanley's research made increasingly clear to him the practical limitations of the then prevailing form of electrical current known as Edison Direct Current (named for its principal proponent). "DC" electricity—the same form generated in household and automobile batteries—required large, cumbersome conductors and provided relatively low voltage levels.

When transmitted over wires at distances greater than a mile, direct current was susceptible to disturbing voltage drops. Edison and other influential industry figures, however, opposed switching to the more practical "alternating current." They feared that the extremely high voltage of "ac" was inherently dangerous and were also concerned for their financial investments in supplying direct current electricity.

In 1885 William Stanley retreated to Great Barrington for another quiet summer in the Berkshire foothills. There he brooded over his poor health from tuberculosis and his failure to convince his mentors of the value of his research findings. A determined Stanley finally decided to give the world a convincing demonstration. In the fall he leased the "old rubber mill" on Cottage Street in Great Barrington and set to work.

Stanley's plan was to use a 25-horsepower steam engine to generate 500 volts on a Siemens alternator. The electric current would then be transmitted along two telegraphlike wires running the length of Main Street. At each of twenty-five subscribers (mostly businesses, including a grocery store and a hotel), he installed an "exhorter" (what we call today a transformer) capable of reducing incoming power to a manageable 100 volts for the purpose of lighting incandescent lamps.

On March 6, 1886, Stanley threw the switch. The system tested successfully, and he gave a public demonstration ten days later. In short order, Stanley's generator was delivering electricity to numerous Great Barrington stores and homes from four o'clock in the afternoon until midnight. Electricity wasn't generated during the day, when it was considered unnecessary. If a Saturday night dance were held at Town Hall, the lights remained on until the band played its last number.

♣ ♟ ♣

At the New England Fair in Worcester, Samuel Messer Jones introduces the predecessor of the roadside diner (1887).

 AMERICAN EATING HABITS REFLECT the nation's peripatetic character. In a country always "on the go," food inevitably must follow. Americans have become accustomed, as a result, to eating anywhere and at any time. When abroad, they bemoan the rather more strict observation of meal hours and the impossibility of finding coffee to go with milk and sugar.

Until the period after the Civil War, however, Americans still ate either at home or in restaurants that usually closed at 8:00 P.M. Industrialization introduced the late shift, and with that, a call for good food served at all hours.

In 1872 in Providence, R.I., Walter Scott created a horse-drawn lunch cart, and from inside it he served eggs, pies, sandwiches, and, of course, coffee long into the wee hours. The copycats quickly followed.

The practice of eating at lunch carts was brought north to

Massachusetts in 1884 by Samuel Messer Jones of Worcester, a cousin of a prosperous Providence lunch cart owner. Unemployed at the time, Jones believed that he, too, could make good money in this new line of the catering business. He was not disappointed.

With his first profits of $800, Jones ordered another, larger cart built according to his own design. His one major improvement was a simple but significant one and was inspired by a particularly long night in the rain: the cart would be big enough so that customers could stand inside while eating.

In the fall of 1887, at the New England Fair in Worcester, Samuel Messer Jones introduced the "night lunch wagon." It was more of a building on wheels than a simple cart, and held a full kitchen as well as stools for diners. For attractive decoration, Jones installed woodwork and stained glass windows with motifs of cake, coffee, and sandwiches.

The immediate ancestor of the roadside diner, an American original, was born.

For the next generation, Worcester was the center of the country's fast-growing lunch cart industry. In 1889 Jones sold his flourishing business to fellow citizen Charles Palmer, who received the first patent for a lunch cart design in 1891.

Thomas Buckley opened his own New England Lunch Wagon Company in 1892 and was in his day the king of the lunch wagon. His firm eventually sold not only wagons but also supplies such as knives, mirrors, linoleum, and glass. In his zeal for the business, Buckley set up nearly three hundred wagons in towns across the United States from 1893 to 1898.

The most popular lunch wagons were only technically portable. Many were installed like mobile homes on a semipermanent basis at busy street corners. As a way to promote his product, Buckley became obsessed with creating more and more elaborate lunch wagons. In the "Tile Wagon," built in 1892, diners gazed at brilliant opal tiles, a brass cash register with intricate filigree, and heroic portraits of Washington, Lincoln, and Columbus.

In 1897 Buckley created what was arguably the first true American diner when he built the $8,000 White House Café on a stationary foundation. Its centerpiece was an impressive soda fountain of Mexican onyx with three dozen syrup dispensers.

Unfortunately for Buckley, the Worcester public was not impressed enough. In short order, the White House Café lost $25,000, and Thomas Buckley went broke. A successor firm, the Worcester Lunch Cart Company, continued to produce diners into the 1930s.

♣ ♥ ♣

James Naismith invents the game of basketball, in Springfield (1891).

THE NEW GAME MIGHT have been called "boxball."

Sometime in mid-December 1891, James Naismith asked a janitor at what is today Springfield College to find a pair of 15-by-15-inch boxes. The custodian instead returned with two half-bushel peach baskets, which Naismith ordered to be tied to the balcony railing at either end of the school gym.

A physical education instructor for the International Young Men's Christian Association (YMCA) Training School, Naismith called his class into the chilly gymnasium. The eighteen young men who were gathered saw the janitor and a companion seated atop ladders arranged beside the hanging peach baskets. "Hunh!" Frank Mahan, one of the students, muttered derisively, "another new game!"

Spurred by a school dean who wanted his students to continue their athletic training indoors after the football season ended, James Naismith had experimented before with "new games." For this latest trial, Naismith drew liberally from lacrosse, soccer, and other existing sports. Lacrosse suggested the original positions of his players, for example, and a soccer ball was used because it was soft and too large to be concealed. Players were not allowed to run with the ball, which had to be tossed from one to another and into a goal. Holding, pushing, and tripping were barred.

Naismith aimed to create a noncontact, indoor sport that provided exercise for the whole body and required sharp mental attention.

Incredibly, the hybrid game of "basket ball" was an instant success. Naismith published his list of simple rules in the school's campus newspaper on January 15, 1892, and local athletic associations were soon clambering for copies. By year's end, the new game had even taken on an international dimension, when it was played for the first time in Mexico and Canada. Basketball soon spread overseas to France, China, Australia, and India.

Setting aside his initial skepticism, Frank Mahan became a devotee of "the new game." In fact, Mahan gets credit as the first person to call the sport "basket ball" (which, at first, was written as two words). "We have a basket and a ball," Mahan irrefutably observed, "so 'basket ball' would seem a good name for it."

The "basket" evolved quickly and the game along with it. Cylindrical baskets of heavy woven wire replaced peach baskets almost immediately. In 1893 these were replaced in their turn by "baskets" with iron rims and braided cord netting manufactured in Providence at the Narragansett Machine Co. Nevertheless, basket nets were not opened at the bottom until 1912. The first true "basket balls," made by the Overman Wheel Co. of Chicopee Falls, replaced soccer balls in 1894, the same year the free throw was introduced.

The first recorded women's basketball game was played barely four months after the first men's game. The teams were mostly drawn from women working in the Springfield Y's stenographers' pool, among them Maude Sherman, who later became Mrs. Naismith. On March 22, 1893, Senda Berenson Abbott introduced basket ball to the women students of Smith College in Northampton. Male spectators were not allowed to watch the bloomer-clad players.

A century after its invention, according to curators at the Naismith Memorial Basketball Hall of Fame in Springfield, basketball has conquered the world. The first two sides of nine players each (reduced to five players in 1895) have multiplied to some 18 million professionals and amateurs who dribble, fake, and shoot their way around the neighborhood court and in enormous indoor arenas.

Lizzie Borden took an ax … (1892).

FALL RIVER LEGEND, A 1948 ballet by Agnes De Mille with score written by Morton Gould; *Lizzie Borden,* a 1965 opera by Jack Beeson; and a 1934 play, *Nine Pine Street,* starring Lillian Gish, are among the list of ambitious works of art that all share for their inspiration the same famous crime. None of these, however, is likely to replace in the public mind four lines of cheap doggerel, composer unknown.

"Lizzie Borden took an ax and gave her mother forty whacks. And when she saw what she had done, she gave her father forty-one."

In all such accounts of the Borden murders, Lizzie is guilty and, frequently, she has done the deed for love. Most importantly to her, however, if not to either artists or posterity, is that Lizzie Borden was swiftly judged "not guilty" by a jury after only ninety minutes' deliberations. Their finding was roundly seconded by those who had followed the case closely.

No less an institution than *The New York Times* made its opinion of the Fall River court proceedings perfectly plain.

"The acquittal of this most unfortunate and cruelly persecuted woman was, by its promptness, in effect, a condemnation of the police authorities of Fall River and of the legal officers who secured the indictment and have conducted the trial," declared a *Times* editorial. "It was a declaration, not only that the prisoner was guiltless, but there was never any reason to suppose that she was guilty." Indeed, Fall River was named as the guilty party in place of Borden. It deserved conviction (in the New York press, at least) of being a slovenly and provincial backwater. "The town is not a large one," the *Times* editorial pointed out bluntly. "The police is of the usual inept and stupid and muddleheaded sort that such towns manage to get for themselves."

Pity the muddleheaded police, though. The scene they found at 62 Second Street the afternoon of August 4, 1892, would have muddled anyone's thinking. According to a contemporary account, Andrew Borden, sixty-nine, lay lifeless on the living room sofa. The president of the Union Savings Bank was a stern-faced Yankee capitalist who had accumulated a large fortune through real estate and other investments. Borden died from a deep wound to the left temple, possibly by the blow of an ax. His left eye was dug out, and a cut extended the length of his nose. Upstairs, Mrs. Borden, sixty-seven and the banker's second wife, lay in a pool of her own blood. She had been similarly attacked. "Hacked to pieces" was how one newspaper headline described her condition. Otherwise, nothing seemed to have been stolen, and the house was not ransacked.

Suspicion fell immediately on someone the papers called "a sturdy Portuguese," a laborer who worked on a farm Borden owned and who had visited his employer earlier in the day to demand wages owed him. Several arrests of suspicious persons were made—one Portuguese man was taken in custody as well as two Russian Jews. "They were locked up simply by way of precaution," noted a report in the *Boston Advertiser*.

The theory quickly took root among the Fall River press and public that the Borden murders were committed by someone who lived in the house—either Lizzie J. Borden, Andrew Borden's thirty-two-year-old daughter from his first marriage, or possibly the family maid Bridget Sullivan.

On August 11, police abruptly arrested Lizzie. Evidence and motive were scant. No ax or murder weapon of any kind was ever found. The state would suggest in court that Lizzie Borden was jealous of her stepmother and was afraid she would not receive a fair share of his father's estate when he died, but it never substantiated the charge.

Because Lizzie Borden said nothing, because she did not cry or show much of any emotion throughout her long ordeal, the prosecution felt that was proof enough of her guilt. The jury decided that it was not.

Lizzie Borden died in 1927, friendless and alone. In her will, the largest single bequest was for $30,000 to the local chapter of the Animal Rescue League.

♣ ♥ ♠

The Boston terrier is recognized by the American Kennel Club as America's first native purebred (1893).

IN THE ROMANTIC EYES of dog breeders, the Boston terrier seems to wear a tuxedo. With a white "blaze" draped across its eyes and a white chest setting off a sleek black coat, the animal's appearance bears more than a passing resemblance to a dog dressed in formal wear. The gruff yet gentle bulldog face even adds an appropriate touch of gravity to its elegant costume. Among fanciers, the Boston terrier is affectionately known as "the American gentleman."

The ancestor of all Boston terriers was a cross between an English bulldog and a white English terrier (a now extinct breed) that Robert C. Hooper of Boston purchased sometime after 1865. Weighing in at thirty-two pounds, "Judge" was considerably larger than his contemporary descendants.

As the now century-old pedigrees note, Judge was later mated to "Gyp or Kate," and quickly enough, the new breed of gentle and playful dogs had grown popular with Bostonians. The city's first dog show was held in 1879, and the dogs were entered simply as "bull terriers." After nearly a decade, however, a separate show category was established for what were had come to be known variously as "round-headed bull terriers," the American bull terrier, and even the bullet head.

Perhaps not surprisingly, the early champions of this unfamiliar breed met with opposition from breeders of true bull terriers who tried their best to discourage introduction of a new and, in their view, unworthy line of dog. Ambitious breeders finally organized themselves in 1889 in Boston as the American Bull Terrier Club. Their opponents charged that the dog was undeserving of the name and not even a typical bull terrier. In fact, the

Boston terrier is decidedly unterrierlike in appearance and temperament.

In 1891, bull terrier breeders and others successfully blocked an application to the American Kennel Club (AKC) for granting the Boston dogs the highly prized "purebred" status. The Bostonians were determined, however, and soon they recast themselves as the Boston Terrier Club of America. In 1893 the AKC relented in its opposition and enrolled the dogs on its official stud list following the breeders' second application. The Boston terrier thus became the first native American purebred dog.

Described as confident, outgoing, friendly, and alert, the Boston terrier is especially popular today with apartment dwellers across the country who appreciate the dog's pleasant behavior as well as its limited requirements for outdoor exercise. Middleweight dogs are quite manageable in size, weighing fifteen to twenty pounds. In addition, Boston terriers are typically long-lived canine companions who reach ages of fifteen years and more.

The first Boston terrier registered with the AKC was Hector, whelped July 19, 1891, and bred by George Huse of Boston. During Woodrow Wilson's administration, a Boston terrier lived in the White House. Helen Keller's pet dog was also a "Boston."

In a 1924 article for the AKC *Gazette,* dog fancier and Boston native Charles C. Kammerer recalled playing hooky from school to visit breeder John Barnard's Beacon Kennels on Myrtle Street. The Boston terrier, he wrote, "will stick to his master in prosperity and poverty; and in health and in sickness. He will sleep on the cold ground when the wintry winds blow and the snow drives fiercely, if only he may be near his master's side. He will kiss the hand that has no food to offer.

"When riches take wings and reputation falls to pieces," concluded Kammerer, "he is as constant in his love as the sun its journeys through the heavens. That is the American gentleman, the Boston terrier."

♠ ♥ ♣

In Springfield, Frank Duryea test-drives the first American gasoline-powered automobile (1893).

AT THE CLOSE OF the nineteenth century, numerous inventors and entrepreneurs across Europe and America contributed to the perfection of the internal combustion engine, the key element in the automobile as we know it today.

Jean Joseph Étienne Lenoir, a Belgian working in Paris, patented an internal combustion engine that burned coke gas in 1860. Improvements in petroleum products steered others to use more volatile gasoline for engine fuel. In 1885 Karl Benz put a one-cylinder, gasoline-powered engine on a three-wheeled vehicle with a steel frame—essentially a motor-tricycle. He sold his first four-wheeled Benz automobile two years later. In 1886 Gottlieb Daimler and Wilhelm Maybach mounted their own high-speed internal combustion engine on a modified carriage chassis. The Daimler Motoren-Gesellschaft opened for commercial automobile production in 1890.

Americans showed a keen interest in the many improvements made to self-propelled vehicles, but especially those powered by steam and electricity. They were relatively late in latching onto the gasoline-powered, internal combustion engine as the technology of choice.

Massachusetts inventors were no different from compatriots in other states. Beginning in 1859, Sylvester Roper of Roxbury produced a series of steam-powered coaches vehicles, including a two-passenger four-wheeler built in 1863. In 1888 Philip W. Pratt built the nation's first electric carriage and operated a manufacturing plant Boston's South End. In Brookline, German emigré Charles Holtzer assembled an electric car in 1892 for a wealthy Bostonian from parts purchased in Europe. The driver was involved in what was probably the state's first automobile accident, also in Brookline, in June 1893.

Gradually, mechanics and inventors in Massachusetts and around the country became frustrated with the limitations on speed and efficiency posed by heavy batteries and steam engines. Internal combustion engines were obviously smaller, lighter, and more powerful. The Americans copied diagrams of German designs published in *Scientific American* and made their own modifications.

Among those fascinated by what the Germans had accomplished were Frank and Charles Duryea, Illinois-born brothers who worked in a bicycle factory at Chicopee. Beginning in 1891, Charles Duryea prepared designs for a one-cylinder, two-cycle engine to be installed on a horse carriage.

When an investor agreed to stake the pair $1,000, the Duryeas rented space at a Springfield machine shop. Frank Duryea, the more mechanically inclined of the brothers, began the car's construction in the summer of 1892, and Charles soon returned to Peoria, Ill. Notwithstanding a bout with typhoid fever that interrupted his labors, Frank Duryea persevered for the next year.

On September 21, 1893, Frank Duryea finally tested his automobile on the road. The noisy car, hampered by a transmission problem, traveled only as far as two hundred feet before stalling. By January 18, 1894, however, Frank Duryea drove six miles round-trip from his shop to his investor's home at a top speed of eight miles per hour.

Eventually reunited, the Duryea brothers formed the Duryea Motor Wagon Company, the nation's first gasoline automobile manufacturer, in 1895. On Thanksgiving Day that year, they won America's first automobile race, from Chicago to Evanston, Ill., and back. The Duryea car averaged slightly over five miles per hour, but it had beaten three Benz automobiles as well as several American-made electric cars. The Duryea Motor Wagon Company folded in 1898 when Frank and Charles argued over division of its ownership.

The most memorable contribution to automobile history from Massachusetts was the Stanley Steamer. The Stanley twins, Francis Edgar and Freelan Oscar, began producing steam-powered automobiles in

Newton in 1897. At an 1898 automobile show in Cambridge, a Stanley Steamer set a world speed record (36 mph). The Stanley Motor Carriage Company closed in 1923.

♣ ♥ ♣

John McDermott wins the first Boston Marathon (1897).

AT THE FIRST MODERN Olympics, held in Athens in 1896, the American field and track squad shared in common their membership in the Boston Athletic Association. Founded in 1887, the BAA attracted to its ranks the vigorous sons of Boston's merchant princes. These athletes had competed as college students, and they wished to maintain their fit conditions even as gentlemen.

Devoted amateurs, the early BAA members disdained those who were paid money or ran in races where betting was allowed. It has been pointed out that this cult of amateurism, though admirable, was one that only wealthy men such as the Boston Brahmins could afford to abide by. Indeed, amateurism likely became a convenient instrument to keep out of sports "the wrong kind of people"—professionals who usually were drawn from among the working class, particularly immigrants.

The marathon derived from the ancient Greek practice of employing fleet-footed messengers to carry important communications from one city to another. In a legend with a historical basis, Pheidippides in 490 B.C. covered twenty-four miles from the Battle on the Plains of Marathon to Athens to bring word of the Persians' defeat. "Rejoice, we conquer!" Pheidippides supposedly declared on his arrival before he collapsed dead.

In 1896, the revival of the Olympics caught the public's attention with the decision to include a twenty-four-mile marathonlike race. The unprecedented running contest promised a romantic spectacle with an appealing hint of danger. Appropriately, a Greek won the race in two hours, fifty-five minutes, and twenty seconds.

On Patriot's Day, April 19, 1897, eighteen men gathered at the starting line in Ashland for the first Boston Marathon, sponsored by the BAA. Six runners represented several New York athletic clubs, including John J. McDermott, a lithographer, who had won the only other U.S. marathon yet held (from Stamford, Conn., to New York City in 1896). The Boston favorite, Dick Grant, was, of course, a Harvard man and a BAA member.

Ten runners finished the course, with the last arriving at the BAA clubhouse on Boylston Street four hours and ten minutes after the starting gun was fired. The winner was John McDermott, who fought cramps and blisters to cross the finish line at two hours, fifty-five minutes, and ten seconds—ten seconds ahead of the Olympic winner's time, and a new world record. Newspaper accounts estimated that twenty-five thousand spectators lined the marathon route, which was rather informally guarded. In the last few hundred yards of the race, McDermott weaved through a funeral procession moving somberly down Massachusetts Avenue.

A Bostonian did not win the Boston Marathon until 1916, when Arthur Ross crossed the finish line ahead of the pack.

♣ ♥ ♣

The first subway in America opens at Park Street Under (1897).

AT THE END OF the nineteenth century, Boston's tremendously popular system of interconnecting electric trolley lines converged downtown along Tremont Street near Boston Common and Old Granary Burying Ground. Streetcars gathered toward the center of the city's bustling business and retail district like metal filings around a powerful magnet.

Eventually even City Hall and the state legislature on nearby Beacon Hill conceded that there was a transit problem in Boston. Surveys were ordered and proposals evaluated. In the meantime, streetcar blockades worsened, and pedestrians despaired of ever crossing safely from Boston Common to their favorite shops on Winter Street.

A number of corrective schemes were considered. One proposal suggested clearing a path for a twenty-five-foot-wide transit "alley" between Washington and Tremont streets. Another advocated widening Tremont Street to improve the flow of trolleycars or otherwise putting up an elevated railway bridge high above the pavement. A variety of plans offered streetcar access to Boston Common either on the surface or along trenches.

At the same time, travelers who visited London, Paris, and Budapest returned with praises for those cities' revolutionary new underground trolley lines. Arguments were made in favor of such "subways" and were recorded in the Boston Transit Commission's first annual report.

"The subway destroys but little property," the commission noted. "The subway eliminates the danger which pedestrians now encounter in crossing tracks; the subway increases traffic capacity by removing from the surface one important class of traffic; the subway relieves the streets of the posts and network of wires necessary in the overhead trolley system; [and] the subway relieves the street of the noise of the streetcar, the rumble and jar of the wheels, the hum of the motor and the clang of the bell."

The Bostonians of the Victorian Age had apparently no reason to be nostalgic for the trolley's ding-ding-ding and clang-clang-clang. They were happy enough, indeed, to find an excuse to put it out of sight, at least along crowded Tremont Street, and they were willing to pay for it. In 1893 and 1894 the state legislature voted to fund a $5 million subway system, and construction work began at Boston Common on March 28, 1895.

On schedule and under budget, the nation's first subway line finally opened on September 1, 1897. The cars ran only the length of the Common, from Park Street to Boylston Street, at first, though by month's end, stations at Scollay Square and elsewhere were opened connecting "Park Street Under" to cars running on the West End Railway Company and the Boston Elevated Railway Company. Eventually a two-mile subway system stretched from Back Bay to North Station.

♣ ♥ ♣

The Boston Pilgrims face the Pittsburgh Pirates in the first "World Series" (1903).

IN 1900, BAN JOHNSON, a former Cincinnati sportswriter, changed forever the character of baseball. As president of what was formerly known as the Western League, Johnson announced that new baseball franchises were set to open the following season in Boston, Philadelphia, Baltimore, and Washington. The Western League—with teams in Cleveland and Chicago, among other midwestern cities—was renamed the "American League."

Johnson had the gall to declare that the American League was to be considered a "major" league on a par with the well-established National League. To ensure that no one questioned its "major league" status, Johnson announced that American League owners would not honor the National League's $2,400 salary cap.

Not surprisingly, 111 of the 182 players for the American League's first season were attracted from the lower paying National League. Triple Crown winner Nap Lajoie, for example, moved across town from the Philadelphia Phillies to the upstart Philadelphia Athletics. Pitcher Cy Young also bolted to the American League team in Boston. By 1903 a truce was reached between the two baseball leagues that ended American League raids on National League teams. Bleacher and standing-room tickets sold that season for fifty cents, while grandstand seats were a buck.

The more peaceful environment begged for an interleague championship contest. The National League pennant winners, the Pittsburgh Pirates, now challenged the American League leaders, the Boston Pilgrims (ancestors of the present day Red Sox), to a "World Series." A nine-game series was arranged with the first three and last two games to be played in Boston and the middle four in Pittsburgh.

The idea of a "World Series" wasn't entirely new. Twenty-one years before, when the term was first coined, the National League champion Chicago team first experimented with such a contest against the American Association champs from Cincinnati. The play in these early "World Series" was erratic, even farcical. The 1885 matchup saw 101 errors in seven games (27 errors were made in the final seventh game). That year's series ended in a draw, with three wins and a tie each for the St. Louis Browns and the Chicago White Stockings.

In the first game of the 1903 World Series (officially recorded as the first such match-up), Boston's Cy Young, a twenty-eight-game-winner in the regular season, was walloped for four runs in the first inning; the Pilgrims eventually lost, 7–3. When the Pilgrims and Pirates returned to Boston for an eighth game, the American League champs held a one-game lead over their National League rivals. A ninth game proved unnecessary, however, as pitcher Bill Dinneen won his third game of the series by a score of 3–0.

A strike threat made by the Boston Pilgrims nearly prevented the first World Series. The players' contracts expired on September 30, and the series was to be played well into October. Team owner Henry Killilea was told he must pay his men two weeks' additional wages as well the entire club's share of the series' gate. Killilea agreed to the extra pay, but successfully held out for a club owner's share of ticket sales. To boost the take, he charged admission to every attending sportswriter and even the owner of the Pittsburgh Pirates.

♣ ♥ ♣

Fenway Court, the home of Isabella Stewart Gardner, is opened with a gala New Year's Eve party (1903).

WHEN NINETEEN-YEAR-OLD BELLE STEWART of New York visited her classmate Julia Gardner of Boston in the winter of 1859, the two young women took chaperoned sleigh rides and attended chaperoned dances. At one dance, Julia's brother Jack took his turn with this bright-eyed but plain-looking visitor. On April 10, 1860, in New York's Grace Church, Isabella Stewart became "Mrs. Jack."

Belle Gardner became the center of social life in Boston because she had a style that flew in the face of the local tradition of not being showy and grand. As much a part of Boston's social circle as the Cabots and Lowells, "Mrs. Jack" nevertheless enjoyed being provocative. She converted to Buddhism for the shock value and walked lion cubs on a leash down Tremont Street. Her portrait by John Singer Sargent sparked comment for the way a string of white pearls around Belle's neck called attention to the deep neckline of her black dress (a usually indulgent Jack Gardner ordered that the painting not be exhibited as long as he lived).

In 1886 Jack and Belle Gardner were persuaded to support a subscription for an extraordinary Harvard scholarship. The recipient, twenty-two-year-old Bernard Berenson, reminded not a few Bostonians of Oscar Wilde, though he was a Lithuanian-born Jew raised in a South Boston slum. Through him, Mrs. Jack purchase her first Italian Renaissance painting of an early period, *The Tragedy of Lucretia* by Botticelli. Berenson had found the earl of Ashburnham, who was apparently strapped for cash, a willing seller at $16,500.

In 1894, "B.B." persuaded the Gardners to have him act as their agent in purchasing some Italian masterpieces. Altogether, the Gardners bought nineteen paintings while touring Europe that year; ten of those old masters they acquired through Berenson.

Only a family of staggering wealth could have kept up such a pace, and the Gardners never flagged. In 1898 alone, Mrs. Gardner bought work by such artists as Raphael, Giorgione, Rembrandt, Cellini, and Masaccio. They quickly joined an art treasure trove that included work by Cranach, Vermeer, and Titian. The Gardners' holdings amounted to one of the greatest private art collections in the world.

In December 1898 Isabella Stewart Gardner lost her husband of thirty-eight years. Even in mourning for Jack, the childless "Mrs. Jack" attracted notice from the public and the press, though few wasted pity on such a widow. With the $2.75 million her father willed his daughter in 1891, and a net bequest of $2.3 million provided at her husband's death, she enjoyed a tax-free annual income from various trusts exceeding $100,000 (in today's dollars, at least $1 million).

With ample funds at her disposal, "Mrs. Jack" bought a lot of land 100 feet by 150 feet on a marshy section of Boston called the Fenway. There she planned construction of a museum to house the collection of painting and sculptures she began to acquire while Jack was alive and happy to indulge her.

Appropriately located on Palace Road, Mrs. Gardner's building project was the extravagant result of a lifetime of international antique-hunting. Rather than a single Italian structure scrupulously reassembled, "Fenway Court" is a Frankenstein's monster of mismatched body parts: Venetian window frames; Roman mosaic floor tiles; Spanish leather wall coverings; and Flemish tapestries. Such features and furnishings provide a suitably rich setting for galleries crammed with an eclectic array of paintings and statues.

Like the worst of her class, Mrs. Gardner possessed a *noblesse oblige* attitude of staggering proportions. When construction of the music room was finished and only the acoustics remained to be tested, Mrs. Gardner ordered from the Perkins Institute for the Blind a load of their schoolchildren to come fill the seats and judge the results. She wanted an audience (other than the players) who could hear the music but not see the room. Its appearance must remain a secret until the entire palace was completed.

Engraved invitations were issued to 150 of Boston's most prominent citizens and a choice selection of others for January 1, 1903. Edith Wharton arrived from New York in a private railroad car. After a concert of Bach, Mozart, and Schubert, Mrs. Gardner finally threw open the doors to the flower-bedecked atrium of Fenway Court. The musicians were shunted out to the wintry night by a back door. The public did not get its first glimpse of the building's majesty until after its owner's death in 1925.

♣ ♥ ♣

Filene's Automatic Bargain Basement opens in Boston (1909).

EDWARD FILENE PROCLAIMED HIS new store to be unlike any other in the crowded downtown shopping area along Washington Street. For one thing, it lay below street level, with access from the newly constructed Washington Street subway tunnel. For another, the merchandise on sale bore strange tickets, which were stamped not only with the price but also with a date.

Filene's Automatic Bargain Basement was a store with the ultimate sales gimmick. Any item on its shelves or racks that did not sell immediately was discounted until it was either sold or given away. According to a scale of reductions prominently displayed at all store entrances, the item's original price was automatically marked down 25 percent at the end of twelve selling days; after eighteen days, the price was cut by 50 percent; after twenty-four days, by 75 percent. If after thirty selling days any item in Filene's Basement had still not found a buyer, it would be given away to charity.

As an enticement to thrifty Yankees, the unusual pricing system worked well. There were those people in the early days who voiced doubts about the authenticity of the much-trumpeted markdown practice, and others wondered if, perhaps, Edward Filene had lost his mind. In short order, however, a uniquely Boston institution was firmly established. Shopping for bargains was suddenly fashionable rather than merely necessary.

Outside the basement's doors, crowds gathered long before the appointed opening hour. They were full of the hope of finding an extraordinary "buy," as if the store contained buried treasure rather than merely clothing, handbags, and toys. Filene's Basement was not profitable for the first ten years, but it has done rather well since. The store has long been a tourist attraction for traveling shoppers.

Buyers for Filene's Basement became legendary for the way they hunted down merchandise marked "second" or "irregular" as well as canceled orders, surplus stocks, and discontinued lines. The store's owners likened these items to odd pieces of diamonds and other precious stones that remain after larger, more expensive gems have been cut and polished.

Anyone who has grown up in the Boston area will likely recall a particularly terrifying visit to Filene's Basement on a vacation day in grade school. No matter how tightly little fingers are wrapped around a parent's hand, somehow they come apart. Suddenly the adult is swallowed up in a swarm of bargain-hunting humanity that encircle a mountain of "famous maker" men's dress shirts.

♣ ♥ ♠

The "Bread and Roses" strike hits Lawrence's textile mills (1912).

WITH NEW YEAR'S DAY 1912, Massachusetts put into force a set of labor laws that had the effect of sending a tidal wave of reform over American industry. The regulations set maximum working hours for women and children at fifty-four hours weekly. In addition, a new law required a minimum wage to be paid female employees that will "supply the necessary cost of living and maintain the worker in health."

For their time, these were progressive, even revolutionary laws. Massachusetts frequently led the nation in labor reform, though the standards first introduced seem ludicrous today. In 1842, for example, the legislature restricted the working day for children to ten hours.

For factory workers, January 11 was to be the first payday under the new laws. In Lawrence, nearly forty thousand toiling workers gravely feared that textile mill owners would use a shortened working week as an excuse to cut wages. Envelopes were distributed, then hurriedly opened, and the workers' worst fears were realized: On average, about thirty-two cents were missing from each paycheck. Among those who typically earned just over $8 weekly, the pay cut was substantial.

Inside the mills, angry words were spoken in Polish, Italian, French, and other tongues. The mostly unorganized workers left their looms in a spontaneous strike, first at the Everett Mills and later at the American Woolen Company.

As a congressional investigation later uncovered, Lawrence was a tinderbox waiting for a spark. Husbands and wives labored side-by-side in the deafening mills, as well as most children over fourteen. "Malnutrition was universal," the committee noted in its report. "The chief articles of diet were oleomargarine, condensed milk, and a cheap meat stew." Factories and housing throughout Lawrence were deemed overcrowded and unsafe.

In the walkout's first days, union organizers rushed to Lawrence. The Industrial Workers of the World (IWW or "Wobblies") sent Joseph Ettor and Arturo Giovannitti from New York to provide a kind of strike management. The pair were soon arrested and confined in jail on trumped-up charges as accessories to murder. The police quickly regretted the plot, for it only served to draw into their midst "Big Bill" Haywood, a highly regarded and experienced Wobblies leader who was met at the Lawrence railroad station by a crowd of fifteen thousand.

The winter of 1912 proved an especially harsh time for a strike. Union leaders and families made the difficult decision to send workers' children to live with families in New York, Philadelphia, and elsewhere. This exodus was interrupted on February 24, when police took nearly 150 children and their parents into custody, provoking yet another round of negative publicity for the authorities. By March 18, the strike was settled. Exhausted workers had won a one-cent-per-hour pay increase and other concessions.

A photograph of a young girl marching in a Lawrence strike parade and carrying a banner that declared, "We want bread and roses, too," inspired James Oppenheim, a radical poet and novelist, to memorialize the strike in verse.

> As we come marching, marching, we bring the greater days
> The rising of the women is the rising of the race.
> No more the drudge and idler—ten that toil while one reposes
> But a sharing of life's glories: Bread and Roses! Bread and Roses!

♣ ❦ ♣

On Opening Day at the new Fenway Park, Boston beats New York (1912).

IN 1911, BOSTON RED SOX boss John I. Taylor announced that the team was pulling away from the beloved Huntington Avenue Grounds, where they were tenants. The Taylor family (who also owned the *Boston Globe* newspaper) held controlling interest in "Fenway Realty Company," which owned a large tract of undeveloped mud flats in the Fenway area. They intended to build their own baseball park there.

A baseball team that owned its own park and the land it sat on, a cash-poor John I. Taylor reasoned, would make a better sales prospect. It was not long after construction at "Fenway Park" got under way that the Taylors sold half ownership in the Red Sox for $150,000 (they held back full ownership of the park itself).

The first major-league baseball game played in the Red Sox's new home field of Fenway Park was an uncharacteristic start for a team cherished today not as winners but as persistent also-rans. On April 20, 1912, the Boston nine beat their visitors from New York in eleven innings, with twenty-seven thousand fans looking on. At the season's end, the Red Sox posted a .691 winning percentage, an American League record not broken until 1927 by the Yankees.

The 1912 Red Sox were marked not by power but by speed on the bases and powerful pitching. Hurler "Smokey" Joe Wood racked up a sixteen-game winning streak through the summer.

The Sox proved to be so spectacular a team, in fact, that there wasn't even a pennant race for fans of the other American League teams to enjoy. The AL favorites and reigning world champs, the Philadelphia Athletics, were stunned to watch Boston ascend to first place on June 18 and stay there until September. The 1912 season ended with a fourteen-game Red Sox lead over the second-place Washington Senators; the Athletics were left behind in third. In October Red Sox went all the way against the New York Giants, winning the World Series in seven games.

Construction at Fenway Park continued throughout the 1912 season. The right-field bleachers were not opened until the World Series. Fenway's now legendary collection of odd angles and cockeyed field dimensions were an organic result of the haphazardly managed work. Offices were laid out and built first, then the park inside them. Finally, fences were put up to close off any open gaps. Designers of the Red Sox's new baseball home even provided a parking lot for fans' automobiles, located behind the right-field wall.

Fenway Park's most distinguishing feature—a thirty-seven-foot wall behind left field known as the "Green Monster"—was not built until 1934. Up to that time, left fielders played in front of a ten-foot sloping embankment where overflow fans were seated for big games.

♣ ♥ ♣

A tank holding 2 million gallons of molasses bursts in the North End (1919).

ON AN UNSEASONABLY WARM afternoon for a New England winter, North End children finished lunch and began returning to school for their afternoon classes. Along Commercial Street, dogs roamed aimlessly and pedestrians coursed distractedly. The elevated train squealed through the air above the neighborhood streets. In that era, automobiles were a rare sight. Much more common were teamsters on delivery rounds.

In offices above the street, men and women responded thoughtlessly to a muffled rumble from outside. They paused at their work and looked up from their desks. The sound was different from the usual city noises of trains and traffic. It had roared, then whistled like the wind.

All at once, windows were blackened as if a curtain were drawn across the front of buildings. A brown liquid with a sickly sweet odor began pouring in through open windows and broken panes. The world was coming to an end in a sticky flood of molasses.

On the corner of Foster and Commercial streets, a ninety-foot tank filled with more than 2 million gallons of molasses weighing over fourteen thousand tons had exploded. The liquid was being used by the Purity Distilling Company for the production of munitions. (Making rum with the molasses was illegal; Massachusetts had recently ratified the Eighteenth Amendment, prohibiting the manufacture, sale, or transportation of intoxicating liquors.)

According to eyewitnesses, the crackle of a thousand machine guns rang out near the tank just after 12:30 P.M. on January 15, 1919. As it ruptured with a tremendous force, the steel structure shattered into bits of deadly shrapnel. One piece sliced through a girder supporting the elevated railway like so much cheese.

Cascading from the ruptured tank, a wave of molasses rose thirty feet in the air. Couples walking arm in arm were torn apart, with death claiming one while the other miraculously escaped. The molasses swept through the street and carried off its victims without pity. Like flies caught on sticky fly-paper, the more people and animals struggled, the tighter the molasses held them in its grip. Often, those who were not immediately drowned, died from suffocation after their nostrils became plugged airtight.

Firefighters pulled unrecognizable brown forms from the molasses. Molasses swirled and bubbled in the street as rescue teams—with molasses up to their waists—struggled to separate the living from the dead. Water from high-pressure hoses was useless to move the mess. Ingenious firefighters discovered that seawater cut the molasses. They were finally able to wash the sickening mess off the streets and into the nearby harbor.

The final casualty count from the bizarre flood recorded 21 people dead, 150 injured. In court, expert witnesses testified that the holding tank was improperly designed and structurally inadequate for the volume of molasses stored inside it. The Purity Distilling Company was ordered to pay more than $1 million in claims to survivors and property owners.

♣ ♥ ♣

Boston police strike gains Gov. Calvin Coolidge national prominence (1919).

IN AUGUST 1919, THIRTEEN hundred Boston police officers voted to enroll their fraternal group, the Boston Social Club, into the American Federation of Labor. The pro-union vote followed on complaints of low wages, unsanitary working conditions, and mandatory overtime with insufficient compensation. The officers were immediately forbidden by their anti-union commissioner to be members of any organization except those for veterans. City officials subsequently found eight officers guilty of disobeying the anti-union rule.

A strike order was called for September 9, effective with the evening roll call. That night, fewer than 10 percent of the force arrived for duty. As darkness gathered, Boston was plunged into chaos: Robbery and looting were rampant.

To ensure the maintenance of order, stalwart citizens prepared to make sacrifices. The Harvard College football coach volunteered his players as police substitutes, saying, "To hell with football if men are needed." Meantime, union sympathizers surrounded police stations to chant their support for strikers and heckle any picket-crossing scabs. National Guards officers on duty in South Boston opened fire on pro-union demonstrators, killing two boys and wounding seven others. In Scollay Square, National Guard cavalry charged a crowd; one woman was shot and a man lay dead.

Massachusetts governor Calvin Coolidge received the lion's share of public credit for breaking the back of the strike. The diffident and laconic Yankee held firmly to a basic principle: "There is no right," Coolidge said, "to strike against the public safety by anyone, anywhere, anytime."

Ironically, the man perhaps most responsible for restoring peace in Boston was AFL president Samuel Gompers. On September 11 he ordered the striking men to return to their posts for the good of all labor causes. A day later, the police union voted to comply with Gompers and public sentiment and they reluctantly returned to work.

With the Boston police strike ended, "Honest Cal" was thrown a lifeline directly from Beacon Hill to Pennsylvania Avenue. In a year's time, Coolidge had won election as vice president on the Republican Party's "return to normalcy" ticket with President Warren G. Harding of Ohio. He ascended to the White House in 1923 on Harding's death and handily won reelection in 1924.

♣ ♥ ♣

The Boston Red Sox sell Babe Ruth to the New York Yankees for $125,000 (1920).

OVER THE 1919 BASEBALL season hangs the shadow of the "Black Sox" scandal. All but forgotten, however, is that the 1919 season saw a dramatic personal achievement, one that heralded the arrival of a new breed of baseball player: the slugger. In Boston, Babe Ruth, a former pitcher turned outfielder, had notched a record twenty-nine home runs. Ruth would nearly double that historic mark in the following season, but not as a player for the Red Sox.

A left-handed hitter, George Herman Ruth was built like a cast-iron statue. He stood 6 feet, 2 inches tall and weighed 215 pounds. Born a bartender's son and raised in a Baltimore tenement, "the young Goliath" became the toast of Boston. The baby-faced twenty-three-year-old carefully maneuvered his wide-body Packard through Boston's narrow streets and was recognized wherever he went. In fact, Ruth was lionized as probably no athlete before him had been. Other men were in awe of Ruth; women found him irresistibly attractive.

In the first fifteen years of the modern World Series, the Boston Red Sox had won four titles, more than any other team. Ruth came to the team in 1914, and his tremendous pitching abilities had made the difference in 1916 and 1918, two championship seasons for the Red Sox. In 1916 the home team defeated the Brooklyn Dodgers, four games to one; in the second, grueling game of that matchup, pitcher Babe Ruth gave up just six hits in fourteen innings on the mound to lead the Sox to a 2–1 victory. Two years later, Ruth pitched $29^2/_3$ scoreless innings, a series record, as the Red Sox beat the Cubs, four games to two.

Even the most casual of American baseball fans were aware that the team with Babe Ruth on their side was the one to beat. In a word, Ruth was priceless. Red Sox owner Harry Frazee, however, saw things differently. Before the start of the 1919 season, Ruth demanded to be paid $10,000. Frazee refused, and "the Babe" threatened to sit out the entire year. The pair finally agreed to a $9,000 salary, and before the season ended, they had renegotiated a three-year contract paying Ruth $10,000 a year.

Making money came as easily to Babe Ruth in those days as hitting home runs. As the only baseball player in the league with his own business manager, he managed to pull in thousands at "barnstorming" exhibition games he played across New England. Ruth even invested in a local cigar factory that rolled its product in colorful paper bands printed with his Ruth's smiling face.

In both crowd figures and revenues, the 1919 baseball season was the best yet seen in major league history. When the season was ended, Johnny Igoe, Ruth's manager, chose his moment to demand even more money for his player. Ruth's salary with the Red Sox would now have to be $20,000 or he wouldn't play at all in 1920.

Once more, Harry Frazee refused. A theatrical entrepreneur, he had bought the Red Sox in late 1916. Despite owning a winner, he quickly found himself in financial hot water with impatient creditors. When an upstart American League team in New York began to throw money around, Frazee signaled that Ruth was for sale.

On January 5, 1920, the owners of the New York Yankees promptly snatched up Babe Ruth for $125,000—more than double the price ever before paid a team for one of its ballplayers. In New York, Ruth would get the $20,000 salary he had demanded in Boston. Ever since Babe Ruth left the team, the Red Sox have never won a World Series. Everyone blames "the Curse of the Bambino."

Jean-Louis "Jack" Kerouac is born in Lowell (1922).

THE CHILD OF FRENCH-CANADIAN parents, Jean-Louis Lebris Kerouac was raised in the Centralville neighborhood of Lowell. This area of the famous mill town was crowded with tenements and known by everyone as Little Canada.

Kerouac's father, Leo Alcide Kerouac, rose from printer to press owner until a 1936 flood of the Merrimack River ruined his business. The son was devoted to his mother, Gabrielle Ange L'Evesque, a devout Catholic who worked intermittently in Lowell's shoe factories. A fastidious housekeeper, "Mémêre" was especially faithful to Thérèse of Lisieux, a Carmelite nun from Brittany whom the church touted as a saint. Her son rejected her faith though he never quite escaped its influence.

Not until he entered grade school did Jean-Louis Kerouac learn very much English, and there begin his transformation into Jack Kerouac. A strong football player in high school and always a hardworking student, he was recruited by Boston College but resisted being taught by Jesuits. Boston also was not far enough away to suit his growing need for independence. Against his father's wishes, Kerouac chose instead to attend Columbia University. In New York City, Kerouac began a lifelong affair with jazz music, an enduring friendship with Allen Ginsberg, and an acquaintance with life's seamy underside.

When he impulsively quit college in October 1941, Kerouac took a job at the *Lowell Sun* as a sportswriter. He struggled with the restrictions and responsibilities of the day-to-day working world. Kerouac preferred the personal and introspective work of serious writing to journalism. As impulsively as he had left Columbia, he left Lowell and moved to Washington, D.C., where he found work as a sheet metal cutter and then at a diner.

In the navy, Jack Kerouac chafed at authority just as he had in civilian life. During a training drill, he laid down his rifle and marched away. He was finally given an honorable discharge for having a schizoid personality and what was called an "indifferent character." After a time as a merchant sailor, Kerouac began to travel and work around the country and in Mexico. Among his many jobs were as a railroad man and forest ranger.

In 1950, the twenty-eight-year-old at last published his first novel, *The Town and the City,* which he had completed while living in a small room at his mother's house in Lowell. Kerouac was already at work on what many consider his masterpiece, *On the Road,* but it was not to be published until 1957.

Before seeing print, The *Town and the City* was heavily edited. The novel was cut by a third of its length, and the rough edges were smoothed. Ironically, Kerouac would later become known not for refined prose but for a rough, even rollicking literary style. In life and in art, he eschewed convention in order to achieve a kind of transcendence.

In *The Town and the City,* Kerouac remade Lowell as "Galloway"— "mill town in the middle of fields and forests." Little else about his boyhood home was changed. For Kerouac, the autobiographical impulse was impossible to resist. His friends and family as well as the town of Lowell went on appearing in his books for the next twenty years.

On the Road crystallized the author's belief in the redemptive quality of physical and spiritual movement. The book became the bible of the "Beat Generation," and Jack Kerouac its apostle (in spite of his own misgivings about the role).

In 1969, Kerouac—sharing a St. Petersburg apartment with his wife and mother while battling a drinking problem—died from internal bleeding brought on by a hernia. He was buried in Lowell's Edson Catholic Cemetery with Allen Ginsberg, Gregory Corso, and others of the Beat Generation by the graveside.

♣ ♥ ♣

In Auburn, Robert Goddard launches the first liquid fuel rocket (1926).

SPRING WAS ONLY A few days away, but snow still covered the rolling fields of rural central Massachusetts on March 16, 1926. A Clark University professor of physics was dressed appropriately as he stood in a field in Auburn where his aunt, Effie Ward, owned a farm. His full-length overcoat was buttoned to the neck, with the collar turned up to his ears against a sharp wind. On his feet, his heavy boots were laced well above the ankles. He wore a tweed cap to protect his hairless head, and a pair of leather gloves supple enough for delicate handiwork.

With Henry Sachs, a skilled machinist, assisting him, Robert H. Goddard was about to accomplish what his favorite authors, Jules Verne and H. G. Wells, had imagined in their science fiction novels. In 1898 Goddard read *War of the Worlds* serialized in the *Boston Post* and began to work out the problem of space flight in his head. Also that year, on October 19, the sixteen-year-old Goddard climbed a cherry tree in his Roxbury backyard and was struck by a tremendous idea that he later described in his diary.

"I imagined how wonderful it would be to make device which had even the possibility of ascending to Mars," he wrote. "When I descended the tree...existence at last seemed very purposive." Goddard celebrated this moment of spiritual rebirth throughout his life as his "Anniversary Day."

In December 1925 Goddard had successfully tested his revolutionary liquid fuel rocket in a static testing track at his Clark laboratory. He had already developed the basic principles of modern rocketry. Goddard was the first to recognize that thrust—and thus propulsion—can take place in a vacuum without air to push against. He was also the first to work out the mathematic ratios of energy and thrust for liquid oxygen, liquid hydrogen, and other fuels.

That morning in the cold, on March 16, 1926, Goddard and Sachs assembled a rocket motor and fuel tanks. The device, encased in a ten-foot-long tubing, was held in place by a sturdy pipe frame. By noon, Goddard and Sachs were joined by Percy Roope, another Clark physicist, and Esther Goddard, who was to make a motion picture film of the historic launch. Aunt Effie stayed warm inside her farmhouse and prepared hot malted milks.

In his diary, Goddard recorded that the launch finally occurred at 2:30 P.M. The rocket rose 41 feet high and landed 184 feet away in a flight of 2.5 seconds. Esther Goddard's camera, which required rewinding after it consumed just 7 seconds of film, unfortunately ran down before ignition. When Goddard wrote his mentor Charles Abbot of the Smithsonian Institution about the experiment's success, he enclosed a photograph of the empty pipe frame that once had held his invention.

♣ ♥ ♣

Nicola Sacco and Bartolomeo Vanzetti are executed (1927).

IN CHARLESTOWN PRISON ON August 1927, two Italian immigrants prepared to go to their deaths in the electric chair. Very few people anywhere truly believed that Nicola Sacco and Bartolomeo Vanzetti were guilty of the crime with which they had been charged and convicted. The more the world agitated for clemency, however, the more the guardians of law and order in Massachusetts became determined to fulfill the court verdict pronounced by Judge Webster Thayer on July 14, 1921.

So that his conscience and the justice system of the commonwealth could appear free from blemish, Gov. Alvan T. Fuller had earlier called for an independent inquiry. Impartial men—the likes of A. Lawrence Lowell, president of Harvard College, and Samuel W. Stratton, president of the Massachusetts Institute of Technology—were asked to serve the commonwealth in its moment of need. The Lowell Committee, as it became known, reviewed what was already well known internationally about the case.

When arrested as "suspicious persons" while riding on a Brockton streetcar on the evening of May 5, 1920, Sacco and Vanzetti were found to be armed—Sacco with a .32 Colt automatic, Vanzetti with a .38 revolver (both weapons were loaded). At the police station they made numerous false statements about their recent movements and about their political affiliations. The pair reluctantly admitted they were anarchists, members of a violent political movement on the rise in the United States following World War I.

Police immediately became convinced that the men were involved in an April 20 holdup at the Slater and Merrill Shoe Factory, South Braintree, in which the company paymaster and a security guard were killed and more than $15,000 in cash was taken.

In court the prosecution spun a complicated web to link Sacco and Vanzetti with the crime. Little material evidence was produced. The district attorney primarily relied on the men's behavior at the time of their arrest. Carrying guns and lying to the authorities, he told the court, indicated a "consciousness of guilt" in connection with the holdup and double murder.

Law-abiding citizens had good reason to fear anarchists and to want them executed or otherwise silenced. In September 1920 an anarchist's bomb exploded at the corner of Wall and Broad streets in downtown Manhattan, killing thirty and injuring more than two hundred. "We will destroy to rid the world of your tyrannical institutions!" anarchists thundered at the nation's trembling capitalists. "Long live social revolution! Down with tyranny!"

As for Judge Thayer, he made various statements outside the courtroom that appeared somewhat injudicious. "Did you see what I did with those anarchist bastards the other day? I guess that will hold them for a while!" is the most widely quoted of such remarks. The Lowell Committee determined that Judge Thayer was guilty of a "grave breach of official decorum."

The Lowell Committee also decided that Sacco and Vanzetti were guilty. Clemency was refused. Finally, on August 23, 1927, Sacco and Vanzetti were executed. "We are proud for death," Sacco wrote in his last hours.

Artists and writers found in the Sacco and Vanzetti case a model for American social injustice in the 1920s. For author John Dos Passos, the injustice perpetrated on the pair of Italian immigrants showed the United States to be "two nations"—one rich, the other poor; one powerful, the other powerless. Painter Ben Shahn sharply evoked the men's pathetic plight in *Passion of Sacco & Vanzetti* (1931).

Frances Perkins is appointed the first woman cabinet member (1933).

WHEN PRESIDENT-ELECT FRANKLIN ROOSEVELT asked her to come to the Roosevelts' Manhattan home several weeks before his inauguration, Frances Perkins had some inkling of what he would ask.

In the days leading up to their meeting, the New York State industrial commissioner became convinced that Roosevelt wanted to nominate her as U.S. secretary of labor, but Perkins confided to close friends that she did not think she was the right person for the job. With the nation mired in its worst economic slump ever, Perkins was convinced that only a man could do the job properly.

But Roosevelt insisted and got his way. Frances Perkins, born in Boston on April 10, 1880, and raised in Worcester, had long distinguished herself as a social reformer and an advocate for the rights of workingmen and workingwomen. On March 4, 1993, she took the oath of office from U.S. Supreme Court justice Benjamin Cardozo as the first woman member of a U.S. presidential cabinet.

The Perkins family were of solid Yankee stock. Moving to Worcester from Boston in 1882, Fred Perkins formed a stationery supply firm with partner George Butler. "Perkins and Butler" soon became a household name across central and western Massachusetts. Eldest daughter "Fanny" Perkins attended Worcester Classical, a college preparatory high school, and entered Mount Holyoke in 1898, where she and classmates played the new sport of basketball in bloomers.

From her graduation in 1902 until she completed graduate studies in social economics at Columbia University in 1910, Francis Perkins concentrated on reform-inspired social work from many angles. She taught for five years at schools in Massachusetts and elsewhere, eventually moving to the Chicago area, where she worked with Jane Addams at Hull House. Later, Perkins directed the Philadelphia Research and Protective Association, which helped immigrant and southern black young women from becoming easy prey for prostitution rings and unscrupulous employers.

These and other dramatic experiences as an activist affected Perkins deeply and prepared her for a second career, in government service. In New York in 1929, then governor Franklin Roosevelt made her state industrial commissioner, where Perkins proved to be a strong voice for unemployment compensation and a greater role for government intervention in the economy.

Under Perkins, federal labor law changed enormously. Her accomplishments directed not only the course of the nation's recovery from the Great Depression but also steered government and labor into a mutually beneficial relationship.

Perkins's achievements as secretary of labor include creation of the Civilian Conservation Corps (CCC); enactment of a federal minimum wage and limits on the working week; and implementation of restrictions on employment of children under sixteen. In 1938, the secretary of labor also drafted the Social Security Act and the Fair Labor Standards Act. In Washington, Perkins served Roosevelt until he died in office in 1945. She was one of only two cabinet members to serve through all four Roosevelt terms.

In a city unfamiliar with women cabinet members, there was some question as to how Secretary Perkins should be addressed. She proposed "Miss Perkins" (although she was married with one daughter, Perkins preferred to go by her maiden name). A referral to *Robert's Rules of Order,* however, prompted the title "Madam Secretary," which Perkins found distasteful. In some unflattering newspaper accounts, Perkins was even derisively called "the madam."

♣ ❦ ♣

Drs. Minot, Murphy, and Whipple receive the Nobel Prize for developing a cure for pernicious anemia (1934).

THE FORCE OF THE word "pernicious" has dissipated considerably since it was first applied in the nineteenth century to a particularly vicious sort of anemia. "Pernicious anemia"—meaning, quite frankly, "deadly" anemia—was perhaps a less frightening diagnosis for the medical community to pronounce. Clinical euphemisms remain common today. Pernicious anemia, for example, has been recast as "Addison's disease." Whatever else they might choose to call it, pernicious anemia is undeniably a killer. Until a cure was found, in fact, pernicious anemia struck down at least as many people as tuberculosis. The disease was an indiscriminate leveler. In 1934, the year Drs. Minot, Murphy and Whipple shared the Nobel Prize in Medicine for finding a cure, Marie Curie (who earlier shared the Nobel Prize in Chemistry with her husband, Pierre, for the discovery of radium) was also a victim.

Today, doctors understand quite clearly that pernicious anemia is caused by a lack of vitamin B_{12}. The deficiency is not a matter of diet but of the stomach's inability to produce certain juices that in healthy individuals can absorb the vitamin from food. Without vitamin B_{12}, red cell production in the bone marrow becomes abnormal, and a deficiency of white blood cells and of platelets occurs. Breathing difficulty; weight loss; memory impairment; and, most characteristically, inflammation of the tongue eventually develop. Over time, the liver, brain, nervous system, and digestive system are severely impaired.

Pernicious anemia affects men and women equally, but it is uncommon in those under thirty-five. Those most at risk include individuals with blood type A and blue-eyed, bulky-framed, light-skinned northern Europeans.

In 1922, a University of Rochester pathologist, Dr. George Hoyt Whipple, discovered that dogs that suffered from a canine form of pernicious anemia could be cured by feeding them large amounts of beef liver. The secret curative ingredient in liver remained a mystery.

Whipple's curious finding came to the attention of Dr. George Richards Minot and Dr. William Parry Murphy of Harvard Medical School. The now common medical notion that disease might result from a deficiency—and might be remedied by addition of what was lacking—was only beginning to be accepted. In his own research, Dr. Minot had already come to the conclusion that iron, which was regularly prescribed for other forms of anemia, was powerless to abate the debilitating effects of pernicious anemia.

"The idea that something in food might be of advantage to patients with pernicious anemia was in my mind [as early as] in 1912," Dr. Minot noted in his Nobel acceptance speech. Thus he seized on the idea that liver held the key to a cure. By 1926 he and Dr. Murphy had demonstrated the effectiveness of a liver treatment for pernicious anemia. Patients were prescribed a steady diet of liver—at least a half pound a day. Later, a liver extract was developed that could be given intravenously. Not until 1948, however, did U.S. and British scientists conclude that vitamin B_{12} was the mystery element contained in beef liver.

♠ ♥ ♠

Edwin H. Land establishes the Polaroid Corporation (1937).

KNOWN AS "THE DOCTOR," Edwin H. Land built a tiny lens manufacturing firm into a billion-dollar company that at its height employed eighteen thousand people. He held 537 U.S. patents, more than any other inventor besides Thomas Edison.

Edwin Herbert Land never graduated from college, but he later taught at both Harvard and MIT. An intensely private individual, Land shed little public light during his life on his childhood experiences as an upper-middle-class Jew growing up in Yankee Bridgeport, Conn. Unlike Edison and the typical image of the wayward genius, however, Land did well in school. He graduated from Norwich Academy in 1926 and immediately enrolled at Harvard College.

A trip to New York City soon placed Edwin Land on the path to success. The seventeen-year-old Harvard freshman was walking along a Manhattan thoroughfare beneath the omnipresent electrified blaze of advertising signs when he conceived of a way to minimize glare from bright lights. A series of polarizing filters, reasoned Land, could control the otherwise unwanted effects of illumination.

The young student abruptly took a leave of absence from his Harvard studies to pursue this inspirational thinking. Land returned to Harvard in 1929 after three years of independent study, and his awestruck professors eagerly made available the sort of sophisticated laboratory he needed to continue his research.

By 1932 Land could announce that he had perfected a manufacturing process for material to polarize light, which he called "Polaroid." With George Wheelright III, Land's physics section leader at Harvard, the twenty-one-year-old inventor formed Land-Wheelwright Laboratories later that year and left Harvard for good. In 1937 the Polaroid Corporation opened in a former tobacco company warehouse in Boston's South End.

The second invention that spurred the myth of Land's innovative genius resulted from a 1943 trip to the Southwest with his wife, Helen, and their three-year-old daughter, Jennifer. After he took the girl's picture with an ordinary film camera, she asked to see it. It wasn't ready, her father told her, but already he was asking himself why not. Land said that he had solved the problem of a one-step photographic process within the hour.

Four years later, on February 21, 1947, "the Doctor" publicly demonstrated an instant picture camera—the first "Land camera." The question on most people's minds was why no one had thought of it before.

At one time or another in his long, busy life, Edwin Land would be compared to both Einstein and DaVinci, though significantly, he was never likened to Ford or Rockefeller. "The bottom line is in heaven," Land liked to say. He could afford to say that, at least well into the 1960s, when the still pioneering Polaroid remained a darling of Wall Street investors. In 1980, however, a chastened Dr. Land was forced to resign as Polaroid's chief executive following the disastrous introduction of Polavision, an "instant" movie system that devoured $68.5 million of investment money.

"The essence of business leadership in America is to be able to turn your back on the demands of the financial world: Its analyses are never profound," he had once announced boldly, yet the business world Land so dearly loathed had, at last, had its way with him. In 1982 "the Doctor" gave up his title as Polaroid chairman, and in 1985 he sold his remaining holdings of company stock. On March 1, 1991, Land died in Cambridge at age eighty-one, more a myth than a man.

♣ ♥ ♣

The Great Hurricane hits, costing millions in damages (1938).

METEOROLOGICALLY SPEAKING, A TROPICAL depression becomes a "hurricane" when the storm's heaviest winds exceed 65 knots (the equivalent of 75 miles per hour or 120 kilometers per hour). Unusually strong hurricanes with sustained winds blowing between 111 and 130 mph are rated as "category 3" storms. In recent memory for New Englanders, Hurricane

Gloria (1985) and Hurricane Bob (1991) were both "category 3" storms.

The last "category 4" storm—with sustained winds between 131 and 155 mph—swept up the northeastern coast on September 21, 1938. The impact of this greatest of all Massachusetts hurricanes was ferocious: By official count, some 650 people were killed in New England and Long Island. The "Great Hurricane of 1938" did not have a name because it was not until 1953 that tropical storms were given names.

Most of the hurricane's victims were drowned when surging waves and overflowing rivers lifted them off their feet and swept them violently into watery graves. Seaside cottages where families were huddled in fear came away from their foundations. Building and occupants were swallowed whole by the churning sea.

Death in the Great Hurricane of 1938 came from freakish accidents as well as the mundane. Chimneys collapsed, and automobiles were overturned like children's toys. The Athol River swirled with tapioca from a factory spill at Orange. Trees and utility poles were snapped in half as easily as matchsticks. Fifteen percent of all mature timber in New England— enough to build two hundred thousand homes—was mowed to the ground by the hurricane's winds.

Of course, there were no weather satellites or other high-tech gadgetry to track the Great Hurricane of 1938. Those who remember the storm recall it as striking without warning, though this does not mean it was entirely unexpected. Government meteorologists were aware of an approaching storm, but they had expected it to follow a curling, coastal track that would keep it safely away from land.

According to meteorologists, the conditions that created the Great Hurricane of 1938 (i.e., a pair of massive high-pressure weather systems with room enough for an errant depression to squeeze between them) occur as often as ten times a year. The principal determining factor is the low-pressure system's original force.

Will another category 4 storm ever again find itself suddenly pumped up like an athlete on steroids? It's only a matter of time, say scientists.

♣ ♥ ♣

The Swift River Valley is flooded to create the world's largest artificial water source (1939).

IN 1895 THE MASSACHUSETTS Board of Health issued a lengthy if inconclusive report on how the state should address metropolitan Boston's persistent water supply problem.

The commonwealth's engineers considered the suitability of water in the Merrimack River and the Charles River (both too polluted); Lake Winnipesaukee in New Hampshire and Sebago Lake in Maine (both too distant and outside of Massachusetts); and numerous other alternatives. The Metropolitan Water and Sewerage Board eventually settled for constructing the Wachuset Reservoir by diverting a Nashua River tributary.

The Wachuset Reservoir was created with a 64-billion-gallon capacity, yet the need for additional reservoir supply was immediately foreseen. By 1928, state engineers began construction on what was to be called the Quabbin Reservoir. Four towns in the Swift River Valley of central Massachusetts—Dana, Enfield, Greenwich, and Prescott—were ordered taken by eminent domain.

Massachusetts authorities had picked the location well. The Swift River Valley was chosen for obliteration because it contained no important businesses and relatively few people. Opposition to the $65 million project did not appreciably slow construction. The timeline for demolition and dam building moved inexorably forward throughout the 1930s.

At the Quabbin Park Cemetery, more than 6,500 bodies were brought from cemeteries across the Swift River Valley and reinterred. The living were not quite so easily relocated. Finally, voters in the four condemned towns held their last town meetings in the spring of 1938. The state legislature subsequently wrote the towns out of existence, effective one minute past midnight, April 28. At the Enfield Town Hall, the firemen sponsored a festive ball to mark the occasion. The very last of the valley's remaining families, however, were not all gone for another year.

On August 14, 1939, the Quabbin began to fill when gates to a dam holding back the Swift River were opened. Workmen continued to demolish buildings left standing in the district well into 1940. On June 22, 1946, the reservoir reached its capacity of 412 billion gallons and was declared full. Work to create the world's largest artificial domestic water source had finally ended. The Quabbin today covers 39 square miles and has an average depth of 51 feet.

Eerie stories that houses can sometimes be seen through the reservoir's waters are entirely fanciful. During a 1965 drought, however, stone foundation steps emerged through the mud and low water that covered what was once Dana, Mass.

♣ ♥ ♣

Ted Williams bats .406 (1941).

IN BASEBALL MORE THAN any other sport, percentages matter. This obsession with statistics is not only a source of endless fascination for fans but also a fundamental element in the game itself. Over the course of a 162-game professional season, baseball managers and their players are as mindful as aluminum siding salesmen that they are in a numbers game.

On Sunday, September 28, 1941, Boston Red Sox outfielder Ted Williams would have seen printed in newspaper sports sections across the country an extraordinary number. The slugger's batting average (calculated as a percentage of hits to total times at bat) stood at the magic ".400" mark. His other important numbers that day, as the Red Sox prepared for a season-ending doubleheader against the Athletics at Philadelphia, were equally impressive: in 444 at-bats so far that season, Williams had punched in 118 runs and notched 36 home runs.

Only seven major leaguers in the twentieth century had previously achieved a season batting average over .400. The last to do so was thirty-one-year-old Bill Terry, playing for the 1930 National League New York Giants, who had whacked his way to .401. In his third major league season with the

Red Sox, Ted Williams was just twenty-three years old (hence his popular nickname, "the Kid"). If the magic number held one more day, he would become the youngest player of the modern era to hit .400 or over for the season.

On baseball cards and in the press, baseball hitters' batting averages are typically calculated to just three decimal places. It sounded like quibbling then, but despite the newspapers, Ted Williams was not quite batting .400 on September 28, 1941. Carried out to a fourth decimal place, his average was .3995. Williams had connected regularly with the ball throughout September, but at nothing like the pace he had set throughout the summer. In fact, after reaching .411 on September 14, his average had slipped precipitously.

For either side, Red Sox or Athletics, the doubleheader to be played on September 28 would have no effect on team standings. The Red Sox had been eliminated from World Series contention two weeks earlier by their archrivals, the Yankees. The Philadelphia Athletics were a last-place team.

In the first game that afternoon, Williams went four-for-five with a home run and three singles and boosted his average to .405. A player more concerned about his place in history might have chosen to protect the number by sitting out the next game. "Never crossed my mind," Williams told *Boston Globe* sportswriter Peter Gammons fifty years later. "I was getting paid, I played. It was as simple as that." For the second game, the slugger went two-for-four. His average rose another notch, to .406. No major leaguer has come close ever since.

For the record, Ted Williams' career statistics read as follows: .344 lifetime batting average (sixth highest); 521 home runs (eighth highest); 1,839 RBIs (tenth highest); and 2,654 total hits. His average fell below .300 only in 1959, when he slumped to a still respectable .254. Altogether, he played nineteen seasons for the Boston Red Sox, with time out for military service in World War II and the Korean War.

Ted Williams played his last game at Fenway Park on September 28, 1960. In his final professional at-bat, he hit an eighth-inning, two-run home run. Williams trotted around the bases as the 10,454 fans cheered, then he disappeared inside the dugout without further fuss. The Red Sox eventually won, 5–4.

Cocoanut Grove nightclub fire kills 490 (1942).

By ONE MAN'S CALCULATION, the dead, the dying, and the barely living were rushed into Boston City Hospital at the rate of one every eleven seconds throughout the long night of November 28, 1942. A weary physician finally telephoned the police and begged authorities that no more of the dead be brought to his crowded emergency ward. The doctor's desperate call came less than an hour after the first fire victims began to arrive.

Many of those relaxing in the Melody Lounge at the Cocoanut Grove that night were attending what had been scheduled as a victory party for the Boston College football team. Instead, they mourned a devastating loss by the Eagles to rivals Holy Cross, 55–12. Young men and women poured into the popular spot at Piedmont Street and Broadway in South Boston. Off-duty servicemen and holiday revelers eagerly joined them for a drink or a dance.

The devastating fire may have been started accidentally by Stanley Tomaszweski, a sixteen-year-old busboy who was working illegally at the Cocoanut Grove. With his father out of work, the $2.47 wage plus tips that Stanley earned nightly was crucial to his family's support. Holding a burning match to help him see, Tomaszweski had diligently replaced a lightbulb hung on a decorative potted palm. According to witnesses, he walked away unwittingly as a smoldering palm frond ignited the ceiling's satin fabric.

An investigation, however, labeled the fire of unknown origin and suggested that the cause could also have been "alcoholic fumes, inflammable insecticides, motion picture film scraps, electric wiring, gasoline or fuel oil fumes, refrigerant gases, [or] flameproofing chemicals."

The fire—actually, a large volume of inflammable gases—raced from its starting point to a distant doorway 225 feet away in fewer than five minutes. Every exit available was partially or completely blocked: a revolving door was jammed; four doors were locked; two recently installed doors opened inward and were useless. Many victims succumbed to poisonous fumes and were not actually burned alive. Indeed, many of those pulled from the inferno were, strangely, not scarred by flames.

Like the *Titanic* disaster, the tragedy of the Cocoanut Grove fire spurred important reforms. Fire codes in Boston and across the country were largely rewritten. In addition, doctors learned to treat severe burn victims more successfully.

♠ ♥ ♣

The computer age dawns in Cambridge laboratories (1944).

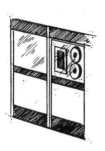

THE MARK 1, A CALCULATING machine more than fifty feet long, was an entirely new species of electromechanical device. Its progenitors were a team of scientists from Harvard, IBM, and the U.S. Navy and led by Harvard's Howard Aiken. More nineteenth-century "analytical engine" than twentieth-century electrical computer, the clumsy creature was even more clumsily named the "Harvard-IBM Mark 1 Automatic Sequence Controlled Calculator (ASCC)."

Mark 1 was programmed in a digital code that was punched onto paper tape and cards. Counterwheels for calculations were electromechanical, with electrical connections between units. The "memory" consisted of seventy-two counters and sixty switches.

According to Aiken, the Mark 1 owed its conception to the desire to minimize time and effort in ever more sophisticated mathematical calculations. As science had increased its ability to measure the physical universe throughout the nineteenth and early twentieth centuries, so the need had grown for accurate computation of lengthy differential equations and other complex formulas.

Concurrently in 1944, the Massachusetts Institute of Technology agreed to build for the U.S. Navy a new generation of real-time aircraft flight simulators. Jay Forrester and other scientists at the school's Servomechanisms Lab pursued at first a clumsy analog device. In 1946 they substituted for that notion "Whirlwind," a digital computer that when construction was completed in 1951 filled thirty-one hundred square feet or several large rooms.

During the Cold War, American military leaders pressed for computer calculating systems capable of monitoring the nation's growing arsenal of aircraft loaded with atomic weapons as well as guarding against attack by Soviet planes. To permit the "real-time" calculations necessary, Whirlwind relied on advances in cathode-ray tube memory. Project scientists gradually grew dissatisfied with CRT memory, however, and by 1953 the MIT team developed a substitute using magnetic cores to store computer memory more reliably and more easily. Computers have long since left the laboratory, and their numbers have increased to epidemic proportions.

♣ ♞ ♠

Jackie Robinson and two others from the Negro leagues try out with the Boston Red Sox (1945).

 ON THE SAME GLOOMY, rainy day in April 1945 on which Franklin Roosevelt died, three players from the Negro leagues prepared for a tryout at Fenway Park: Kansas City Monarch shortstop Jackie Robinson; Cleveland Buckeye speedster Sam Jethroe; and all-star second baseman for the Philadelphia Stars Marvin Williams. Trying to ignore the shattering news of FDR's death, they trotted onto the field in their Negro leagues uniforms for a workout of hitting, fielding, and baserunning.

The brave trio were brought to Boston on something of a dare. Black sportswriters, including John Wendell Smith of the *Pittsburgh Courier,* an

African-American newspaper, hoped to persuade the major leagues to give up their "whites only" policy.

Smith approached Boston city councilor Isadore Muchnick, who played an integral role by threatening to prevent the Red Sox from continuing to enjoy a blue laws exemption that allowed them to play on Sundays unless they consented to give Robinson, Jethroe, and Williams a tryout. Muchnick, a white man, represented a predominantly minority district, and clearly his integrationist's stand was intended to win him votes.

Robinson, Jethroe, and Williams showed off their baseball skills as best they could among a group of white tryouts. None of them was ever contacted by the Red Sox again.

Major league baseball had been integrated for a dozen years when infielder Pumpsie Green became the first African American to wear a Boston Red Sox uniform. Green is remembered by local fans for his role in finally integrating major league's last all-white team, though little else. He played four seasons with the team, from 1959 to 1962, then left the majors altogether after one year with the New York Mets, in 1963.

Pumpsie Green was the first black Red Sox player, though not the first African American to play major league ball for a Boston team. When the city hosted both American League and National League teams, Sam Jethroe, twenty-eight, joined the Boston Braves in 1950 and won National League rookie of the year honors.

♣ ♣ ♣

Under indictment for mail fraud, James Michael Curley wins election for a fourth term as mayor of Boston (1945).

BORN NOVEMBER 20, 1874, of Galway-born immigrants in an archetypal cold-water flat on Northampton Street in Roxbury, James Michael Curley was orphaned at ten years old. At eleven the boy took his first job, hawking newspapers on Washington Street. His political career began in 1899 with

a term as Boston city councilor. He later served as Boston mayor; Massachusetts state representative; Massachusetts governor; and U.S. congressman.

Of all his titles, Curley arguably cherished that of "Mr. Mayor" most. Curley was first elected to the chief executive's post at City Hall in 1914 and was defeated and reelected frequently for the position throughout the next thirty years.

In the legend of James Michael Curley, his most memorable election battle was that fought in 1945. Curley already held office as U.S. representative for the state's Eleventh District in Charlestown, but the lure of City Hall proved irresistible.

Indeed, not even indictment by a federal grand jury for using the mails to defraud could stop him from pursuing a fourth term as "His Honor." That it also did not prevent Bostonians from voting for him in record numbers is not surprising either. He won nineteen of twenty-two city wards with a larger margin than any mayoral candidate before him. Conveniently for his mayoral campaign, the congressman's trial in a Washington, D.C., court did not begin until December 1945. The indictments charged that Curley had served with two others as officers of the Engineer's Group, a mining syndicate in name only; the several partners in the Engineer's Group were accused of misrepresenting themselves to potential clients and spending retainers recklessly. A 1943 series of indictments against them was dismissed on technicalities, but the government rebounded with new charges that stuck.

Shortly after his inauguration in Boston, Curley returned to Washington and received the jury's verdict: guilty. The seventy-one-year-old politician faced a maximum sentence of forty-seven years and a $19,000 fine; he received six to eighteen months and a $1,000 fine.

Curley refused to resign either from Congress or as mayor of Boston. He tried his best, in fact, to behave as if nothing had happened. In 1947 an appeals court upheld his conviction. Justice had at last pulled James Michael Curley under its slowly grinding wheels.

Even as his lawyers railed that jail would prove a death sentence for their ailing client, Mayor Curley went to the federal penitentiary in

Danbury, Conn., on June 26, 1947. Later that year, just days before Thanksgiving, President Harry Truman commuted his sentence. Two days after leaving prison, the mayor was back in his City Hall office. He completed his term but was never elected to office again.

♣ ♥ ♣

WBZ-TV, New England's first television station, goes on the air (1948).

NOW THAT TELEVISION DOMINATES America's political arena as well as the private lives of its citizens, few people can imagine a world without instant replay, live courtroom coverage, and the infomercial. In Massachusetts, centuries of peace were ended abruptly with six words: "WBZ-TV is now on the air!"

Newsman Arch MacDonald shouted that announcement at 10:00 A.M. on June 9, 1948, on what is remembered at the station as "T-day." The first regularly broadcasting television station in Massachusetts began its first day with a test pattern that ran for two hours before going off the air at noon. The test pattern returned for another hour at 5:15 P.M. Finally, at 6:15 P.M., a balding and bespectacled Arch MacDonald appeared. He read fifteen minutes of local and national headlines (the same station now carries more than four hours of news programming daily).

The history of the electronic media in Massachusetts neatly parallels the course of the twentieth century and includes several national "firsts." In 1901 Guglielmo Marconi, the inventor of the wireless telegraph, built an oceanside transmitting station near South Wellfleet at what is today the Cape Cod National Seashore. President Theodore Roosevelt and King Edward VII exchanged transatlantic greetings from the Marconi Station on January 19, 1903.

The nation's first radio program was broadcast at Brant Rock in Marshfield, Mass., on December 24, 1906, using a 429-foot transmitting antenna. The Christmas Eve entertainment included the spoken call "CQ" (code for "seek you" and meant as an open invitation for listeners to tune in) followed by a song, the reading of verse, a violin solo, and a request for listeners to write with comments and reception reports.

Radio station WBZ, then located in Springfield, officially became the country's second commercial radio station on September 19, 1921 (the station call letters migrated to Boston in 1924). Earlier that year, in May, WNBH had gone on the air in New Bedford, but without a license (the 1,000-watt AM station is still broadcasting). The country's oldest public radio station is WFCM-FM, Williamstown, which began broadcasting in 1940.

The development of television accelerated rapidly in the 1930s and culminated in a demonstration at the 1939 New York World's Fair featuring President Franklin Roosevelt. Over the next two years, experimental stations began to operate in New York, Philadelphia, and Chicago, but the coming of World War II halted further progress. The industry recovered after 1945, although slowly. By 1948 thirty-six stations operated across the country with 1 million television sets in use.

When Arch MacDonald concluded the news at 6:30 P.M. on June 9, 1948, he introduced WBZ-TV's inaugural program with a somber announcement. The station had prepared in advance a short film of congratulatory messages from a trio of the city's religious leaders, including Roman Catholic archbishop Richard Cushing; Very Rev. Edwin van Etten, dean of Cathedral Church of St. Paul (Episcopal); and Dr. Joshua Liebman of Temple Israel. Fewer than forty-five minutes before the program was to be broadcast, the station learned that Dr. Liebman had suddenly died. With a delicacy that now seems quaint, station management considered canceling the program but decided ultimately to continue and inserted a special tribute to the deceased.

"T-day" continued with a variety of programs from NBC-TV's national schedule, including A. A. Milne's "The Fourth Wall" on *Kraft Television Theater*. The day's transmissions ended at 11:10 P.M. after ten minutes of local news. According to WBZ-TV, more than a hundred thousand New Englanders had watched throughout the day.

♣ ♥ ♣

A holdup of a Boston Brink's armored car nets thieves $2.7 million (1950).

SEVEN MEN ENTERED THE Brink's, Inc., offices at 165 Prince Street in the North End just after 6:30 P.M. on January 17, 1950. They converged on a counting room, where employees worked diligently at tagging heavy sacks of cash and payroll checks and entering figures in their ledger books. The seven men waited for their victims to take notice of them. Finally, one of the robbers spoke impatiently: "Hands up!"

The Brink's employees turned to where the order had originated. They saw a strange and frightening sight: Each of the seven men was identically dressed in chauffeur's cap, peacoat, and dark trousers. All wore flabby, hideous rubber masks like the sort sold at carnivals and joke shops.

After they had opened the office's principal vault, the Brink's employees were tied hand and foot and their mouths taped tightly shut. The masked gunmen then tore at money sacks, sorting out worthless checks from hard cash as well as "good" (used) money from "bad" money (new bills in serial order). One of the men worked frantically but unsuccessfully to pry open a plain metal money box.

In less than an hour, the thieves prepared to leave. They loaded sack after sack of loot onto a waiting truck. At 7:27 P.M., an alarm finally sounded. Boston police and a few ambitious journalists converged within minutes on the garage and offices at the corner of Commercial and Prince streets, where Brink's was headquartered. The excitement and confusion created a chaotic crime scene, and much of the evidence was disturbed.

With each passing minute, official estimates of the take from Brink's that night leaped higher. The first figure mentioned was $100,000, but that quickly multiplied ten times over by the time of the late news. Until then, the largest single robbery of hard cash in modern U.S. history was $427,000, from Brooklyn's Rubble Ice Company in 1932.

At a 2:00 A.M. press conference, a Boston police superintendent announced what made journalists and the public gawk in awe: that $1 million in cash and $500,000 in securities were believed missing from

Brink's. Left behind, police estimated, was another $1 million in cash, including a General Electric payroll of $880,000 in the metal money box with the stubborn lock. Later the tally mounted further: Gone were more than $1.2 million in currency and more than $1.5 million in checks, money orders, and securities.

In a race with the statute of limitations over the next six years, the Boston Police Department and the Federal Bureau of Investigation spent close to $29 million on their investigation. Law officials attempted to interview every known criminal in Greater Boston. Convinced that the robbery was an "inside job," Brink's administered lie detector tests to the victimized employees of 165 Prince Street (five of the six Brink's men involved eventually suffered breakdowns following the robbery).

In December 1955, fewer than three weeks before the Brink's gang members would have been beyond the hand of the law, Joseph James "Specs" O'Keefe began to yield to FBI pressure. A career Boston criminal who had spent most of the five years since the robbery in jail on one charge or another, "Specs" was straining under a mountain of legal bills. Despite repeated pleas for help, O'Keefe had received next to nothing from his partners in crime.

On January 6, 1956, with eleven days remaining, "Specs" O'Keefe started his confession. Eight men were tried and convicted that August and sent to Walpole State prison for long prison terms. In July 1971 Tony Pino, the last of the living Brink's robbers, left on parole after serving a fifteen-year Walpole prison stretch.

♣ ♥ ♣

Martin Luther King, Jr., begins his doctoral studies at Boston University (1952).

THE YOUNGEST PERSON EVER awarded the Nobel Peace Prize, Martin Luther King, Jr., was a deeply religious man whose vision of equality for all has forever shaped the nation and the world. At twenty-three, he was already an intellectual prodigy when he came to study at Boston University's campus on Commonwealth Avenue.

When he was fifteen years old, King had entered Morehouse College in Atlanta under an admissions program for especially gifted students. After graduating there, he spent three years at Crozer Theological Seminary in Chester, Pa., where he earned a second bachelor's degree, in divinity. He finished first in his class at Crozer and won a $1,300 scholarship toward further studies.

With his family's support, King chose to pursue a doctorate at Boston University's School of Theology. He planned to work with Edgar Sheffield Brightman, an exponent of the philosophy of "personalism," which professed God's personal involvement in everyone's life and extolled the virtues of personal idealism.

With Dr. Brightman as his guide, King undertook a rigorous examination of Hegel's *The Phenomenology of Mind*. His mentor fell fatally ill after a year, however. King's new adviser was L. Harold DeWolf, who led his student through investigations of a broad range of subjects, from Christian ethics and the philosophy of religion to a comparative study of world religions, including Islam and Hinduism. King also studied at Harvard, where he mastered the works of existentialists.

Eventually King adopted a Hegelian outlook on human nature, one that reconciled in his mind the fact that human beings are capable of both good and evil and will always remain so. Already aware of pacifism through the teachings of Gandhi and the writings of Thoreau, Martin Luther King also focused his philosophical and spiritual questions to the proper pursuit of social justice. At Boston University's School of Theology, Dean Walter Muelder and Professor Allan Knight had written eloquently on pacifism. With their help, King came to hold that nonviolence was the only acceptable form of political resistance.

From his apartment in the South End on Columbus Avenue, Martin Luther King ventured to his classes at BU by day and relaxed in the evenings at local jazz clubs. A friend introduced him to Coretta Scott, who had come from Alabama to study at the New England Conservatory of

Music as a singer. In 1953 the pair were married at the home of Scott's parents in Heiberger, Ala.; King's father, a Baptist minister, performed the ceremony.

For his dissertation, Martin Luther King chose to write "A Comparison of the Conceptions of God in the Thinking of Paul Tillich and Henry Nelson Weiman." These two theologians arrived at diametrically opposite conclusions about the nature of God: Tillich believed that God was outside of things; Weiman, that God had involvement in all things. King chose to accept parts of each man's philosophy. "In this way, oneness and manyness are preserved," he wrote.

Martin Luther King received his Ph.D. from Boston University in June 1955. The scholar quickly proved himself capable of far more than intellectual musings. Appointed pastor of a Baptist church in Montgomery, Ala., King rose to national prominence in December of the same year as leader of a black boycott of the city's segregated bus system.

♣ ♥ ♣

Artist Norman Rockwell moves to Stockbridge (1953).

FROM HIS STUDIO ABOVE a market on Main Street, the artist enjoyed what he called a "peep show" of small-town activity. The scenes unfolding outside provided him with inspiration, and the people enacting them frequently became his models.

Norman Rockwell and his family moved to Stockbridge, Mass., on the edge of the Berkshires, from Arlington, Vt., in November 1953. They came for the most unlikely of reasons for an artist given to showing the world not as it was but as he wished it to be. Mary Rockwell had earlier begun receiving psychiatric care at the Austin Riggs Center in Stockbridge, fifty miles south of Arlington. When the strain of traveling to appointments became too great for her, the Rockwells decided to move in order to be close to Mary's doctors. Eventually Norman joined her in analysis, though the notion seems out of character for the realistic painter of allegorical American moments—from *Saying Grace* to *After the Prom*. Rockwell, however, contained many more intriguing contradictions than any of his paintings.

Born in 1894 in New York City, Norman Rockwell sold his first illustration to *The Saturday Evening Post* in 1916. Over the next half century, he contributed a total of 317 *Post* covers. Their sentimental subject matter complemented the magazine's conservatism and nativist politics.

In World War II Rockwell defined the country's notions of patriotism through a gentle brand of agitprop. Posters depicting the "Four Freedoms" (Freedom of Speech, Freedom of Worship, Freedom from Want, and Freedom from Fear) were reprinted and distributed by the Office of War Information for its War Bonds sales campaigns.

Except for their realistic details, a Rockwell image from the 1930s is all but indistinguishable in technique or form from any executed in the Stockbridge years of the 1950s and 1960s.

What did noticeably change following his move to Stockbridge was the artist's decision to take up the controversial subjects of racism, poverty, and social injustice. He also traveled widely, including visits to the Soviet Union and Ethiopia. On a 1958 round-the-world jaunt paid for by Pan American World Airways, Rockwell stopped at Istanbul, Beirut, Bangkok, and Hong Kong, among other places. His sketches of exotic daily life disappointed his sponsors, who would have preferred a bit more glamour.

In 1961 Rockwell submitted a sympathetic portrait of Marshal Tito, the Yugoslavian Communist dictator, one that presented him as the only person capable of bringing together Croats, Serbs, and Bosnians. The rabidly anti-Communist *Saturday Evening Post* refused to publish it, so Rockwell leapfrogged to its rival *Look*, where he contributed a series of paintings on the civil rights movement.

In 1960, when he painted *Golden Rule* (an illustration holding up the ideal of the human family), Rockwell was able to prove to himself that even a country town like Stockbridge held its share of cultures. The work shows an international gathering of faces he gathered from throughout Stockbridge and the outlying area.

In 1967 Rockwell mythologized Stockbridge's Main Street for a holiday illustration in *McCall's*. *Christmas in Stockbridge* shows the east section of Main Street with the Red Lion Inn at the far right. More than a quarter century later, the archetypal New England village has only subtly changed.

♣ ♥ ♣

Playwright Eugene O'Neill, sixty-five, dies in his room at the Shelton Hotel, Boston (1953).

AFTER WILLIAM SHAKESPEARE AND George Bernard Shaw, Eugene O'Neill is the world's most widely translated and produced playwright. His writing career spanned four decades, and the accolades he earned included the Nobel Prize in Literature in 1936 and four Pulitzers, for *Beyond the Horizon* (his first Broadway production, in 1920); *Anna Christie* (1922); *Strange Interlude* (1928); and *Long Day's Journey into Night* (1956, awarded posthumously). Such professional success, however, never could dispel from O'Neill's tortured thoughts either his agonizing childhood memories or a deep spiritual disquiet.

Born in a New York hotel in 1888, Eugene O'Neill was the son of actor James O'Neill, who was nationally known for his portrayal of the count of Monte Cristo in a play adapted from the Dumas novel. When he was too old to accompany his parents on the road, Eugene was sent to boarding schools and later attended Princeton. He left the university after his freshman year and lived a sailor's life in Buenos Aires, Liverpool, and New York. Finally, at twenty-four, O'Neill chose the more sedentary existence of a newspaper reporter, but he had contracted tuberculosis and soon was confined to a sanitarium. There he pledged himself to become a playwright.

In the summer of 1916 in a stuffy, shack-turned-stage by the waterfront, the Provincetown Players produced *Bound East for Cardiff,* a one-act play O'Neill had written about life at sea. Members of the same avantgarde group formed the Playwrights' Theater that fall in Greenwich Village, and over the next four years they produced several other early plays by O'Neill.

Four decades later, Eugene O'Neill made a pitiable picture of a miserable and heartbroken old man. He had abandoned in frustration a planned cycle of eleven plays, to be performed on eleven consecutive nights, and following several generations of an American family from the nineteenth century to the modern era. Only one of these plays, *A Touch of the Poet,* was completed before a nervous illness left O'Neill physically unable to hold a pencil.

Eugene O'Neill was three times married, twice divorced. A disinterested father in his youth, O'Neill watched bitterly in his last decade as his children failed to live up to his expectations. His eldest son, Eugene, Jr., began a promising beginning career as a scholar at Yale, then fell into radicalism and alcoholism, committing suicide at forty. Another son, Shane, suffered from various emotional illnesses and lived in near poverty with his young wife. Tragically, the couple's first child, Eugene, suffocated while asleep in the makeshift crib his parent had made of a bureau drawer. O'Neill's only daughter, Oona, was written out of the playwright's life permanently when, at eighteen, she married Charlie Chaplin, a man only a year younger than her own father.

With his third wife, Carlotta Monterey, Eugene O'Neill marked his sixty-fifth birthday on October 16, 1953, at the Shelton Hotel, on Bay State Road near Kenmore Square. His condition rapidly deteriorated over the next several weeks, and finally pneumonia set in. Before he fell into a coma on November 26, O'Neill managed to pull himself up from bed and yell, "I knew it! I knew it! Born in a goddam hotel room and dying in a hotel room!"

The curtain fell at last on November 27. The widow followed her husband's instructions to avoid publicity, and she delayed the burial until December 2, when Eugene O'Neill was laid to rest at Forest Hills Cemetery.

The world's first successful human kidney transplant operation is performed (1953).

IN A NEWSPAPER PHOTOGRAPH, the Herrick twins stand at the front entrance of the old Peter Bent Brigham Hospital (now Brigham and Women's Hospital) on Huntington Avenue. The pair wear matching gray overcoats; Ronald and Richard both have their hands thrust deep in the pockets, presumably to ward off a sharp December wind. It was a sunny day, in any case. The twins cast identical sharp shadows on the portico pavement.

Handsome young men with neatly brushed dark hair, the twenty-three-year-old Herricks appear equally at ease and in good health. But careful scrutiny of their faces and frames points to a fatal difference. Ronald is thin, with chiseled facial features. Richard's upper body is larger, and his face is swollen. His bloated condition is known as edema or dropsy—a retention of body fluids—and is the telltale symptom of the kidney dysfunction that was slowly killing him.

Sadly, fatal kidney disease is not uncommon in men and women in their twenties and thirties. Humans are born with a pair of kidneys and can survive with only one fully functioning. If both kidneys become damaged by disease or injury, however, the body will suffer massively debilitating impairment. As kidney function deteriorates, the patient becomes weak and anemic. Fluids collect in the body's tissues and, most dangerously, in the lungs. Waste products that cannot be effectively removed cause the heart and the linings of the stomach and colon to be inflamed. High blood pressure also results from the strain on the heart's function.

In 1953, the "mechanical kidney," which cleansed the body of waste and excess fluids by a process called "dialysis," was a new and relatively untested treatment. At the Brigham, physicians and researchers had experimented with transplanting healthy human kidneys, but without success. In the first such operations, the kidney was transplanted into the patient's thigh so it could be removed quickly and without major abdominal surgery in case of problems.

The surgeons learned the hard way that the body will attack a transplanted organ as it would any foreign object. Dr. Joseph E. Murray, a native of Milford, Mass., and a skilled plastic surgeon, sought ways to short-circuit this rejection process. He theorized that it would not happen if an organ were transplanted from one identical twin to another. In a sense, such an operation would trick the body's natural defenses.

On December 23, 1954, Dr. Murray removed a kidney from the healthy Ronald Herrick and transplanted it in the abdomen of his brother, Richard. The operation's success led Murray and other researchers to continue transplanting organs and later to develop antirejection treatments. This included low-dose radiation at first, and in 1962, immunosuppressive drugs such as azathioprine. For his pioneering medical work, Dr. Murray shared the 1990 Nobel Prize in Medicine with E. Donnall Thomas, a Seattle-based researcher.

Richard Herrick lived seven years before succumbing to congestive heart failure brought on by his original kidney disease. Over the generation since that first kidney transplant, such life-saving operations have become almost commonplace.

♣ ♥ ♣

Malcolm X opens Muhammad's Mosque 11 (1954).

THE MAN WHO RETURNED to the streets of Roxbury and Dorchester for the first time in seven years was entirely transformed. Malcolm Little, who had served seven years in Charlestown Prison and Norfolk Prison Colony for burglary, was reborn as Malcolm X, a minister in the Nation of Islam led by the charismatic Elijah Muhammad in Chicago. He exchanged his "slave name" for "X," indicating the unknown African tribe of his ancestors. He also adopted the sect's strict rules of behavior and personal habits.

In Boston, Malcolm X began to preach the fiery message of Hon. Elijah Muhammad among the city's African-American community. The principal teachings of the Nation of Islam at that time rested on a belief in the racial superiority of Africans and a great fury over the mistreatment they had endured in America and elsewhere from white people, whom Elijah Muhammad considered a race of devils. Malcolm X also spoke powerfully to his audiences of the injustices of slavery, segregation, and poverty. Among those who listened most intently to Malcolm X was Louis Walcott, the New York-born son of a single mother from Barbados; he had grown up on Roxbury's Shawmut Avenue.

Even as racism was not unfamiliar to them, black separatism was not a new idea to either Malcolm X or Louis Walcott. At meetings of the Universal Negro Improvement Association at the Toussaint Louverture Hall on Tremont Street, a young Walcott heard Marcus Garvey call on African Americans to support a "Back to Africa" movement. Growing up in Omaha, Nebr., Malcolm X was likewise impressed by Garveyism. His father, a Baptist minister, was an outspoken member of the Universal Negro Improvement Association.

At Boston's English High School, Louis Walcott distinguished himself as a student, athlete, and musician. As a track star, his abilities in the relay race consistently made English a winner in school athletics throughout the late 1940s. As a violinist, Walcott won trophies for his excellent playing and even performed on television for *The Ted Mack Original Amateur Hour*. With his brother Alvin (today a highly regarded jazz musician) on piano, Louis Walcott gave popular music recitals. He even proved talented as a calypso singer and was an understudy to Harry Belafonte.

In 1954 Minister Malcolm X founded Muhammad's Mosque 11 at 10 Washington Street, Dorchester. Louis Walcott converted to the Nation of Islam a year later. As Malcolm X's assistant, he was known as Louis X until Elijah Muhammad later renamed him Louis Farrakhan. Malcolm X was reassigned to organize a Nation of Islam temple in New York City, and ultimately Louis Farrakhan rose to replace him as minister of Mosque 11.

Before his assassination in 1965, Malcolm X reshaped the militant nature of his Islamic beliefs and fell out of favor with Elijah Muhammad. A pilgrimage to Mecca had left Malcolm X convinced of the possibility of peace among the world's races.

Louis Farrakhan has been more steadfast in his radical convictions. He remained loyal to the Nation of Islam founder even after allegations surfaced that Elijah Muhammad had broken his own codes of asceticism by having sexual relations with several of his secretaries. Today he is the sect's leader throughout the United States.

♣ ♥ ♠

The basis for a female contraceptive ("the Pill") is discovered at the Worcester Foundation for Experimental Biology (1954).

IN 1950, MARGARET SANGER, a pioneer feminist and advocate of family planning, joined Katherine Dexter McCormick, a philanthropist who was the second woman to graduate from the Massachusetts Institute of Technology, in an effort to encourage development of a safe, easy, and reliable method of contraception.

The two women sought out Dr. Gregory Pincus, cofounder of the Worcester Foundation for Experimental Biology and an expert in mammalian reproduction. With a check from McCormick for $40,000—the first installment on what grew to nearly $2 million in such gifts made under the umbrella of Sanger's International Planned Parenthood Foundation—Dr. Pincus began research with his colleagues Dr. John Rock, a Harvard professor of gynecology, and Dr. Min Cheuch Chang, an authority on fertilization.

The Worcester Foundation research teams tested dozens of synthetic compounds on rats and rabbits. These efforts eventually led in 1954 to the discovery of an artificial steroid hormone. Depending on the dosage, the hormone was capable either of increasing a woman's chance of conceiving or of preventing ovulation altogether.

By 1957 the Worcester Foundation announced that an oral contraceptive—a white pill the size of an aspirin tablet—had been clinically tested on women in Boston, Puerto Rico, and Haiti with great success. In April 1960 the hormone—trademarked as Enovid—was approved for use by the U.S. Food and Drug Administration. Despite unpleasant and usually harmless side effects such as bloating and dizziness, "the Pill" quickly became a popular method of birth control around the world.

Founded by two Clark University professors, Gregory Pincus and Hudson Hoagland, the Worcester Foundation has continued to perform pathbreaking research in a wide range of fields, from cancer to nervous disorders. Understandably, it has never quite escaped from the notoriety gained when the Pill was introduced. The Worcester Foundation, regardless of its name, has long been based in the neighboring town of Shrewsbury.

Following its introduction, the Pill provided ammunition for the sexual revolution of the 1960s. Once women became freed from the constraints of reproductive biology, they could begin to behave differently. A woman using the Pill saw herself as sexually independent; previously, only men enjoyed that type of freedom.

The Worcester Foundation scientists did not foresee the Pill's impact on sexual mores, nor did they even ask themselves about the potential for such social impact. As a Catholic, Dr. Rock even found himself under attack from the church's hierarchy for violating God's will. Dr. Chang, for his part, said that he considered himself only a basic research scientist with a specialty in fertility. He was interested in population control, not changes in human sexual behavior. "We're scientists and we did it for curiosity," he said. "It was not for people to have a good time."

♣ ♥ ♣

The Boston Redevelopment Authority gives eviction notices to residents of the West End (1958).

IN THE 1950S, THE Boston Redevelopment Authority (BRA) justified its wholesale taking of the West End neighborhood with concerns for the health and safety of residents. The West End's narrow streets and congested tenements made not for a thriving neighborhood, the BRA declared, but a vermin-infested firetrap. Rather than exterminate the pests, the agency proposed to raze virtually every structure for several square blocks.

This urban renewal program transformed the character of Boston's center. Replacing the old world of the West End was a brave new world: Government Center—a collection of modern offices including Boston City Hall and the John F. Kennedy Federal Building—and luxury apartments at neighboring Charles River Park.

An element of moral righteousness may have played a role in the BRA's choosing to begin its renewal efforts in this old corner of the city. Scollay Square, and historically the West End, had long been centers for gambling dens, burlesque halls, and brothels. Once the West End and Scollay Square were "renewed" (in the same fashion that Godzilla "renewed" Tokyo), the BRA was prepared to move along for the obvious sequels: the North End and Back Bay. The agency had plans prepared to modernize the North End with a more rational street plan and to construct high-rise apartment blocks at various corners along Commonwealth Avenue.

Experts and pundits of the day roundly supported the BRA's renewal plans. Admittedly, the threats to safety and health posed by overcrowding in unsafe buildings were genuine. West Enders—chiefly the poor, the elderly, and newly arrived immigrants—could recall a recent national polio epidemic and the catastrophic Cocoanut Grove fire of 1942. A new, cleaner, safer, modern city center would prove a catalyst for boosting Boston's fortunes, which everyone could see had fallen on hard times.

The seven thousand West End residents put up weak resistance to the BRA. Many doubted that the city would carry out such an awesome threat as a neighborhood's wholesale destruction.

On April 25, 1958, registered letters of eviction from the city arrived at homes and businesses throughout the West End. As Christmas approached that year, nearly half of the area's families had moved from the area or were relocated. Demolition began in full force the following spring. By the summer of 1960, the West End was reduced to ashes, stones, and splinters. The Harrison Gray Otis House and the West End Church, both designed by Charles Bulfinch, were among the very few buildings considered worth saving.

♣ 🦃 ♣

Massachusetts senator John Fitzgerald Kennedy is elected thirty-fifth president (1960).

THE KENNEDY ADMINISTRATION, SEEN through rose-colored glasses, was the era of Jack's charm and Jackie's elegance. In this "Camelot," the White House was tastefully redecorated and Pearl Buck and Robert Frost were invited to dinner. The youngest elected president in American history, a handsome man brimming with wit and vigor, led the nation to a New Frontier. Meanwhile, his children played hide-and-seek in the Oval Office.

It would not require X-ray vision, however, to see through to Camelot's dark underside. In a winning campaign tactic, the decorated war hero had condemned the Eisenhower administration for permitting a "missile gap" to open between the United States and the Soviet Union. Once in office, he confronted military enemies, both real and imagined, in

Vietnam, Cuba, and Berlin. For two weeks in October 1962, nuclear war became a possibility, not just a remote threat.

The 1960 election, which put John Fitzgerald Kennedy in the White House, virtually redefined American politics. Television, particularly a series of broadcast debates, was credited with giving the warm and affable Kennedy a distinct advantage over his Republican opponent. Viewed through the camera lens, at least, Richard Nixon was much less attractive and hence considerably more unelectable. Ever since, presidential aspirants have risen and fallen according to their ability to project a winning television image.

Virtually forgotten is that Kennedy confronted early in his candidacy a question unthinkable today: whether a Roman Catholic could or even should be elected to the nation's highest office. How Kennedy won over the doubters and even some of the bigots makes a remarkable study.

At the turn of the century, John "Honey" Fitzgerald, Rose Kennedy's father, had pretty well flattened the idea that a Catholic and an Irishman never could become mayor of the city of Boston. Irish and Italian politicians in the predominantly Catholic cities of the Northeast followed him in their inevitable rise to political power carried on a tidal wave of irresistible numbers.

Across the country, however, on the midwestern prairies and in the southern hills, bigotry against "Papists" was almost as strong as hatred of blacks. The fear remained with many that, in a conflict of loyalty toward one's country and faithfulness to one's religion, a Catholic American might betray the United States in favor of the commands of the Roman pope.

In Wisconsin, in September 1959, the Kennedy presidential campaign began in earnest. It swiftly met with anti-Catholic prejudice. "I can't vote for Kennedy," registered Democrats around the state declared, "he's a Catholic."

For its primary polls, the *Milwaukee Journal* divided voters into three categories: Democrat, Republican, and Catholic. The votes were counted according to the candidates' names, and Kennedy received more popular votes than any candidate in the state's history. He had soundly beaten Midwesterner Hubert Humphrey on his own turf, but Kennedy had noticeably failed to carry the state's four predominantly Protestant districts.

Kennedy faced a final grueling test next in West Virginia, where registered voters were 95 percent Protestant and the latest polls showed Humphrey ahead by nearly two to one. On the campaign trail, the Massachusetts senator asked a question daunting for even the most hardened West Virginians: "Did forty million Americans lose their right to run for the presidency on the day they were baptized as Catholics?" In a not so subtle reminder of his record as a war hero, he declared, "Nobody asked me if I was a Catholic when I joined the United States Navy."

The Appalachian Mountain state's Democratic primary became a vote for tolerance (i.e., for Kennedy) or for intolerance. That Hubert Humphrey was an impeccably tolerant man made little difference, and Kennedy swept West Virginia by 60 percent to 40 percent. In November the Democratic Party candidate defeated Richard Nixon by only 119,450 votes out of 69 million cast, but the point was made: An Irish Catholic from the commonwealth of Massachusetts was elected to the White House.

♣ ♥ ♣

The "Boston Strangler" begins a twenty-one-month rape-and-murder spree (1962).

THIRTEEN WOMEN, RANGING IN age from nineteen to eighty-five, shared a common death at the hands of the Boston Strangler. His methods terrorized Boston women along with the city's fathers, brothers, and boyfriends for an agonizing period from June 1962 until January 1964.

The Boston Strangler gained access to his victim's apartment without apparent forced entry, and when he had chosen the appropriate moment, he attacked viciously. The bizarre killer typically tied his victim to her bed, where she was raped repeatedly. Then he strangled her with her hosiery, which he tied in a trademark bow under her chin. Once, the Strangler had beaten his victim with a lead pipe; he also stabbed two women, one with a jackknife, another twenty-two times with a fork.

To the public's horror, the Boston Strangler seemed to come and go at will. He even managed to strike on the day following President John Kennedy's assassination. Massachusetts attorney general Edward Brooke organized a special Boston Strangler investigative bureau in an attempt to answer the crimes with a solution (in 1966, Brooke became the first African American elected to the U.S. Senate since Reconstruction).

In early 1965, police arrested Albert De Salvo for breaking and entering. The Chelsea native was sent for examination to the state's mental hospital at Bridgewater. After De Salvo reported to his guards that he was hearing voices, he was committed to Bridgewater indefinitely.

Boston Police remembered Albert De Salvo as the "Measuring Man" who had seduced and sexually abused a series of women in the late 1950s. Claiming to represent a Hollywood talent agency, the smooth-talking "Measuring Man" carried a clipboard and measuring tape and gained entry to women's homes to record their "vital statistics." Arrested on an unrelated charge in March 1960, De Salvo confessed to being the Measuring Man, but the police did not consider him a dangerous sex criminal because the attacks were not violent. De Salvo served eleven months of a two-year sentence on a simple breaking-and-entering conviction and was released in April 1962.

At Bridgewater, De Salvo began telling a fellow inmate, George Nassar, about a series of grotesque murders he had committed. Nassar, a Mattapan gas station attendant, was himself charged in a brutal slaying and was even under suspicion as the Boston Strangler. Eventually he told his lawyer about the strange conversations with De Salvo.

Nassar's lawyer was thirty-two-year-old F. Lee Bailey. The up-and-coming defense attorney conducted a series of interviews with De Salvo, who revealed to him details in the Strangler murders that were otherwise known only to police.

With Bailey representing him, De Salvo pleaded not guilty by reason of insanity to a series of rape charges unrelated to the Strangler killings. In his account of the case, Bailey wrote that he simply wanted De Salvo to wind up in a psychiatric hospital rather than a prison. The jury, however, returned guilty verdicts on all counts.

For lack of evidence, no charges were ever formally brought against De Salvo for the Boston Strangler crimes. In 1973 he was murdered in his Walpole prison cell.

♣ ♚ ♣

Bill Russell is the first African-American to be a head coach in the NBA (1966).

THE MAN REMEMBERED BY one opponent as "an eagle with a beard" dominated his sport as few before or since. Bill Russell entered the National Basketball Association after leading the University of San Francisco to the 1956 NCAA championship and making the U.S. Olympic basketball team a gold medal winner that summer.

With his intelligence, grace, and extraordinary athletic ability, Russell was expected to lead the Boston Celtics to victory in like manner. Indeed, the Green were NBA champions in Russell's first season, and over the next thirteen years, the Celtics repeated that performance eleven times.

Along the way, Russell virtually redefined the sport according to his own terms. At six feet, ten inches tall, he conceded several inches to most NBA centers, though never a single point. Russell rebounded endlessly, and he blocked shot after shot after shot. As a high school player, Russell had learned to jump higher than other players. Capable of elevating four feet off the ground, he became accustomed to staring down at the top of the basket rim. Along with USF teammate and roommate K. C. Jones, Russell introduced to basketball a hitherto unknown third dimension. The pair of "rocket scientists in sneakers," as they were called, refocused the game from action on the floor to action in the air.

Some sense of Russell's abilities may be gleaned from his first meeting on the parquet floor of Boston Garden with Wilt Chamberlain of the NBA Philadelphia Warriors. The sold-out crowd watched the seven-foot, one-inch rookie and the three-year veteran meet at center court for an awkward pregame handshake. Chamberlain was a flamboyant presence beside the serious Russell.

For the next four quarters of basketball, Russell and Chamberlain put their various talents to work for their respective teams. Russell became the first to block a previously invincible one-handed jump shot by Chamberlain. Throughout the game the Celtic stubbornly continued to put himself between Wilt and the basket.

By the final buzzer, Wilt Chamberlain had managed to outscore Bill Russell, 30–22, though he had to do it with twice as many shots from the field. Man-on-man, Chamberlain beat Russell in just four of twelve tries. The tireless Celtic center outrebounded his Warrior opponent by a dramatic 35–28. Most importantly, however, the Celtics won the game. Over the next couple hundred games pitting Russell against Chamberlain, the Celtics won two of three.

In 1966 Bill Russell became player-head coach of the Boston Celtics, the first African American to hold such a position in the NBA. Russell retired from the Celtics in May 1969 following a four-games-to-three Celtics' victory against the Los Angeles Lakers in the NBA championship series. The 1969 title was the tenth in eleven seasons for the Celtics.

♣ ♛ ♣

Baseball fans awake from their "impossible dream" when the Red Sox lose the seventh and decisive game of the World Series (1967).

IN APRIL, WHEN THE 1967 baseball year began, the Boston Red Sox were given odds of 100 to 1 to be World Series champs. A lot can happen in a baseball season; six months later, the World Series hung in balance as a Fenway Park crowd looked on.

In 1966 the Red Sox finished in ninth place in the American League, twenty-six games behind the pennant-winning Orioles; the Birds had subsequently taken the World Series in four straight games, the last three as shutouts. The Bosox hadn't fared much better than last place throughout most of the 1960s, even with the slugging abilities of Carl Yastrzemski to help them.

What changed the team's attitude and reputation in 1967 was the appointment of Dick Williams as manager. Williams, a former Red Sox player, was determined to be a winner. He came across to his team, the press, and the Fenway fans as arrogant, headstrong, maybe even authoritarian when he declared he would do anything to win. Williams even took from Yaz the title of Red Sox captain.

However, to everyone's surprise and delight, the 1967 team responded by doing what Williams asked of them: win. Now-legendary players such as George Scott and Tony Conigliaro, as well as Yaz, Jim Longborg, Mike Andrews, Rico Petrocelli, and Reggie Smith performed at their best. Yastrzemski was on his way to a Triple Crown—with league-leading numbers in RBIs, home runs, and batting average. Longborg, too, showed himself a winner that season and ended by capturing the Cy Young Award, pitching's top honor.

That the Boston Red Sox stood just one game away from a World Series victory—their first since Babe Ruth left the team before the 1920 season—was reason for wonder and for dread. In 1946, their last World Series, the Red Sox had also faced the St. Louis Cardinals. That matchup went seven games, with the Cardinals' Enos Slaughter scoring the winning run from first when Red Sox shortstop Johnny Pesky hesitated in relaying a throw to his catcher. Would the Curse of the Bambino strike again?

For the decisive seventh game, October 12, 1967, Jim Lonborg was pitching for the Red Sox and Bob Gibson was on the mound for the St. Louis Cardinals. Both pitchers had already won two series games each for their respective sides. Nine innings of baseball would determine who were champions. With three days' rest, St. Louis pitcher Bob Gibson (a future

Hall of Famer) proved unbeatable. The Red Sox went hitless for five innings before "Scotty" tripled. The game ended with the score Cardinals 7, Red Sox 2.

♣ ♞ ♣

Entered as "K. Switzer," Katherine Switzer is issued an official number in the "men only" Boston Marathon (1967).

THE RULES DID NOT permit women to run. It was as simple as that. And after seventy years as an all-male race, the Boston Marathon was not about to go "coed" without a fight.

Of course, discrimination had nothing to do with it. It was just plain obvious that a woman couldn't run a marathon, so why let any of them bother?

As it turned out, a twenty-three-year-old Roberta Gibb had furtively run in the 1966 Boston Marathon and completed the course in three hours, thirty minutes. With help from her mother, who lived in Winchester, Gibb arrived that April morning in Hopkinton along with the other (male) runners. She slipped into the pack and ran the distance without fanfare or much attention at all. In fact, reports that Gibb finished the race were met with skepticism.

Stories circulated that women had run in Boston Marathon races as early as 1951, but most men dismissed such accounts. After all, the Boston Athletic Association rules did not permit a women to run. And this was because a woman could never finish a marathon.

In 1967 the Boston Athletic Association (BAA) held to tradition and distributed official entry numbers only to male runners. Number 261 was accordingly assigned to K. Switzer. Must have been Kenneth Switzer, right?

Wrong. It was Katherine Switzer, a twenty-year-old student at

Syracuse University who claimed she always wrote her name like that—
"K. Switzer"—and that she hadn't meant to trick anyone when she completed the BAA runner's application.

All the same, that drizzling April morning in Hopkinton, K. Switzer let her coach claim her number. She also wore a hood that concealed her face until after the starting pistol had fired.

As she later told a sportswriter, K. Switzer next remembers Jock Semple tearing after her. More than anyone in his day, Semple—BAA coach and trainer to various runners—was the personification of the Boston Marathon. "Get out of my race!" he yelled as he made to remove the "261" from Switzer's back.

Suddenly it was Semple who had to fend off an attacker as one of Switzer's companions threw Semple what was described by those present as a body check. Press photographers on hand at the starting line caught all the action. And despite the commotion, K. Switzer kept on running—all the way to the finish line at the Prudential Center, in fact.

For the next several years, several women ran as "unofficial" entries in the Boston Marathon. In 1972, seventy-five years after the first such race, Ninan Kuscik became the first "official" women's winner.

♣ ♥ ♣

South End urban renewal opponents organize a "tent city" to publicize calls for affordable housing (1968).

THE PARKING LOT ON Dartmouth Street was strangely transformed on April 27, 1968. At the lot's entrance driveway, a rural free delivery mailbox was staked into the ground near the attendant's cabin. Canvas tents were pitched where pedestrians and motorists typically expected to find neat rows of shiny automobiles. Scrap lumber shacks stood feebly among the tents like playhouses constructed by children. Someone had brought a hibachi and had begun flipping hamburgers.

This "Tent City" was the makeshift headquarters for a remarkable protest by the Community Assembly for a Unified South End (CAUSE) that would endure for twenty years and, ultimately, change the character of inner city development in Boston. The leaders of CAUSE, including the charismatic Mel King, had brilliantly escalated their activism with the sort of irreverent and attention-getting protest common in the late 1960s. They were demanding that "urban renewal" address the housing needs of poor, mostly minority city dwellers.

A crowd of weekend thrill-seekers gathered to inspect the protest on its second day. The day before, nervous police had clashed with CAUSE protesters and arrested twenty-three people. Early in the morning on Saturday, the police had returned, apparently eager to make a second round of arrests. They soon retreated, however, disappointing the reporters and those bystanders who had waited patiently for some excitement.

In 1968, few Americans could be blamed for believing that the year would likely prove to be a memorable one for momentous political tumult and upsetting social upheaval. Civil rights leader Martin Luther King, Jr., had been tragically assassinated just three weeks earlier, on April 4. In the meantime, the ongoing Democratic presidential primary campaign had become an impromptu referendum on the Vietnam War.

According to CAUSE leaders, about one hundred low-income families once lived in apartments that stood on the parking lot where "Tent City" had encamped. These people's homes had been demolished to fulfill the ambitious plans of the Boston Redevelopment Authority (BRA) for "urban renewal." To underscore their opposition to those plans, protesters decorated "Tent City" with posters reading, "BRA Go Away."

Indeed, Mel King, Michael Kane, and other CAUSE activists were challenging city government to reconsider its priorities. Instead of promoting costly housing projects such as the glitzy high-rises on the waterfront and the luxury apartment towers in nearby Prudential Center, they asserted, the BRA and related city agencies should ensure that only comparably affordable new housing would replace what had been torn down.

CAUSE had asserted what was previously unthinkable. Up to this point, BRA planners had mostly behaved as if they were free to reengineer

Boston as a city without giving a thought for the thousands of citizens their schemes inevitably displaced. The West End had fallen entirely to the wrecking ball as a result, and large sections of other Boston neighborhoods were also attacked.

In 1984, activists achieved a reversal when the Flynn administration designated them as the project's developers. What eventually replaced "Tent City" was a thoughtful town house complex on a human scale. Officially named "Leighton Park," the development, in the shadow of Copley Place, had created housing for several hundred low-income and moderate-income families, including some of those who lost homes in 1968.

♣ ♥ ♣

On Chappaquiddick, Mary Jo Kopechne drowns in an automobile accident while driving with Sen. Edward Kennedy (1969).

FATAL AUTOMOBILE ACCIDENTS ARE a tragic fact of contemporary American life. Their frequency, however, does not diminish the individual power of each sudden death on the road to cause lasting grief. More than a quarter century after her death, the family of a young woman from rural Pennsylvania say they still keenly feel their loss. At the same time, the nation remains just as keenly absorbed by the manner of her death. Television writers and serious novelists alike have examined the incident from a myriad of angles and have found in it the quintessential elements of an American tragedy.

On July 18, 1969, as Armstrong, Aldrin, and Collins approached their historic rendezvous with the moon, Massachusetts senator Edward M. Kennedy traveled to Martha's Vineyard to attend the Edgartown Regatta.

Then as now the island off the southern flank of Cape Cod was a popular summer resort for the wealthy and the well placed.

"The Vineyard" is a pair of islands that lie so close together they almost touch, and only the most detailed maps even bother to make this distinction clear. After the regatta concluded, Senator Kennedy left the main island at Edgartown and crossed the short distance to Chappaquiddick Island by a quaint ferry.

Then a vigorous thirty-seven, Edward Kennedy had ascended to the throne of a powerful political dynasty. He was not as sharp as Jack, perhaps, and not as charismatic as Bobby, yet all the same, he presented a forceful political figure. Elected to the Senate in 1962 at just thirty years old, the youngest of the Kennedys had risen in stature more by virtue of the tragedy of his brothers' violent deaths than owing to any substantial accomplishments of his own. The pundits and the party faithful were already saying that the 1972 Democratic presidential nomination was Ted's for the asking a full three years before the convention.

Owing to its isolation, Chappaquiddick is something of an enclave within an enclave. The area's exclusivity, in keeping with Yankee tradition, is evident mostly in its simple character. Kennedy drove a late-model Oldsmobile east along wooded Chappaquiddick Road toward the island's center. At a gray-shingled cottage, he joined a dozen other guests for a festive summer barbecue party.

According to his later testimony at an inquest, Senator Kennedy left the barbecue party at 11:15 P.M. With a passenger, Mary Jo Kopechne, he drove to catch a ferry back to Edgartown, where they each had hotel rooms.

According to his statements, Senator Kennedy mistakenly turned right rather than left about a half mile from what has become known in local lore as "the party house." The error sent his Oldsmobile onto a narrow dirt road. Another half a mile later, as Kennedy drove across Dyke Bridge, his car suddenly went over one side and into Poucha Pond.

The senator managed to extricate himself from the sinking Olds, but his passenger was not so lucky. Mary Jo Kopechne survived for a short time by breathing air trapped inside the sedan, but eventually suffocated.

In the meantime, Edward Kennedy left the scene and went back to the party house. He did not report the accident until ten hours later, the next morning. Kennedy subsequently called this strange behavior "irrational, indefensible, inexcusable, and inexplicable." The senator pleaded guilty to leaving the scene of an accident; he was given a two-month suspended sentence, and his license was revoked for a year. His presidential ambitions were forever crushed.

♣ ♟ ♣

At a bank holdup in Allston, police officer Walter Schroeder is shot and killed by a quintet of self-described revolutionaries (1970).

HIT BY A BULLET in the back, forty-two-year-old patrolman Walter A. Schroeder fell mortally wounded to the parking lot pavement of the State Street Bank branch office at 300 Western Avenue, Allston. He was rushed to nearby St. Elizabeth's Hospital, and an appeal for blood was broadcast over police radio. The father of nine children, Schroeder lived within walking distance of the hospital where he died on September 23, 1970, yet another domestic victim of the Vietnam War.

The five who planned and executed the Allston bank holdup were Stanley Bond, William Gilday, Katherine Ann Power, Susan Saxe, and Richard Valeri. Bond, Saxe, and Valeri entered the bank shortly after it opened and forced cashiers to hand over $26,000 in cash. Saxe held a .30 carbine on three terrified bank employees while Gilday and Bond grabbed the loot. Shots were fired inside the bank, although no one was injured.

Meanwhile, Gilday was outside in the parking lot, revving the lead getaway car; Power waited several blocks down the road in a "switch car." It was Gilday who gunned down Patrolman Schroeder in the parking lot. Power did not learn of the incident until she returned to her Back Bay apartment and listened to radio news bulletins.

Even before Patrolman Schroeder was buried, the daring Boston bandits were placed on the FBI's "Most Wanted" list. Not surprisingly, the women received a large share of public attention not only because of their sex but also because their grinning faces on post office "wanted" posters came to represent the troubled state of American youth. Susan Saxe and Katherine Anne Power were Brandeis University graduates, Class of 1970. They had been prominent on the Waltham campus as antiwar activists, and Saxe was also a well-regarded student who graduated *magna cum laude.*

By comparison, the men involved in the case were far less interesting to journalists as characters in a morality play. Despite his pretensions to be a revolutionary, Stanley Bond was more of criminal than anything else. The convicted bank robber was captured in Denver with most of the Boston bank cash. He later died in a Massachusetts prison, the victim of his own homemade bomb. Gilday was arrested quickly, too, and sentenced to life imprisonment for the policeman's murder. Valeri was arrested after a Philadelphia bank holdup, and he subsequently turned state's evidence against his companions.

The bank holdup was not the group's first strike. They had earlier broken into a Newburyport armory, where they seized weapons to be used in their "revolutionary activities." Their goal was to force an American military withdrawal from Vietnam, and with that, an end to the war there against Communist insurgents.

When Susan Saxe finally surrendered to authorities in 1976, the Vietnam War was over. In 1993, after more than twenty years as a fugitive, a guilt-ridden Katherine Ann Power finally surrendered.

♣ ♥ ♣

The Boston Globe joins *The New York Times, The Washington Post,* and other newspapers in publishing the "Pentagon Papers" (1971).

UNDER THE EDITORIAL LEADERSHIP of Tom Winship, *The Boston Globe* was in the vanguard among the nation's media in calling for an end to

American involvement in the Vietnam War. As early as 1967, its editorial pages urged the Johnson administration to enter negotiations toward a peace settlement, and in October 1969 the *Globe* became the second newspaper in the country to favor an American troop pullout.

A special task force organized in 1967 by then secretary of defense Robert S. McNamara had prepared a forty-seven-volume study, *History of U.S. Decision-Making Process on Vietnam Policy, 1945–1967.* The report's authors, including Daniel Ellsberg, traced how the Truman administration had indirectly supported French action in Indochina and that direct American involvement in Vietnam began during the Eisenhower era. In 1971, Ellsberg removed portions of the Top Secret report from files at the Rand Corporation and sent copies to several influential newspapers. He hoped their publication might lead to an end to the war.

When the "Pentagon Papers" began appearing in June 1971 in *The New York Times,* the attending shock in the Nixon White House was likely equaled by the despair felt at the *Globe*'s headquarters on Morrissey Boulevard. Despite having reported three months earlier on their existence, in a front-page article, the *Globe* was left without a single page of the Pentagon Papers to print.

On Winship's insistence, reporter Thomas Oliphant began a search for Daniel Ellsberg, coauthor of the "secret Indochina report," who was living in Cambridge as a senior research associate at the MIT Center for International Studies. Oliphant's orders were to convince Ellsberg that the *Globe,* too, deserved to have the Pentagon Papers.

Over the several days after the Pentagon Papers were first published, Tom Oliphant made complicated arrangements with Ellsberg, who had gone into hiding, to receive publishable material. On June 21, two *Globe* staffers waited simultaneously at telephone booths in Harvard Square and in Newton. According to plan, they reported their positions to Tom Winship, who relayed the two telephone numbers and locations to a mysterious contact called "Bosbin." In turn, "Bosbin" would contact one to say the papers were on their way (the delivery went to Newton). The *Globe* gleefully printed its own edition of the Pentagon Papers the next morning along with an interview with Ellsberg.

Immediately, the Nixon Justice Department, under Attorney General John Mitchell, moved to prevent further publication of the Pentagon Papers. The court order that Attorney General Mitchell received was the first instance in U.S. history of "prior restraint"—essentially, censorship of unpublished articles. On June 30 the U.S. Supreme Court lifted the restraining order. Ellsberg was later charged with espionage, but the charges were dropped. In 1972 the *New York Times* received the Pulitzer Prize for its role as the first to bring the Pentagon Papers to light.

More than the breach of national security, it was the conclusion arrived at in the Pentagon Papers that shook the foundation of American government: Democratic and Republican administrations alike, the report found, had often lied or misled Congress and the public about the conduct of the war; in addition, vital military and political decisions related to the war were illegally kept secret.

♣ ♥ ♣

Nixon 49, America 1 — Massachusetts is the only state in the Union to vote for McGovern (1972).

ON A COLOR-KEYED MAP showing the results of the 1972 presidential elections, the vote count for the Electoral College appears like a jigsaw puzzle missing a small but essential piece. The votes for every state are given over to one candidate, the incumbent Republican president, Richard Nixon. The single exception among all the fifty is tiny Massachusetts. The commonwealth's voters contradicted their compatriots and voted for the president's Democratic opponent, Sen. George McGovern. No American election since the days of Franklin Roosevelt had ended with as lopsided a decision.

According to the final published tallies, Nixon won the national popular vote by nearly two to one (47,170,000 to 29,171,000, or 61 percent to

37 percent). In the Electoral College, the margin was even wider, with Nixon receiving 520 votes to McGovern's 17. Massachusetts accounted for 14 of the Democrat's votes, with the District of Columbia, then voting in its first presidential election, adding another 3. In the commonwealth's popular vote, McGovern won decisively, with 1,332,000 votes (54 percent) to Nixon's 1,112,000 (45 percent).

Richard Nixon and George McGovern held fundamentally different political views. They saw the responsibilities of government toward citizens as well as what should be the appropriate international role for America from opposite ends of the spectrum. On a crucial point like the Vietnam War, Nixon had shown reluctance to withdraw U.S. troops, while McGovern was a long-standing opponent of continued American military involvement there.

From his position on the left, McGovern also called for a guaranteed annual income—essentially, a plan to redistribute wealth according to moderate socialist principles. In 1973, President Nixon had implemented wage and price controls—themselves the fiscal weapons of moderate socialists in battling inflation—yet the Republican remained a solid ally of business and capitalism.

As the odd state out in the election, Massachusetts became an easy target for conservative ridicule and a symbol of liberal righteousness. Republicans and others took to referring to the commonwealth as the "People's Republic of Massachusetts." Democrats and their allies, on the other hand, took a kind of sanctimonious pride in the state's rejection of Nixon, particularly as the Watergate scandal began to unfold. Bumper stickers declared, "Nixon 49, America 1," or more famously, "Don't Blame Me, I'm from Massachusetts."

Within less than two years after his landslide victory, Richard Nixon faced impeachment in Congress and almost certain removal from the White House. On August 9, 1974, he became the first U.S. president to resign his office. The citizens of Massachusetts found it difficult to resist shouting, "We told you so!"

♣ ❦ ♣

The Godwulf Manuscript, the first "Spenser" detective novel set in Boston, is published (1973).

WHILE TEACHING SOMETHING CALLED "The Literature of Violence" at Northeastern University in the early 1970s, Robert B. Parker was quietly working undercover. He was determined to carry out a secret project, one certain to shake up the academic world, where he had always felt like an intruder. This subversive professor had begun writing a detective novel.

Crime was a field this particular professor, at least, was already familiar with. It was not that he had worked as a police officer or as a private detective or even ever had been a victim of crime. For his insights on the underworld, Parker looked to the masters—Chandler, Hammett, and Macdonald. He read and studied them, in fact, the way a fledgling artist visits a museum and patiently stares at work by DaVinci, Rembrandt, or Raphael.

The son of a telephone company executive who was raised in New Bedford, the young Robert Parker attended Colby College and served in the Korean War. Married to his college sweetheart, Joan Hall, he helped support his family with hack writing jobs even as he continued his studies. At Boston University, Parker earned his Ph.D. with a doctoral dissertation on the detective novel. He claimed to have written the dissertation in two weeks. The novels, he has said, take a little longer (about forty days, with up to five pages as his daily quota).

Not surprisingly from a scholar of the genre, Parker created a detective who seems obviously out of the same cold bloodline as Philip Marlowe and Sam Spade. "Spenser" (no first name is ever given) is a former boxer and a former cop, something of a chest thumper à la Hemingway.

Nevertheless, Spenser likes to cook, he has a delicate view of romance, and he is not unaware of such finer details as the occupation of his namesake, the fairly obscure sixteenth-century author of *The Fairie*

Queene. As the alternately erudite and hard-boiled detective says in *Early Autumn,* "Name's Spenser, with an S, like the poet. I'm in the Boston book. Under Tough."

Robert Parker has said he considers Spenser a Renaissance man, but this is a Renaissance man who has an office in the Combat Zone. In fact, the Boston gumshoe is more vulnerable and more human than either image—of a Renaissance man or a hard-boiled detective—typically suggests. Spenser resembles a postwar *film noir* character, but he has taken sensitivity training. In addition to a feminist girlfriend with a Ph.D., for example, Spenser also acquired a sidekick, Hawk, who is African American.

Obviously, this all has made for an attractive formula. Four years after *Godwulf* was published, Robert Parker was able to leave teaching to write full-time on a six-figure income. A television series, *Spenser: For Hire,* starring Robert Urich as Spenser and Avery Brooks as Hawk, ran from 1985 to 1988 and was syndicated internationally.

Robert Parker has written other "non-Spenser" books, including *Three Weeks in Spring,* a moving account of his wife's bout with breast cancer. Spenser, however, remains for him, just as Sam Spade was for Dash Hammet and Holmes for Conan Doyle, a kind of shadow personality who defines Robert Parker as much as Parker defines him.

♣ ♥ ♠

Pulitzer Prize-winning poet Anne Sexton commits suicide at her Weston home (1974).

WITH A GLASS OF vodka in her hand and wearing her mother's fur coat, Anne Sexton, forty-five, walked into the garage at her Weston home on Black Oak Road on Friday afternoon, October 4, 1974. She slipped behind the wheel of a 1967 Mercury Cougar, started the motor, and switched on the radio. A little while later, a neighbor found her dead.

Anne Sexton was obsessed by death and had attempted suicide at least twice before her doctor suggested in 1957 that she try writing as a form of therapy. Ten years later, she received the Pulitzer Prize in Poetry for *Live or Die*.

Born in Newton in 1928 and raised in Wellesley, Anne Harvey eloped and married Alfred Sexton when she was nineteen. Dark-haired with elegant patrician features, Sexton had worked briefly as a fashion model with the Hart Agency in Boston, appearing at department stores and at promotional events. Her marriage was rocky from the start, though the couple eventually had two children, Linda and Joy.

In the 1950s, Boston and Cambridge became the Mount Olympus of American poetry. Beacon Hill, Back Bay, and Harvard Square were home to such dazzling members of the literary firmament as Robert Lowell; W. S. Merwin; Maxine Kumin; Sylvia Plath; Richard Wilbur; Adrienne Rich; George Starbuck; and, following the 1960 publication of her first volume, the critically acclaimed *To Bedlam and Part Way Back*, Anne Sexton. After attending a poetry writing class by Robert Lowell, Plath, Sexton, and Starbuck often gathered at the Ritz Carlton bar.

On the day she killed herself, Sexton had lunch with Maxine Kumin, who was editing Sexton's latest book, *The Awful Rowing Toward God,* and who was probably the last person to see Sexton alive. Kumin told the *Boston Globe* two days later that Sexton's depression over her recent divorce was probably not the direct cause of her decision to commit suicide. "It was not him [Sexton's husband]. Life had a depressing effect on her," Kumin observed.

In describing the creative act of poetry writing, Anne Sexton said, "It's like the potter. She starts with a lump of clay. Suddenly a pot. I start with a lump of clay. Just words from a dictionary. Suddenly a pot." Sexton also said that poetry gave her a "fleeting sense of power" with which she could momentarily put down death.

♣ ☙ ♣

An antibusing demonstration photograph wins the Pulitzer Prize (1976).

IN 1965, A STATE committee determined that a racial imbalance existed throughout Boston's public school system. Rather than address the problem, however, the Boston School Committee, led by Louise Day Hicks, ignored the commonwealth's findings while more schools than ever fell into "racial imbalance."

Unable to withstand the injustices of institutional discrimination, a group of black parents in Boston and the NAACP finally sued for redress in Federal District Court in March 1972. A year later, a lengthy opinion by Judge Wendell Arthur Garrity declared Boston's schools "unconstitutionally segregated."

Garrity's ruling set in motion a process that would inevitably see racially imbalanced schools integrated by busing students from one section of the city to another. No court was powerful enough, though, to mandate citizens' cooperation in such a plan.

In the working-class Irish Catholic neighborhoods of South Boston and Charlestown, residents resisted what they called "forced busing." They portrayed themselves as victims of social engineering perpetrated by "outsiders" and by a legal system unfairly tilted against them.

In their wrath, many white residents kept their own children home from school as busing began in September 1974. Some organized protest marches and demonstrations; others threw stones at school buses carrying black students to previously all-white schools. Their anger focused not only against blacks, the obvious racial target, but also against "one of their own"—Sen. Edward Kennedy, who had nominated Garrity for the federal bench and who had declared his support for court-ordered busing.

On September 9, 1974, Senator Kennedy arrived at a City Hall rally of busing opponents to explain his position. He first was heckled, then chased off the stage. Kennedy escaped the crowd by hurrying inside the nearby Government Center federal office building named for his brother Jack.

Seven months later, on April 5, 1976, anti-busing demonstrators once again came to vent their anger at City Hall plaza. Into their midst marched Ted Landsmark, an attorney and executive director of the Contractors' Association of Boston, a trade group representing African Americans in the city's building industry. The demonstrators—mostly white high school students—could not resist the temptation to scapegoat Landsmark. They surrounded him, knocked him to the ground, and kicked him.

As Landsmark rose to defend himself, a man carrying an American flag on a pole raced toward him. Among those watching was Stanley Foreman, a *Boston Herald* photographer. He framed the sickening scene in his lens just as the white figure with the flagpole speared his defenseless black victim. Landsmark suffered a broken nose and other injuries; Foreman's photograph won a Pulitzer Prize. The shocking image deeply shamed a city that once touted itself the Cradle of Liberty.

♣ ♥ ♠

First album released by rock group "Boston" achieves platinum status in just eleven weeks (1976).

"THEY'RE REALLY ROCKIN' IN Boston," Chuck Berry once sang in the 1950s, but the notion was hardly one that bore up to scrutiny. Throughout the first two decades of the rock and roll era, Boston remained in the shadow of such centers of music and style as Detroit, Philadelphia, and San Francisco.

Not that the record industry and local musicians didn't try to put the Hub on the rock and roll map. In the mid-1960s, something called the "Bosstown Sound" was hyped. The forced name consciously echoed the successful "Mersey Beat" of the Beatles and other British invasion bands, though the "Bosstown Sound" failed to spark any lasting national excitement. In Cambridge, the Harvard Square youth culture had already made its preference clear for folk music and beat poetry.

"Dirty Water" by the Standells, released in 1966, anticipated the sardonic humor of punk rock as well as the seamy obsessions of grunge. In a malicious ode to pollution, the Standells invited their audience to join them "down by the banks of the River Charles" along with "lovers, muggers, and thieves." The chorus proclaimed proudly, "Love that dirty water/Oh, Boston, you're my home!"

For many years, rock fans across Massachusetts had little reason other than the perverse "Dirty Water" to associate their native Commonwealth with their favorite music genre. Embarrassingly, "Massachusetts" was sung by the BeeGees, a déclassé British pop group.

In 1976, Gov. Michael Dukakis proclaimed "Massachusetts," written and sung by adopted native son Arlo Guthrie, as the official state folk song (the legislature concurred in 1981). The lovable Berkshire Hillbilly, however, was too mild a figure to be a genuine rock hero. The far noisier Aerosmith and the blues-inspired J. Geils Band made the local airwaves in the early 1970s, but their national reputations required time to mature fully.

Into the breach in 1976 stepped a most unlikely candidate for rock superstardom. Tom Scholz, twenty-nine, was an MIT graduate with a day job at Polaroid Corporation in Cambridge, where he labored on a top-secret project designing the electromechanical hardware for an instant movie camera. At night, Scholz spent hours playing guitar and recording his own rock songs with a Scully twelve-track and the help of some friends. Scholz made twenty-five copies of one tape and sent them to major record labels. Seven companies replied with form rejection letters.

In October 1975, Charlie McKenzie, an ABC records promotion director, happened to be visiting a record warehouse in Woburn, Mass. The warehouse manager was Paul Brouseau, Scholz's cousin. As he recalled later, McKenzie heard music from Brouseau's office and asked who it was playing. In a month's time, Scholz and four other musicians were signed to an Epic Records deal under the band name "Boston."

The eponymous first album by "Boston" was released on August 23, 1976, with "More Than a Feeling" as the lead single. It became the fastest selling album by a new artist in the history of recorded music, "going platinum" (indicating the sale of 1 million units) in just eleven weeks.

♣ ♥ ♣

A blizzard blankets the commonwealth with record amounts of snow (1978).

FOR ANYONE OLD ENOUGH to remember it, the Blizzard of '78 will remain the yardstick by which all subsequent snowstorms are measured.

"The most destructive storm in the history of the commonwealth," as a report by the Massachusetts National Guard later called it, began on February 6 and ended thirty-two hours, forty minutes later. By then, 27.1 inches of snow had been dumped on Boston. As much as forty-eight inches of "the white stuff" had fallen in other communities across the state.

For six days, Gov. Michael Dukakis imposed a ban of all but emergency vehicles from the roads. President Jimmy Carter declared eight Massachusetts counties as major disaster areas. All five thousand members of the National Guard were pressed into service. Army units were dispatched for the massive evacuation and rescue effort necessary.

In Boston, the snow accumulated at the record rate of an inch every hour. High winds piled snow in drifts as high as fifteen feet. Tides rose twenty feet above normal.

For those commuters who abandoned offices and factories early that first afternoon and tried to return home along city streets and suburban highways, the falling snow became an invincible nemesis. On a long stretch of Route 128 near Needham, an estimated three thousand cars were trapped. Many people spent the long, cold night stranded in their vehicles. At least two people died from carbon monoxide poisoning when snow clogged their cars' exhaust pipes. Altogether, twenty-nine were killed, including five crewmen of a Gloucester boat who were attempting to rescue those aboard a Greek tanker that had gone aground.

Tides swept homes away along the Massachusetts coast, particularly in seaside communities surrounding Boston such as Hull, Scituate, and Revere. Resulting erosion literally rewrote the map of Cape Cod.

The Army, National Guard, and local police and firefighters evacuated ten thousand people from their homes, cars, and workplaces. At public shelters, seventeen thousand people received food, clothing, and warm beds.

Several unusual meteorological and astronomical factors contributed to creating the legendary "Blizzard of '78." On February 6, a "new moon" saw the earth's natural satellite moving in to perigee, or the closest point in its orbit around our planet. In addition, the moon was in a rare alignment with the earth and sun. Both factors cause tides to rise above normal heights.

Meanwhile, on earth, a pair of low-pressure systems began to converge over Cape Hatteras, N.C. One moved down from Canada and carried arctic air, with temperatures as low as 40 degrees Fahrenheit below zero. The other had traveled from the tropical Atlantic, where it was formed in warm Gulf Stream air. The resulting double-strength "nor'easter" headed for Massachusetts like a runaway train driven by two powerful locomotives.

Final calculations put total losses from the Blizzard of '78 at close to $1 billion. The Federal Disaster Assistance Administration quickly distributed $38 million in emergency grants to Massachusetts residents and business owners.

♣ ♥ ♣

Rosie Ruiz wins the Boston Marathon but is later denied the title (1980).

IN THE FIRST TWO marathons of her running career, Rosie Ruiz posted outstanding finishing times.

For the September 1979 New York Marathon, her first race, Ruiz covered the 26 miles, 385 yards through the boroughs in 2:56:29, good for 23rd place among all women and 663rd overall.

Then, seven months later, Ruiz came out of nowhere to win first place

among women in the 84th Boston Marathon. At 2:31:56, she had run the Boston race in record time for a woman and posted the third fastest woman's time anywhere.

Indeed, the Cuban-born long-distance runner, who left her family and came to America in 1968 as a young girl, had shown the dazed Boston crowd quite a remarkable improvement over her New York finish time. Ruiz gouged 25 minutes off her previous mark.

How had Rosie Ruiz done it? Boston Athletic Association officials wanted to know immediately after the award ceremonies. What was special about her training regimen? How could she possibly improve her time in the New York Marathon by 25 minutes in the Boston race?

One possibility was that Boston had a better subway system.

As became clear almost immediately to officials and other runners, Rosie Ruiz knew nothing either of running or of training for a marathon. According to one official, she was not even familiar with basic running terms. As she crossed the finish line and snapped the tape, Ruiz gave away her con as she wore what another official considered too heavy a shirt for the day's unseasonably warm weather.

It got worse after that. Far worse. Rosie Ruiz's name was never recorded at any checkpoints along the route from Hopkinton to Prudential Center. No runners in the race recalled seeing Ruiz pass them on the course.

In addition, monitoring charts and ten thousand high-speed photographs taken throughout the race's final ten miles showed another runner, Jacqueline Gareau of Montréal, as clearly the lead woman. Rosie Ruiz was neither listed on the charts nor seen in the photographs.

In the meantime, Susan Morrow, a New York photographer and freelance clothing designer, had told journalists that she recognized Ruiz from television as the same woman runner she had met at the West Fourth Street subway station the day of New York City's Marathon. The pair allegedly rode the train together to Columbus Circle and walked to the finish line in Central Park, where Ruiz left Morrow.

BAA officials pondered what to do for a week before final voting in a secret ballot at the organization's annual dinner to strip Ruiz of her title. The following day, April 29, Gareau was declared the race's new champion, with a winning time of 2:34:26.

At that press conference, BAA director Will Cloney was asked if the reversal meant Ruiz was a liar and a cheat. "I wouldn't use that term for another human being," he replied with proper Bostonian grace. His counterpart with the New York Marathon, Fred Lebow, was far less restrained, however, in his characterization of the woman who worked a day job as an administrative assistant at Metal Traders, Inc., in mid-Manhattan. "We're sure she's a fraud," Lebow declared. As far as anyone knows, Ruiz has never admitted wrongdoing.

♠ ♥ ♣

U.S. oceanographic research vessel *Knorr* returns to Woods Hole after discovering the *Titanic* (1985).

ON APRIL 15, 1912, at about 2:20 A.M., survivors in lifeboats watched with awe and horror as the *Titanic* lifted its stern high in the air. Movable items inside the ship rushed toward the sinking bow with a thundering roar. The massive hull split in two from the strain, then the ends dove separately beneath the waves, headed for the ocean bottom. Of 2,224 men, women, and children who made up the list of passengers and crew aboard the *Titanic*, 1,515 perished that night.

The *Titanic* may have been the largest luxury liner of its era, but the search for its remains was the equivalent of looking for the proverbial needle in a haystack. A senior scientist at the Woods Hole Oceanographic Institute, Dr. Robert Ballard, had substantial experience finding such "needles." The underwater geologist began working at WHOI (known by its neighbors as "Whooey") in 1973, where he was a member of the *Alvin* Group. The *Alvin* is a small, three-person submarine originally built in 1964, and at the time, capable of diving six thousand feet (in oceanographic terms, a fairly shallow depth). In 1973, however, the *Alvin's* steel hull was replaced with one made of a more rugged titanium alloy. The retrofit meant that the sub's diving range was more than doubled, to thirteen thousand feet, or about the ocean's average depth.

In a relatively short time, Dr. Ballard gained a reputation as one of the world's leading marine explorers. He made numerous daring dives in various submersibles that helped to expand the frontiers of oceanographic research. Near the Galápagos Islands, for example, he discovered giant hot air vents nine thousand feet below the water's surface where tube worms and other strange creatures thrived in an otherworldy environment.

In 1980 Dr. Ballard began development of a new generation of submersible equipment capable of transmitting real-time video photography from the ocean floor. Towed at the end of a fiber-optic cable, the *Argo* was an unmanned submersible equipped with video cameras and capable of cruising above the ocean floor at one or two knots; if the *Argo* spotted something interesting, its companion, the robot "Jason," could investigate the scene at close range with its own video.

As a suitable test for the *Argo,* Dr. Ballard chose to search for the *Titanic* in the same vicinity where others had come away frustrated. The last people to have seen the great ship were those lucky few crowded on its lifeboats in the chilly North Atlantic about four hundred miles south of Newfoundland. Using the known points of the *Titanic's* last reported position and where lifeboats were recovered, the ship lay somewhere within a twenty-five-square-mile area.

Three weeks of searching the ocean bottom in August 1985 had not yielded Dr. Ballard and the crew of the oceanographic research vessel *Knorr* the trophy they sought. At about 1:00 A.M. on September 1, 1985, after viewing miles of mud lying at more than thirteen thousand feet, the *Argo's* camera caught sight of what could only be *Titanic* debris. With the aid of a 1911 photograph taking during the *Titanic's* construction, researchers identified it as one of the ship's massive boilers. Portholes and railings also were seen clearly.

On September 9 the *Knorr* returned to Nantucket Sound, swarmed by air and at sea by helicopters, light planes and pleasure boats. Beside the famous headlines of *"Titanic* Lost" were now placed the equally remarkable words *"Titanic* Found."

♣ ♥ ♣

Thieves remove $200 million in paintings from the Isabella Stewart Gardner Museum in the largest art theft in history (1990).

LIKE WOLVES DRESSED IN sheep's wool, the art thieves wore police badges and uniforms.

On Sunday, March 18, 1990, at 1:15 A.M., a pair of bogus officers banged at a side door to the Isabella Stewart Gardner Museum. They yelled to the guards inside that there was a report of a suspicious disturbance in the area, and they asked to be let in.

Within minutes, the feckless museum guards were prisoners bound with electrical tape, and the museum's sophisticated surveillance system was disabled. In the language of 1940s comic books, the "phony flatfoots" went to work. They spent two hours inside the Gardner before vanishing like smoke from a chimney. Eleven paintings by European masters—each universally agreed to be priceless—were carried off into the Fenway night.

Gone was *The Concert* by Jan Vermeer, the seventeenth-century Dutch artist whose entire known body of work numbers only thirty-two paintings. Ripped from its frame was *A Lady and Gentleman in Black* by Rembrandt as well as a self-portrait etching and *The Storm on the Sea of Galilee,* Rembrandt's only seascape.

Gone, too, were *Landscape with an Obelisk* by Rembrandt's pupil Govaert Flinck; *Chez Tortoni* by Édouard Manet; and five pieces by Edgar

Degas. A Shang Dynasty (1200–1100 B.C.) bronze beaker, the museum's most ancient object, was also taken.

Pressed to place a dollar figure on the theft, museum officials determined the pieces were worth at least $200 million, a figure that made the Gardner theft the most lucrative art heist in history. The works had not been insured, as the premiums would have been greater than the museum's $2.8 million operating budget. The theft was the most sensational in the art world since the 1911 lifting of the Mona Lisa from the Louvre (the DaVinci masterpiece was recovered two years later).

The choices made during the theft left observers wondering whether the thieves followed a very specific shopping list. Why leave behind a Rubens or a Giotto or a Raphael or some other more important Rembrandt?

Some observers suggested that the stolen art was intended for an eccentric Japanese collector. Others theorized the paintings would be used by Colombian drug dealers as a commodity form of payment, an alternative to cash. FBI agents hunted for clues inside the museum, while curators waited to receive a ransom demand.

The thieves, however, have proven reticent. To date there is still no trace of them or the abducted art. The $1 million reward offered by auction houses Christie's and Sotheby's remains unclaimed. Visitors at the Gardner will find only tersely worded cards—"Stolen, March 18, 1990"— where once hung the precious Rembrandts, the Vermeer, and the Degas pieces.

The well-known terms of Mrs. Gardner's will—that every object in her house remain as it was when she died, or else the museum's entire contents must be sold—remain faithfully observed. Paintings, sculpture, and *objets d'art* are not shielded behind Plexiglas nor otherwise protected. The art the eccentric Bostonian collected in her lifetime is as vulnerable as ever.

♣ ♥ ♣

Facing arrest for the murder of his wife, Charles Stuart leaps from the Tobin Bridge to his death (1990).

CAROL DIMAITI STUART, A well-liked lawyer for a suburban Boston magazine publishing firm, was pregnant with her first child when she was shot in the head on October 23, 1989, as she rode with her husband, Charles Stuart, through Boston's Mission Hill neighborhood. The incident occurred shortly after the couple left a nighttime birthing class at the Brigham and Women's Hospital for their Reading home.

According to Charles Stuart, an African-American male with a raspy voice and beard entered their car while it was stopped at a light at the intersection of Huntington Avenue and Francis Street. The thief supposedly demanded Stuart's wallet and became upset when his victim did not comply. He then ordered Charles Stuart to drive into Mission Hill, where the pair were robbed and shot. Carol Stuart was fatally shot in the head; Charles was seriously wounded in the stomach. Carol's child, Christopher, was delivered by cesarean section but later died.

In a dramatic call on his car telephone that was recorded and replayed repeatedly on radio and television, a bleeding Stuart had directed police to the murder scene. The chilling tale of a young white couple from the suburbs terrorized in the city by a ruthless black man absorbed the attention of the media, the police, and the public. Mission Hill was surrounded by detectives and news cameramen.

A homeless man named Alan Swanson was soon arrested but released three weeks later. Another man, William Bennett, who had a criminal record, was said to have boasted to Mission Hill neighbors that he was the gunman. Bennett was duly captured, and Charles Stuart subsequently identified him as the assailant in a police lineup.

Overwhelming public sympathy helped to obscure the doubts cast almost immediately on Charles Stuart even as he recovered from his wounds.

Police investigators wondered why he had driven in what was obviously the wrong direction on leaving the hospital that fatal night. At the hospital, physicians and others asked themselves why Carol was shot in the head while Charles was shot in the stomach. Skeptical journalists also inquired why the attack on two whites should receive so much attention when the murder of a poor black man on the same evening had received comparatively little notice.

The mystery surrounding Carol Stuart's murder was abruptly solved early on January 4 as police approached a car parked on Tobin Bridge. The car was unlocked, with the engine running. On the front seat lay Charles Stuart's driver's license and a handwritten note.

In late October, Charles Stuart had written an emotional love letter from a hospital bed where he was recovering from gunshot wounds. "Now you sleep away from me," the grieving husband wrote to his murdered wife in moving words read at her funeral by a mutual friend. "I will never know again the feeling of your hand in mine, but I will always feel you. I miss you and I love you."

On January 4, however, Stuart wrote in a different tone as he prepared to leap to his death in the Mystic River. "I love my family," the note read. "The last four months have been real hell.... All the allegations have taken all my strength."

In fact, the "allegations" were the sworn testimony of his brother, Matthew Stuart. On January 3, Matthew Stuart told police that Charles had masterminded his wife's brutal murder to gain the proceeds of several life insurance policies in her name. His brother, Matthew swore, had shot his wife and then turned the gun on himself. Matthew Stuart met Charles at the scene and received from him a Gucci bag with orders to "take this to Revere." Inside the bag were the murder weapon as well as several pieces of Carol Stuart's jewelry, including an engagement ring, which Matthew kept, before tossing the bag and its contents into the Pines River.

At first, Matthew Stuart told police he had not immediately understood his brother's motive for the strange string of events but had gradually came to realize what happened. The startling end to the Stuart case found

Bostonians and, indeed, Americans everywhere, deeply ashamed at their own credulousness. The bizarre conclusion to a notorious murder case proved, yet again, that truth is stranger than fiction.

♣ ♥ ♠

The 275th episode of *Cheers* is broadcast, ending the popular TV series (1993).

WHAT IN THE WHOLE history of the commonwealth has given rise to "more fame than Paul Revere's ride, as much hometown pride as the Boston Red Sox, and more pseudointellectualism...than a Harvard Square café"?

The answer, recorded in a solemn proclamation by Gov. William Weld, is the one-word name of a long-running television sitcom: *Cheers*.

Starring at one time or another Kirstie Alley, Ted Danson, Kelsey Grammer, Woody Harrelson, Shelley Long, Bebe Neuwirth, Rhea Perlman, John Ratzenberger, and George Wendt, *Cheers* survived eleven seasons on NBC, beginning in 1983 and winding up 275 episodes later on what became known among camera-hugging Massachusetts politicians as *"Cheers* Day."

Standing on the steps of the State House, Governor Weld expressed his official regret that never again could he watch "Carla insult another customer, see Sam welcome another patron to his bar, see Norm run up his tab or hear Cliff bore us with another story." Weld, a descendant of Puritans and political heir of John Adams and John Hancock, then handed out one by one a blue folder with the *"Cheers* Day" proclamation to the assembled members of the cast.

John Ratzenberger, who the night before had thrown the ceremonial first pitch at a Fenway Park Red Sox game, paraphrased Yogi Berra.

"Thank you," he told the crowd, "for making this day necessary." Rhea Perlman could not muster anything like the comeback viewers might have expected from her character, Carla. "You make such a big deal out of this," said Perlman with shocking honesty for anyone in shouting distance of the Great and General Court of Massachusetts.

Inside the State House lobby, the governor's staff had ordered a replica of the *Cheers* bar in museumlike detail. Several blocks west, on Beacon Street, a reviewing stand for cast members and other attending dignitaries stood opposite the Bull & Finch Pub, the much-revered "real" inspiration for the *Cheers* television bar.

As locals well knew and as patient tourists eventually discover after waiting long hours in line, the Bull & Finch really looks nothing at all like the bar seen on *Cheers*. Certainly it was not the sort of place where anyone knew your name—unless you first handed over a credit card.

As was to be expected from those outside the limelight on "*Cheers* Day," the state's Democratic Party objected that the Republican governor had spent taxpayers' money to build the phony State House bar. Jay Leno, a Massachusetts native, seized the moment for some much-needed self-publicity for the flailing *Tonight* show.

At the end of the night, gaiety prevailed. Making up for the sourness of fellow Democrats, Senate president William Bulger was effusive in his tributes and resolutions at what the newspapers called a "raucous" legislative ceremony. Bulger even handed over his prized gavel to "Carla"—that is, Rhea Perlman.

♣ ♥ ♣

Eugenia Moore, one of the "Framingham Eight," has her life sentence for murder commuted (1993).

THE THIRTY-FOUR-YEAR-OLD BUS DRIVER finally could not take it any longer. In 1985, Eugenia Moore felt trapped in an abusive relationship with

Alfred Phillips, her former live-in boyfriend. He had beaten, stalked, and threatened before, but now Phillips had gone so far as to attack Moore while she was driving for the Massachusetts Bay Transportation Authority.

The night of the bus assault, Phillips came up behind Moore as she got into her car. Moore drew out the knife she carried for self-defense and stabbed Phillips dead. When the judge in her trial refused to admit as defense evidence Moore's history of suffering "battered women's syndrome," she was convicted of second-degree murder and sentenced to life in prison at the state's prison for women in Framingham.

Moore was not alone at Framingham. At least seven other women imprisoned there claimed they had killed their husbands or boyfriends in self-defense after the men repeatedly beat and abused them. Massachusetts advocates for women's rights took up the cause of the "Framingham Eight" and began to seek pardons for their crimes. On February 14, 1992, the legal team of the Task Force on Battered Women and Self-Defense submitted eight petitions for commutation to the Massachusetts governor.

Ironically, the governor who eventually recommended pardoning Eugenia Moore was elected, at least in part, on his reputation as a tough prosecutor and supporter of capital punishment. A former U.S. attorney, the Republican William Weld nevertheless found that there was sufficient evidence in the record to support Moore's pleas for justice.

Weld became the first Massachusetts governor to accept "battered women's syndrome" as a defense for murder, though he followed the lead of governors in seven other states who had earlier granted clemency to nearly forty battered women convicted of assault or murder.

On April 29, 1993, the Massachusetts Governor's Council accepted Governor Weld's recommendation and the unanimous suggestion of the Advisory Board of Pardons by voting to free Eugenia Moore after she had served more than seven years of her sentence (she would not have been eligible for parole until 2001).

Defending Our Lives, a documentary about the Framingham Eight, won the 1994 Academy Award in the Short Documentary category.

Massachusetts filmmakers Margaret Lazarus and Renner Wunderlich, in collaboration with Stacey Kabat of the advocacy organization Battered Women Fighting Back, explored the nature of domestic violence in the United States by focusing on the cases of the Framingham Eight.

To date, four women of the Framingham Eight (including Moore) have had their sentences commuted.

Bibliography

Aesculapian Boston: A Guide to Places of Medical Historical Interest. Boston: Paul Dudley White Society, 1980.

Alberston, Alice Owen. "Maria Mitchell, 1818–1889." *Vassar Quarterly.*

Amory, Cleveland. *The Proper Bostonians.* New York: E. P. Dutton, 1947.

Avrich, Paul. *Sacco and Vanzetti: the Anarchist Background.* Princeton, N.J.: Princeton University Press, 1990.

Axelrod, Alan, and Charles Phillips. *What Every American Should Know About American History.* Holbrook, Mass: Adams, 1992.

Bailey, F. Lee, with Harvey Aronson. *The Defense Never Rests.* New York: Stein & Day, 1971.

Ballard, Dr. Robert. *The Discovery of the* Titanic. New York: Warner/Madison, 1987.

Banning, Evelyn. *Helen Hunt Jackson.* New York: Vanguard Press, 1973.

Bearse, Ray, ed. *Massachusetts: A Guide to the Pilgrim State.* Boston: Houghton Mifflin, 1970.

Beatty, Jack. *The Rascal King.* Reading, Mass.: Addison-Wesley, 1992.

Behn, Noel. *Big Stick-up at Brink's.* New York: G. P. Putnam's Sons, 1977.

Benson, Richard, and Lincoln Kerstein. *Lay This Laurel.* New York: Dover Books, 1973.

Benzaquin, Paul. *Fire in Boston's Cocoanut Grove.* Boston: Branden Press, 1959.

Bishop, Jim. *The Days of Martin Luther King, Jr.* New York: G. P. Putnam's Sons, 1971.

Blanchard, Paula. *Margaret Fuller: From Transcendentalism to Revolution.* New York: Delacorte Press, 1978.

Boettinger, H. M. *The Telephone Book.* Croton-on-Hudson, NY: Riverwood Publishers, Ltd., 1976.

Bradford, William. *Of Plymouth Plantation.* New York: Modern Library College Editions, 1981.

Brant, Irving. *The Bill of Rights: Its Origin and Meaning.* Indianapolis, Ind.: Bobbs-Merrill, 1965.

Brown, Richard D. *Massachusetts: A Bicentennial History.* New York: W. W. Norton, 1978.

Butterfield, Roger. *The American Past.* New York: Simon & Schuster, 1947.

Charters, Ann. *Kerouac: A Biography.* San Francisco: Straight Arrow Books, 1973.

Chase, Owen. *Narratives of the Wreck of the Whale-Ship* Essex. New York: Dover, 1989.

Clark, Judith Freeman. *From Colony to Commonwealth.* Northridge, Calif.: Windsor Publications, 1987.

Coleman, Ken, and Dan Valenti. *Impossible Dream Remembered: The 1967 Red Sox.* Lexington, Mass.: Stephen Greene Press, 1987

The Commemorative Guide to the Massachusetts Bicentennial. Dublin, N.H.: Yankee, 1975.

Conuel, Thomas. *Quabbin: The Accidental Wilderness.* Amherst: University of Massachusetts Press, 1981.

Covey, Cyclone. *The Gentle Radical: Roger Williams.* New York: Macmillan, 1966.

Creamer, Robert W. *Babe: The Legend Comes to Life.* New York: Penguin Sports Library, 1974.

Cumming, William P. *Seafaring in Colonial Massachusetts.* Boston: The Colonial Society of Massachusetts, 1980.

Curtis, Edith Roelker. *A Season in Utopia: The Story of Brook Farm.* New York: Thomas Nelson & Sons, 1961.

Davidson, Edward, ed. *Selected Writings of Edgar Allan Poe.* Boston: Riverside Editions, 1956.

Davison, Peter. *The Fading Smile: Poets in Boston, from Robert Frost to Robert Lowell to Sylvia Plath, 1955–1960.* New York: Alfred A. Knopf, 1994.

Derderian, Tom. *The Boston Marathon.* Champaign, Ill.: Human Kinetics, 1994.

Dickey, Glenn. *The History of the World Series Since 1903.* New York: Stein and Day, 1984.

Douglas, Frederick. *Narrative of the Life of Frederick Douglass, an American Slave*. New York: Penguin Books, 1987.

Edmonds, Anne Carey. *A Memory Book: Mount Holyoke College, 1837–1987*. South Hadley, Mass.: Mount Holyoke College, 1988.

Faber, Doris and Harold. *We, the People: The Story of the United States Constitution*. New York: Charles Scribner's Sons, 1987.

Farr, Francine, and Lee Rand. *A Diary of the Visits of Frederick Douglass to Nantucket Island*. Boston: The Museum of Afro-American History and the Nantucket Atheneum, 1991.

Federal Writers' Project. *WPA Guide to Massachusetts*. New York: Pantheon Books, 1983 (originally published in 1937).

Finch, Christopher. *Norman Rockwell's America*. Pleasantville, N.Y.: Reader's Digest Association, 1976.

Frank, Gerold. *The Boston Strangler*. New York: New American Library, 1967.

Franklin, Benjamin. *Autobiography of Benjamin Franklin*. New York: Modern Library, 1944.

Franklin, John Hope, and Alfred A. Moss, Jr. *From Slavery to Freedom*. New York: McGraw-Hill, 1994.

Frederickson, George M., ed. *Great Lives Observed: Wm. Lloyd Garrison*. Englewood Cliff, N.J.: Prentice-Hall, 1968.

Galton, Lawrence. *The Disguised Disease: Anemia*. New York: Crown, 1975.

Gifford, Barry, and Lawrence Lee. *Jack's Book: An Oral Biography of Jack Kerouac*. New York: St. Martin's Press, 1978.

Gillmer, Thomas. *Old Ironsides*. Rockport, Me.: International Marine, 1993.

Greene, John. *Creation of the Quabbin Reservoir: The Death of the Swift River Valley*. Athol, Mass.: Transcript Press, 1981.

Gutman, Richard; Elliott Kaufman; and David Slovic. *American Diner*. New York: Harper & Row, 1979.

Haley, Alex. *The Autobiography of Malcolm X, as told to Alex Haley*. New York: Random House, 1964.

Hardy, Stephen. *How Boston Played*. Boston: Northeastern University Press, 1982

Harris, Leon A. *Only to God: The Extraordinary Life of Godfrey Lowell Cabot.* New York: Atheneum, 1967.

Higgins, David. *Portrait of Emily Dickinson: The Poet and Her Prose.* New Brunswick, N.J.: Rutgers University Press, 1967.

Holmes, Pauline. *A Tercentenary History of the Boston Public Latin School.* Cambridge, Mass.: Harvard University Press, 1935.

Hopkins, Donald R. *Princes and Peasants, Smallpox in History.* Chicago: University of Chicago Press, 1983.

Howe, Henry. *There She Is, Behold Her.* New York: Harper & Row, 1971.

Jackson, Robert B. *The Gasoline Buggy of the Duryea Brothers.* New York: Henry Z. Walck, 1968.

James, Henry. *The Bostonians.* New York: Bantam Books, 1984 (originally published by Macmillan in 1886).

Johnson, Frederick. *The Boylston Street Fishweir.* Andover, Mass.: Papers of the Robert S. Peabody Foundation for Archaeology, 1942.

Johnson, Thomas. *Emily Dickinson: An Interpretive Biography.* New York: Atheneum, 1955.

Keller, Helen. *The Story of My Life.* New York: Airmont, 1965.

Kennedy, Lawrence. *Planning the City upon a Hill: Boston Since 1630.* Amherst: University of Massachusetts Press, 1992.

Kent, David. *The Lizzie Borden Sourcebook.* Boston: Branden Publishing, 1992.

The Martin Luther King, Jr., Companion. New York: St. Martin's Press, 1993.

Kirker, Harold and James. *Bulfinch's Boston.* New York: Oxford University Press, 1964.

Kumagia, Kasho. *Spenser's Boston.* New York: Otto Penzler Books, 1994

Labaree, Benjamin Woods. *The Boston Tea Party.* New York: Oxford University Press, 1964 (repr., Boston: Northeastern University Press, 1979).

Langguth, A. J. Patriots: *The Men Who Started the American Revolution.* New York: Simon & Schuster, 1988.

Lehman, Milton. *This High Man: The Life of Robert H. Goddard.* New York: Farrar, Straus, & Giroux, 1963.

Lieb, Frederick G. *The Boston Red Sox.* New York: G. P. Putnam's Sons, 1947.

Linden-Ward, Blanche. *Silent City on a Hill.* Columbus: Ohio State University Press, 1989.

Lovett, James D'Wolf. *Old Boston Boys and the Games They Played.* Boston: Riverside Press, 1907.

Lowell, the Story of an Industrial City: A Guide to the Lowell National Historic Park. Washington, D.C.: National Park Service.

Lukas, J. Anthony. *Common Ground.* New York: Random House, 1985.

Manchester, William. *One Brief Shining Moment.* Boston: Little, Brown, 1983.

Marson, Philip. *Breeder of Democracy.* Cambridge, Mass.: Schenkman, 1963.

Martin, George. *Madam Secretary.* Boston: Houghton Mifflin, 1976.

Mason, Julian, ed. *The Poems of Phillis Wheatley.* Chapel Hill: University of North Carolina Press, 1989.

McClung, Robert. *The Gypsy Moth: Its History in America.* New York: William Morrow, 1974.

Memoir of Susan Dimock, Resident Physician of the New England Hospital. Boston, 1875.

Messerli, Jonathan. *Horace Mann.* New York: Alfred A. Knopf, 1972.

Middlebrook, D. W. *Anne Sexton.* Boston: Houghton Mifflin, 1991.

Middlekauf, Robert. *The Glorious Cause.* New York: Oxford University Press, 1982.

Miller, Perry. *Jonathan Edwards.* New York: W. Sloane Associates, 1949.

———, ed. *The American Puritans: Their Prose and Poetry.* Garden City, N.Y.: Anchor Books, 1956.

Moore, Harry T. *Henry James.* New York: Viking Press, 1974.

Morison, Samuel Eliot. *History of Harvard University.* Cambridge, Mass.: Harvard University Press, 1935.

Morgan, Edmund S. *The Birth of the Republic, 1763–1789.* Chicago: University of Chicago Press, 1956, 1977.

Oates, Stephen B. *Let the Trumpet Sound: The Life of Martin Luther King, Jr.* New York: Harper & Row, 1982.

O'Connor, Thomas H. *Bibles, Brahmins, and Bosses.* Boston: Trustees of the Boston Public Library, 1991.

———, *Building a New Boston.* Boston: Northeastern University Press, 1993.

Olshaker, Mark. *The Instant Image: Edwin Land and the Polaroid Experience.* Briarcliff Manor, N.Y.: Stein & Day, 1978.

Reid, William J., and Herbert G. Regan. *Massachusetts: History and Government of the State.* New York: Oxford Book, 1956.

Richmond, Merle. *Phillis Wheatley.* New York: Chelsea House, 1988.

Roman, Joseph. *King Philip: Wampanoag Rebel.* New York: Chelsea House, 1992.

Roper, Laura Wood. *F.L.O.: A Biography.* Baltimore: Johns Hopkins University Press, 1973.

Russell, Howard S. *Indian New England Before the* Mayflower. Hanover, N.H.: University Press of New England, 1980.

Schama, Simon. *Dead Certainties.* New York: Alfred A. Knopf, 1991.

Schapp, Dick, ed. *Babe: The Legend Comes to Life.* New York: Penguin Sports Library, 1974.

Smith, Edward Conrad, and Harold J. Spaeth, eds. *The Constitution of the United States, with Case Studies,* 12th ed. New York: Barnes & Noble Books, 1987.

Smith, Philip Chadwick Foster. *The Empress of China.* Philadelphia: Philadelphia Maritime Museum, 1984.

Smith, Robert. *Babe Ruth's America.* New York: Thomas Y. Crowell, 1974.

Snow, Edward Rowe. *Romance of Boston Bay.* Boston: Boston Printing, 1944.

Starkey, Marion. *The Devil in Massachusetts.* New York: Alfred A. Knopf, 1949.

Swift, Lindsay. *Brook Farm: Its Members, Scholars, and Visitors.* New York: Macmillan, 1900.

Szatmary, David P. *Shays' Rebellion: The Making of an Agrarian Insurrection.* Amherst: University of Massachusetts Press, 1980.

Tharp, Louise Hall. *Mrs. Jack: A Biography of Isabella Stewart Gardner.* Boston: Little, Brown, 1965.

Tourtellot, Arthur Bernon. *The Charles*. New York: Farrar & Rinehart, 1941.

Ungar, Sanford J. *The Papers & the Papers: An Account of the Legal and Political Battle over The Pentagon Papers*. New York: E. P. Dutton, 1972.

Utley, Robert Marshall and Wilcomb E. Washburn. *Indian Wars*. New York: American Heritage Library, 1977.

Walton, Donald. *A Rockwell Portrait: An Intimate Biography*. Mission, Kans.: Sheed, Andrews, & McMeel, 1978.

Ward, Geoffrey C., with Ken Burns and Ric Burns. *The Civil War*. New York: Alfred A. Knopf, 1990.

Weston, George. *Boston Ways*. Boston: Beacon Press, 1957.

Whitehill, Walter Muir. *Boston: A Topographical History*. Cambridge, Mass.: Belknap Press, 1959, 1968.

Wildes, Karl L., and Nilo A. Lindgren. *A Century of Electrical Engineering and Computer Science at MIT, 1882–1982*. Cambridge, Mass.: MIT Press, 1985.

Williams, Selma R. *Divine Rebel: The Life of Anne Marbury Hutchinson*. New York: Holt, Rinehart, & Winston, 1981.

Winslow, Ola Elizabeth. *John Eliot: "Apostle to the Indians."* Boston: Houghton Mifflin, 1968.

Winsor, Justin. *The Memorial History of Boston, Including Suffolk County, Massachusetts, 1630–1880*. Boston: J. R. Osgood, 1880–81.

Yool, George Malcolm. *1692 Witch Hunt: The Layman's Guide to the Salem Witchcraft Trials*. Bowie, Md.: Heritage Books, 1992.

Zobel, Hiller B. *The Boston Massacre*. New York: W. W. Norton, 1970.

Zophy, Angela Howard, ed. *Handbook of American Women's History*. New York: Garland, 1990.

Index